WAR, JUDGMENT, AND MEMORY
IN THE BASQUE BORDERLANDS, 1914–1945

THE BASQUE SERIES

War, Judgment, and Memory in the Basque Borderlands, 1914–1945

SANDRA OTT

University of Nevada Press ▲▲ Reno and Las Vegas

The Basque Series
University of Nevada Press, Reno, Nevada 89557 USA
Copyright © 2008 by University of Nevada Press
All rights reserved
Manufactured in the United States of America

Library of Congress Cataloging-in-Publication Data
Ott, Sandra.
    War, judgment, and memory in the Basque borderlands,
1914–1945 / Sandra Ott.
        p. cm.
    Includes bibliographical references and index.
    ISBN 978-0-87417-738-1 (hardcover : alk. paper)
    1. Pays Basque (France)—History—20th century. 2. World
War, 1914–1918—France—Pays Basque. 3. World War, 1939–
1945—France—Pays Basque. I. Title.
    DC611.B319O88   2008
    944'.716081—dc22   2007040984

The paper used in this book is a recycled stock made from 50 percent post-consumer waste materials and meets the requirements
of American National Standard for Information Sciences—
Permanence of Paper for Printed Library Materials, ANSI/NISO
Z39.48–1992 (R2002). Binding materials were selected for strength
and durability.

FIRST PRINTING

17   16   15   14   13   12   11   10   09   08
5   4   3   2   1

For my beloved sister, Sharon Ott

CONTENTS

ILLUSTRATIONS

PHOTOGRAPHS *(following page 130)*

FIGURE

MAPS

Anthropologists who have conducted fieldwork in France rarely devote more than a few pages to the two world wars, which profoundly altered French culture and society in the twentieth century. Few ethnographers mention the German Occupation in their analyses of village life and its recent past (Wylie 1974; Zonabend 1978).[1] The ethnographic gap may derive in part from ethical issues and the reluctance of informants to talk about local experiences, actions, and events that pitted the French against their fellow citizens during 1940–45. In some parts of France villagers rarely, if ever, saw Germans or Allied soldiers and never suffered the physical damage caused by combat and bombings. Yet, as Laurence Wylie shows in his account of one such village in the Vaucluse, the war nevertheless had a devastating effect on intracommunity relations there. Wylie describes a wartime atmosphere of bitterness, deprivation, and distrust among villagers, who were deeply divided by suspicion, jealousy, and personal animosities. The formation of a maquis in the area exacerbated tensions among local citizens. No violence, arrests, or "serious denunciations" occurred in the village, but intracommunity quarrels turned people against each other to such an extent that feuding factions continued to exist after the war ended (Wylie 1974: 27–30).

One can only wonder what archival research might reveal about those lingering antagonisms and their wartime roots. As my own research in the northern Basque Country has revealed, departmental and other wartime archives contain a wealth of ethnographic material that enables in-depth explorations of complex, delicate issues such as denunciation, local betrayals, collaboration, and collaborationism.[2] For the anthropologist, the archives also have much to teach about the mundane concerns of everyday life under occupation, the conflicts and tensions that existed before the Germans arrived, and the web of relationships in which local citizens became entangled as they tried to cope with their unusual circumstances.

As Richard Cobb (1983: 108) once observed, it is difficult to "recapture something of the familiarity, even the sheer banality of day-to-day relations" between people who experienced the Occupation. Certain local studies, memoirs, wartime correspondence, and works of fiction do, however, give a human dimension to the choices people faced during 1940–45.[3] The literary and cultural critic Tzvetan Todorov (1996) provides a dramatic account of civil war in one French town, where the local resistance group made an ill-fated attempt to liberate their community in June 1944. Resisters executed their hostages (collaborationists) and triggered a reprisal by *miliciens* and German soldiers, who rounded up and killed Jewish citizens in the town. Todorov's examination of the events that culminated in such tragedy raises important moral questions about the ethics of conviction and the ethics of responsibility in wartime, a theme in my own study of Basque resistance groups and their relationship with civilians.[4]

In his study of several different communities in the Loire valley, social historian Robert Gildea (2002) explores the diverse and often surprising ways in which the occupation affected the lives of citizens who were neither "Good French" nor "Bad French" but often a mixture of the two. Like me, Gildea was interested in the varied and often contradictory experiences of ordinary citizens and the strategies they used to cope with their circumstances. His research shows that Franco-German relations were not always as brutal as people often portray them. Some Germans and French citizens learned how to live together. Gildea also found that "the dark years" of occupation were not always characterized by hunger, cold, and fear. The French also "demonstrated imagination, resourcefulness and Gallic cunning in order to make the Occupation liveable" (ibid.: 419). My own local study of Basques under the Occupation reveals a similar picture and offers some new insights into Franco-German relations at a grass-roots level.

Another eminent British historian of Vichy and the Occupation, H. R. Kedward, was likewise interested in the experiences of ordinary people, especially those who became *maquisards* in southern France. In his classic study of rural resistance, Kedward investigates the nature and life of the maquis, which he analyzes as "both a choice and as a necessity in the face of increasing German pressure and demands" (1994: vi). Kedward shows how the maquis was an "inventive adaptation of everyday lives to new forms of wartime survival" (ibid.: 284). His analyses of the maquis and the "culture of the outlaw" demonstrate that the maquis inverted the traditional rule of law under Vichy in the name of higher justice (Diamond and Kitson 2005: 2–3). His theoretical work on the inversion of power relationships under Vichy and occupation has special relevance to my own research on class and ethnic conflict in the Basque town of Maule.

Robert Gildea and H. R. Kedward combined the techniques of history and anthropology by drawing upon wartime archives and extensive interviews with people who had direct experience of the Occupation. Their works inspired me to write this local study of Basques under occupation and to fill a major gap in the existing literature about a little known corner of France, Iparralde, literally "the northern side" of the seven provinces that constitute the Basque Country (Euskal Herria).[5] I focus on the easternmost, mountainous province of Xiberoa (Soule, in French), one of three Basque provinces located in the French state in the western Pyrenees. Located in the Spanish state, Nafarroa (Navarre) lies to the south and the Occitan province of Béarn lies to the north and east of Xiberoa in France.

I have returned to Xiberoa every year since 1976 and thus have had a rare opportunity, as an ethnographer, to maintain close friendships there and to create new ones with a wide range of Basques across the province. During leave from my duties as an administrator at the University of Oxford in 2000, I became interested in the Resistance and Occupation in Xiberoa and spent several weeks there working on a project that dealt, in part, with Xiberoans' experiences during 1940–44. When I took up my academic appointment in the Center for Basque Studies at the University of Nevada, Reno, in 2002, I began the research upon which much of this book is based. I concentrated on Xiberoa for various reasons. I had numerous well-established contacts there and spoke their dialect of Basque. The French edition of my monograph about a Xiberoan shepherding community (Ott 1993a) and a documentary film I made there with Granada Television (1986) had been well received by Xiberoans as a record of practices and rituals that had become obsolete and as a means of recovering aspects of a past that they wanted to remember. Many Xiberoans had already linked me with the preservation of *la mémoire,* a process of remembering the past that is valued in France for what it has to teach younger and future generations. The province also offered an opportunity to study the impact of both Vichy and German rule in a Pyrenean borderland.

I did fieldwork in Xiberoa for a period of eight months, at different stages, between the spring of 2003 and February 2005. I was primarily based in the Xiberoan capital, Maule, where I lived in the house of a couple who often shared their memories of the Occupation with me. I spent three weeks in the village of Sustary and another three weeks in Urdos.[6] To complement my fieldwork, I spent eight weeks working in the departmental archives of the Pyrénées-Atlantiques in Pau, where I concentrated on classified documents relating to Vichy, the Occupation, and post-Liberation trials of suspected collaborators and collaborationists.[7] In 2003 I also spent two months in the provinces of Lapurdi (Labourd) and Behe Nafarroa (Lower Navarre). Both provinces came under German control soon after Philippe Pétain signed France's armistice in June 1940. Only Xiberoa fell under Vichy rule in the so-called Free Zone, until Germany occupied all of France in November 1942.

As happened elsewhere in France, Xiberoan Basques responded in a variety of ways to the opportunities that life under Vichy and German occupation presented and the threats posed not only by those regimes, but also by fellow citizens and by strangers who passed through the territory (Gildea 2002). In both towns and countryside, the experience of war and occupation tested the resilience of local values and institutions and often undermined accepted standards of human conduct. In some Xiberoan communities, war and occupation also led to the suspension and, in some cases, demise of long-standing local customs and social practices. In order to understand how traditional sociocultural practices conditioned Basques' responses to resistance, collaboration, and the process of liberation from 1940 until 1945, I trace the roots of the Xiberoan moral community to Basque customary law and then chart the legacy of political conflict and socioethnic tensions from the first decades of the twentieth century until the post-Liberation period.

ACKNOWLEDGMENTS

First of all, I would like to thank the Xiberoan people who kindly shared their memories, family photographs, unpublished memoirs, private archives, their homes, hospitality, and friendship with me. I could not have written this book without their assistance, trust, and encouragement. The fieldwork upon which the book is based spans thirty years. Many of the Xiberoan Basques who first talked to me about their experiences during the Occupation have now passed away; I remain extremely grateful to them. Of the sixty people who worked closely with me during fieldwork in 2003–2005, I owe special thanks to M. Joanny, who introduced me to a wide range of former Secret Army resisters and sympathizers, as well as to some of their critics. Through her, I met M. Micki Béguerie, a former resister who kindly arranged for me to meet CFP veterans and generously included me in their annual commemorative gatherings at Ospitaleku. I also thank the Xiberoan playwright M. Jean-Louis Davant, whose detailed knowledge of Xiberoan resistance greatly aided my research. I am very grateful as well to M. Jean de Jaureguiberry, the late M. André Barbe-Labarthe, M. Georges Recalt, and M. Georges Althapignet, veteran resisters who shared their memories of the Occupation with me. M. Jojo Malharin generously lent me his father's substantial collection of private-correspondence and military reports about the Resistance (CFP) in Xiberoa.

Special thanks are also owed to Mme Madalon Rodrigo Nicolau and M. Román Pérez, who provided invaluable information about trans-Pyrenean relations and the experiences of Navarrese and Aragonese people who settled in the Xiberoan capital, Maule, during the 1920s and 1930s. M. and Mme Amigo offered many insights into relations between factory owners and workers in Maule. I also thank Mme Odette Huerta for having made two scrapbooks for me with photos and narratives about her two brothers, both of whom she lost as a result of the war. I am equally indebted to the late Mme Marie-Louise Lasserre Davancens, who bravely told me about her experiences during the Occupation and in the Nazi camp at Ravensbrück. I also cherish the many hours I spent listening to Mme Rosemary Siedenburg, who participated in the Normandy landings in 1944 and whose husband was interned at Gurs during the Occupation. I owe special thanks as well to Giselle Lougarot and Poyo and Odile Althabegoity, Denis Cassard and Marie-Antoinette Cassard Althabegoity, Jean Duhau, Dominique Baptiste, Rufino Jaureguy,

Paul Fagoaga, and to the family, who have included me in their household since we first met in 1979, and whom I dearly love.

Several local educators also deserve special acknowledgment. I am greatly indebted to M. Robert Elissondo, a history teacher who recorded several elderly Xiberoans and shared their narratives with me. M. Elissondo kindly read and commented on several chapters of this book. The director of the Collège de Saint-François in Maule, M. Christian Espeso, invited me to several educational events at the school. I owe special thanks to two teachers at the college, M. Joël Larroque and Mme Luxi Etxecopar Camus, for their assistance with my research and generous hospitality. M. Larroque provided detailed comments on several chapters, for which I am most grateful. A retired school teacher, M. Pierre-Paul Dalgalarrondo, let me copy twenty tapes of interviews recorded by local history enthusiasts during the 1960s and 1980s, in which people described their experiences during the 1930s and under occupation.

I am also very indebted to colleagues whose encouragement, advice, and constructive criticism helped me make a difficult transition from university administration back into academia. I shall always be immensely grateful to the late Rodney Needham, my friend and mentor of many years, and to Simon Collison, a long-standing loyal friend who unselfishly provided much needed moral support as I made important personal and professional transitions at the start of my research. In 2000 Geoffrey Thomas generously granted me leave from my position in the Department for Continuing Education at the University of Oxford and thus played a vital role in relaunching my academic career. His ongoing support is greatly valued. Special thanks are owed to Gloria Totoricagüena, former director of the Center for Basque Studies at the University of Nevada (Reno), for her encouragement, support, and friendship. I am also very grateful to my other colleagues at the Center: Jill Berner, Kate Camino, Argitxu Camus Etxecopar, Bill Douglass, Xabier Irujo, and Joseba Zulaika. I would like to give special thanks to William A. Christian for his friendship and mentorship. I am grateful for the time and energy spent by Francesca Cappelletto, Rob Zaretsky, Yves Pourcher, and Bill Kidd in reading and commenting upon draft chapters of this book. I appreciate Sarah Fishman for encouraging me to join French history societies in this country and for including me on conference panels. I value the copyediting performed by Sarah Nestor. Joanne O'Hare, Charlotte Dihoff, and Sara Vélez Mallea's support and interest in my work have been indispensable. My greatest debt of intellectual gratitude is to Rod Kedward and Robert Gildea, whose studies of the Resistance, Vichy, and the Occupation have long inspired me and whose guidance and detailed comments on my work have helped me tremendously.

I am grateful to the Center for Basque Studies at the University of Nevada, Reno, for having funded many of my research expenses during 2003–2005 and to the College of Liberal Arts for a generous Scholarly and Creative Activities Grant awarded to me in 2006. I am also grateful to Martine de Bois-deffre, the minister of culture and communication, by delegation, and the director of archives in France for having granted me permission to consult classified documents in the departmental archives of the Pyrénées-Atlantiques and to the staff responsible for those archives in Pau. I am very grateful as well to Matt Sauls for his instructive comments on several chapters, his patience with me while I wrote this book, his intellectual curiosity, and his many kindnesses. Lastly, I extend my heartfelt thanks to my sister, Sharon Ott, and to Matt for their encouragement, friendship, and love.

AF   The Action Française was a neoroyalist and ultranationalist movement founded by Charles Maurras at the end of the nineteenth century and was the dominant voice of extreme right-wing politics until the 1930s. Many of its members joined the right-wing league, the Croix de Feu. The ideological influence of the AF lingered under Vichy.

AD, P-A   The departmental archives (Archives Départementales) of the Pyrénées-Atlantiques are located in Pau.

AS   The Armée Secrète (Secret Army) played a military role in the Unified Movements of the Resistance (MUR) from the winter of 1942–43. In Xiberoa, as elsewhere in France, AS groups included sedentary resisters who operated from home, as well as from combat units and maquis.

BCRA   The Bureau Central de Renseignements et d'Action, de Gaulle's intelligence network for Free France, worked closely with the section of the British SOE that sent money and weapons to French resisters.

CDL   The Comité Départemental de Libération (Departmental Liberation Committee) of the Basses-Pyrénées operated in clandestinity from the beginning of 1944, following a directive in November 1943 from the National Council of the Resistance (Conseil National de la Résistance), which united French resistance under Charles de Gaulle.

CFLN   Established in Algiers, the Comité Français de Libération Nationale was formed after the Allied invasion of North Africa. Rival generals Giraud and de Gaulle became its co-presidents in May 1943. De Gaulle took over sole leadership of the CFLN in the spring of 1944.

CFP   Responsible for Region 4 (Toulouse) of an urban-based resistance movement (OMA, l'Organisation Métropolitaine de l'Armée), General André Pommiès formed the Corps Franc Pommiès in early 1943 and mainly recruited former officers in the Armistice Army. The CFP operated in the Gers, Haute-Garonne, the Ariège, the Hautes-Pyrénées, the Basses-Pyrénées, and the

	Landes. Its military mission was to remove the Germans from French territory.
CGT	The Confédération Générale du Travail was a socialist trade union confederation that amalgamated with its rival communist trade union (CGTU) in 1936. In May 1943 CGT representatives participated in the formation of the National Council of the Resistance, which drew together diverse resistance movements under the leadership of Jean Moulin.
CNR	Formed in May 1943 through the efforts of Jean Moulin, the Conseil National de la Résistance (National Council of the Resistance) united the Resistance under Charles de Gaulle and established the role of resistance in the liberation of France.
FFI	The Forces Françaises de l'Intérieur (the French Forces of the Interior) brought together all armed resistance groups into one military organization at the end of 1943. As happened elsewhere in France, departmental and regional FFI leaders in the Basses-Pyrénées were not appointed until late spring 1944.
FTP(F)	In the first months of 1942, French communists brought together the various communist resistance movements, forming the Francs-Tireurs et Partisans (Français). Its resisters took extensive military action against the Germans in 1943–44. Both the CFP and Secret Army resistance groups in Xiberoa feared that the FTP would promote a communist revolution at the Liberation.
GC	Founded in 1940 by the essayist Alphonse de Châteaubriant, the Groupe Collaboration, the largest collaborationist movement in France during the Occupation, promoted Franco-German collaboration through cultural activities.
LFC	In August 1940 the Légion Française des Combattants merged the numerous veterans' associations that were formed during the Third Republic. The Legion pledged its support for Pétain and actively promoted the values of Vichy's National Revolution.
LVF	Leading collaborationists in Paris formed the Légion des Volontaires Français contre le Bolchevisme in October 1941 with the approval of the Nazis. Members of the LVF fought alongside German troops on the eastern front.
OMA	In December 1942 a group of officers in the Armistice Army of Vichy created a clandestine resistance group, the Organisation Métropolitaine de l'Armée, initially commanded by General Henri-Honoré Giraud in North Africa. In late June 1943 OMA created an "action group" in London and received weapons and

ammunition from the Special Operations Executive (SOE), part of the British secret service. In May 1944 OMA became known as ORA, the Organisation de Résistance de l'Armée. Other resistance organizations often referred to the OMA as the ORA and as the New Army.

ORA   The Organisation de Résistance de l'Armée (the Resistance Organization of the Army) replaced the resistance movement known as l'Armée Nouvelle or the New Army, started within the Armistice Army after the defeat of June 1940. ORA became active after Germany occupied the Free (Vichy) Zone in November 1942. Organized by career officers and run on a professional military basis, ORA initially backed General Giraud rather than de Gaulle as the head of the Resistance; its mission was military, not political.

PCF   The Parti Communiste Français (French Communist Party) was created as a result of the Tours Congress of the Section Française de l'Internationale Ouvrière (SFIO, the French Socialist Party) in December 1920. A majority of party members voted in favor of affiliation with the Comintern and formed a new party, which became the PCF in 1921.

PPF   The Parti Populaire Français (the French Popular Party) was an extreme right-wing group formed by Jacques Doriot in 1936. After 1940 the party (as the Mouvement Populaire Français) adopted a fascist platform and became one of the most extreme collaborationist movements in France.

PSF   In 1936 Colonel François de La Rocque turned the ultra-right-wing Croix de Feu into a political party, the Parti Social Français, which vigorously promoted Pétain and the values of the National Revolution.

SD   The German security service, Sicherheitsdienst, closely collaborated with its twin organization, the Gestapo, which used intelligence information provided by the SD.

SFIO   In order to comply with the Second International, the Section Française de l'Internationale Ouvrière was founded in 1905, following the merger of two French socialist parties. In 1920 the 18th Congress of the SFIO led to the creation of the French Communist Party (PCF).

SOE   The Special Operations Executive was a British intelligence organization that sent British agents into France to aid the Resistance and defeat Germany.

SOL   Joseph Darnand, among other militant members of the Legion (LFC), created the Service d'Ordre Légionnaire in 1940. Officially recognized by Vichy in January 1942, the SOL operated as a paramilitary force in the unoccupied zone, which, in January 1943, became Vichy's infamous police force, the Milice.

SS   The Schutzstaffeln or SS, organized by Heinrich Himmler, were armored divisions in France that aimed to eradicate resistance groups. The SS division, Das Reich, was stationed in Mont-de-Marsan in the Landes, northwest of Xiberoa.

STO   The Service du Travail Obligatoire, obligatory work service in Germany, replaced the scheme known as the Relève, which promised that one French prisoner of war would be released for every three volunteers who offered to work in German factories. In February 1943 the STO required most Frenchmen between the ages of twenty and twenty-three to enter compulsory labor service in Germany. Deeply unpopular across France, the STO spurred many young evaders to join the Resistance.

UGT   In the 1930s the Unión General de Trabajadores firmly supported Spanish socialism and was one of the most organized workers' movements in Europe at the time. Members of the Spanish bourgeoisie respected the efficiency of the Unión and its reasonable approach to labor disputes.

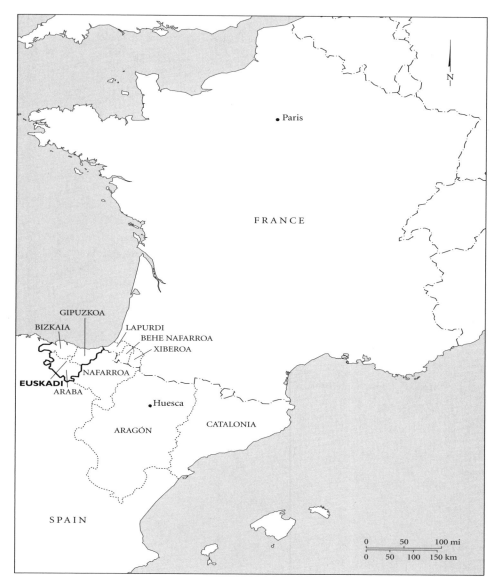

Map 1. The Basque Country and adjacent territories in France and Spain

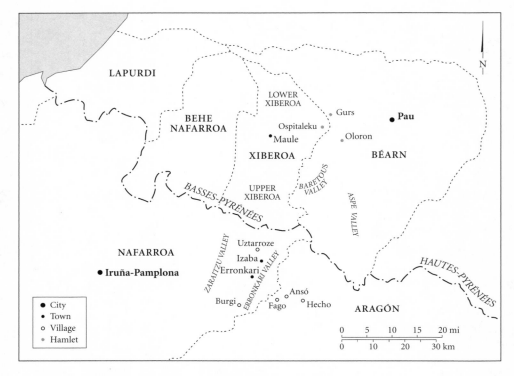

LAPURDI

BEHE
NAFARROA

LOWER
XIBEROA

Gurs

Ospitaleku

•Maule

Oloron

• **Pau**

BÉARN

XIBEROA

UPPER
XIBEROA

BARÉTOUS
VALLEY

BASSES-PYRÉNÉES

ASPE VALLEY

NAFARROA

ZARAITZU VALLEY

Uztarroze

Izaba

Erronkari

ERRONKARI VALLEY

• **Iruña-Pamplona**

HAUTES-PYRÉNÉES

Ansó

Burgi

Fago

Hecho

ARAGÓN

N

● City
● Town
○ Village
● Hamlet

| 0 | 5 | 10 | 15 | 20 mi |
| 0 | 10 | 20 | 30 km |

Map 2. Pyrenean borderlands: Xiberoa, Nafarroa, Aragón, and Béarn

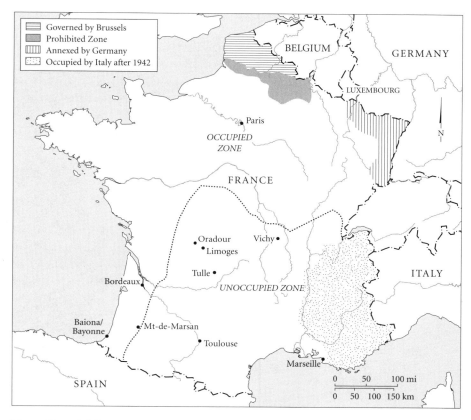

Map 3. Occupied France, 1940–1945

WAR, JUDGMENT, AND MEMORY
IN THE BASQUE BORDERLANDS, 1914–1945

Introduction

During the spring of 1977, I spent most mornings copying parish records in a chilly, musty room in the town hall of a Pyrenean borderland community in the northern Basque province of Xiberoa. In an adjacent office, the priest spent most of his time on the telephone, talking to the authorities about the welfare of local citizens, their schools, roads, and agricultural subsidies, and employment opportunities for young people who did not wish to remain on the family farm. In keeping with local custom, the priest played a dual role as the community's spiritual and secular leader. As the town-hall secretary, he effectively controlled relations between his parishioners and outsiders, including representatives of the French state. The priest enjoyed arguing with departmental and cantonal officials and was quite proud of his success as a negotiator and a defender of both individual citizens and the wider community. He greatly admired his predecessor, who had mediated the delicate relations between his parishioners and the Germans who occupied the community continuously from December 1942 until late August 1944.

When I opened the slightly damp, leather-bound book of death records for 1943, I found an entry for one young shepherd, Tomas Garat. Beneath his name, the priest had written in tiny letters: "died in Buchenwald, November 1943, twenty-one years old." When I returned to the farmhouse in which I lived, I told my hostess, Gabrielle, what little I knew about Tomas Garat. She told me that he was a clandestine guide who regularly took fugitives across the mountains into Spain during Vichy rule and the German Occupation. "One night, the Germans caught Tomas taking four Jews to the Spanish border. They took Tomas to the Gestapo headquarters in Sustary and then deported him to Buchenwald in the summer of 1943. I don't know what happened to the poor Jews." After a long pause, she added: "We can't blame everything on the Germans, Sandy. We hated them, for what they did to people and *for being here.* But we ourselves were responsible for some of the terrible things that happened." Gabrielle was twenty-eight years old when the Germans arrived in her mountain community one cold December day in 1942, by which time her fiancé had already spent two years in Germany as a prisoner of war.

During the course of my fieldwork, several other survivors of the Occupation echoed Gabrielle's resentment about the long-term presence of the Germans in their mountain valley (A. Carricart, M. Idiart, M.-L. Lascombes

1978: pers. comms.). Such resentment arose in part from the Germans' requisitioning of property, which had more than economic value for the local people. Their resentment also derived from notions of space and belonging, recurring themes in this book. Although Gabrielle's remark about responsibility (*ardüra*) struck me forcibly at the time, I did not fully appreciate it until 2003–2004, when questions about responsibility arose repeatedly as elderly Xiberoans recalled events and experiences during the Occupation and afterward. As they made clear, responsibility entailed individual acceptance of the consequences of one's actions.

By the spring of 1977, Gabrielle and I had established an evening routine that included watching the news on television and then sitting beside the open fire. Gabrielle took a keen interest in my learning Basque and in my ethnographic research. Taking up her knitting or some unfinished sewing, she always sat opposite me while I wrote my field notes and often quizzed me about what I had learned that day. One evening our conversation returned to the Occupation, and I mentioned the Garat family. From another local woman, I knew that Tomas Garat's father had also been arrested and deported by the Germans. By revealing such knowledge, without identifying my source, I hoped that Gabrielle might be persuaded to tell me more about the tragedy. Once people knew that I had gained a basic understanding of a delicate local matter, they often felt more disposed to give me details. As one woman explained, the burden of responsibility rested with the first person to divulge information that a household or the wider community regarded as confidential (A. Carricart 1977: pers. comm.).

Gabrielle eventually told me that a local man had "sold" (*saldu*) Tomas to the Germans. Among Xiberoans who experienced the Occupation, selling someone to the enemy constituted the most despicable kind of betrayal, not simply because the act entailed reward (or the promise of it). When a denouncer and the denounced belonged to the same community, the act violated rules of conduct requiring members of a community to trust one another and uphold solidarity in the face of opposition from outsiders (*arrotzak* or strangers). When Gabrielle identified the denouncer of Tomas Garat in 1978, she asked me not to judge the man, who knew Tomas and his family well. "You are not a 'here person' (*hebenkua*), Sandy," Gabrielle explained. "You weren't born here, so you don't have a right to judge the person who betrayed Tomas. Only we have that right as members of this community."

During my first years of fieldwork in Xiberoa, my intellectual interests did not focus on twentieth-century wars, the Resistance, or the German Occupation. In the 1970s I concentrated on the institutions, values, and complex systems of exchange that ordered secular and spiritual life in rural Xiberoan communities (Ott 1993b). Basques with direct experience of the Occupation often used the war as a point of reference when they talked about the ways in which life there had changed in their lifetimes. People referred to the German Occupation as "the black time" (*denbora beltza*). Many informants insisted that it was too soon to talk about what had happened during that period. They felt too close to their recent past, to which the present remained painfully and awkwardly connected in spite of their attempts to forget and to forgive wrongdoing. Yet a core of men and women who had endured the Occupation wanted me to appreciate the dangers they had faced, their anxieties and hardships. In rare moments of privacy, they told me about tragic cases in which people had triggered German aggression against themselves and their fellow citizens. Uneasy relatives sometimes interrupted such conversations and usually terminated them by saying that "Sandy doesn't need to know such things." People talked much more freely when the social process of remembering the war focused on practices that gave stability and order to the community. They were eager for me to appreciate that the Basques had sometimes coped effectively and imaginatively with the Occupation.

More than thirty years have now passed since my first conversations about local denunciations in Xiberoa and the right of "here people" to judge wrongdoers in their midst. In 2003 word spread quickly across Xiberoa that I wanted to write about the Resistance, even though I tried to impress upon people that my interests broadly focused on trans-Pyrenean relations, the impact of Vichy and German occupation on Xiberoans and their society, and the process of liberation. I was interested in the experiences not only of resisters, but also of ordinary citizens who had simply endured those often difficult and strange years. Xiberoan resistance had a prominent place in the popular imagination for two main reasons: first, the public dimension of social remembering has long been dominated by veterans of the two main, rival resistance groups that operated in Xiberoa during 1943–44. Second, a play about Xiberoan resistance (*The Maquis of Xiberoa*), written by a Xiberoan and performed by amateur Xiberoan actors in 2001, had given rise to heated debate, in public and private spheres, about "what really happened" during the summer of 1944, when resisters took military action against the Germans and several Xiberoan communities became victims of reprisal.

During 2003–2004, Xiberoans watched my growing network of contacts with great interest and began to fill in gaps. They introduced me to people who had survived deportation to Nazi camps, to evaders of Vichy's obligatory work service (STO), and to the loved ones they had left behind. I met former prisoners of war, clandestine guides who passed fugitives across the Pyrenees, couriers for the Resistance, and former members of the numerous escape and intelligence networks that operated across Xiberoa. My research on trans-Pyrenean relations led me to former Spanish Republican exiles who had sought refuge in Xiberoa to escape Franco's forces, and I became interested in relations between Xiberoans and displaced populations in the 1930s and early 1940s, including Jewish refugees who remained in Pau for the duration of the Occupation.[1] Through a local Catholic school in Maule, I met Jewish people who had been helped by Xiberoans during Vichy and the Occupation. I also worked closely with fifty-two other people who had lived through the turmoil of the 1930s and 1940s with no claims to heroic deeds or miraculous escapes from enemy hands. I had known some of them since 1976, and many lamented that I was now "too late" to make a comprehensive study of the Occupation, since so many people "who knew what happened" had died (M. Eyheramendy 2003: pers. comm.; K. Irigaray 2001: pers. comm.).[2]

As I listened to twenty-first-century survivors of Vichy and German occupation, I was struck by the frequency with which people displayed two conflicting tendencies: the need to question the legitimacy of moral and legal judgments made more than sixty years ago, and the desire to refrain from moral judgment about fellow citizens altogether. During the social process of remembering their past, informants regularly reminded themselves, and me, that life was not normal during the German Occupation. People did things that they would never do in ordinary circumstances, and it was thus unfair to judge them. Yet, informants constantly engaged in a process of moral judgment as they talked about the dilemmas Xiberoans had faced and assessed the choices they had made. Informants often focused on controversial figures whose actions had divided entire communities in the late 1930s and 1940s: local elites who played instrumental roles in the arrest and deportation of communists; mayors whose relations with the Germans were variously classified as collaboration or as successful mediation for the public good; resisters from elsewhere in France whose reckless actions jeopardized the safety of the local population; and ordinary civilians who used the Germans for economic gain, to settle personal scores, or simply to survive.

During the first half of the twentieth century, the Basque province of Xiberoa was a place of refuge, conflict, transit, exile, and foreign occupation. At the liberation of France in 1944, many Xiberoans confronted ongoing local divisiveness rooted in the interwar years and faced new conflicts arising from legal and civic judgments made during Vichy and German occupation. This book traces the roots of their divided memories to local and official interpretations of what constituted legitimate judgment, legitimate behavior, and justice during those troubled times. I deal with two processes of judgment. One process operated through legal justice (*legetarzün* in Xiberoan

Basque, *légalité* in French) based upon the written laws of the state and administered by its judicial system. The other process operated through popular justice (*züzenbide,* which conveys the notion of doing what is right, legitimate, justifiable; *légitimité*), based upon the unwritten moral codes and practices of a community and administered by the informal courts of public opinion, rumor, and certain ritualized forms of public humiliation and condemnation (such as the charivari).

As happened elsewhere in the Pyrenees, a Xiberoan community had a long-standing right to judge its own citizens and to address wrongdoing that threatened local order and stability. That dual, community-based right underpinned Xiberoans' wish to manage their own justice and intracommunity conflicts without intervention from the external authorities. In certain other circumstances, Xiberoans chose or were forced to seek legal justice and be judged by outsiders. I show how Xiberoans tried to manage justice and conflict during the interwar years and the 1940s and explain why some Xiberoans still question the legitimacy of civic and legal judgments made more than sixty years ago. The moral community provides an analytical tool with which to understand the process of community-based judgment. Drawing upon archives, memoirs, and fieldwork, I show how distinctions between insiders and outsiders defined the boundaries of the moral community in spatial and linguistic terms, in social and symbolic acts, in customary law, in trans-Pyrenean treaties, and in popular culture. Membership in a moral community entailed a shared habitus, compliance with certain moral codes and behavioral norms, and validation by public opinion.

Xiberoan customary law obliged citizens to protect two primordial Pyrenean institutions from internal and external harm: the house (*etxea*) and the community (*herria*). During the 1930s and 1940s, that obligation took on a new meaning for the holders of civic, moral, and military authority responsible for the safety and well-being of Xiberoan communities. In the moral community of traditionally conservative Basques, potential sources of harm included exiled Spanish Republicans, Jewish refugees, communists, Freemasons, anticlerical schoolteachers, and the Germans who occupied Xiberoa from early December 1942 until late August 1944. In the chapters that follow, I consider the ways in which certain mayors, priests, notables, resistance leaders, and ordinary citizens responded to insiders and outsiders who, in their judgment, threatened Xiberoan lives and property.

Four different Xiberoan communities provide a local focus for my examination of borderland Basques and their responses to war, occupation, and displacement: the small industrial town of Maule, the nearby hamlet of Ospitaleku, the market town of Sustary, and the mountain commune of Urdos on the Franco-Spanish border. Located fifteen miles north of the international boundary, Maule had a resident population of approximately four thousand people in 1936 and was the province's main industrial and commercial center. The town also served as the cantonal seat for Lower Xiberoa, where a further six thousand people lived in outlying villages and the rural countryside (Viers 1961: 40). Maule was a culturally diverse town in which ethnic, political, and socioeconomic differences often gave rise to tensions between the indigenous Basque population and the town's immigrant "Spanish" community long before the Germans arrived. The Germans occupied the town for much of 1943–44 and often clashed with the rival resistance groups that operated in the province. In nearby Ospitaleku two inns, a medieval church, and a cluster of farmhouses formed the heart of the hamlet, whose citizens gained their livelihood through small-scale agriculture and trade with townspeople. Although German patrols and convoys often passed through the surrounding countryside, rural hamlets such as Ospitaleku usually had little contact with the enemy. In the summer of 1944, however, the Ospitaleku people were deeply divided by the brief presence of a maquis in their community. In search of the *maquisards* and their supporters, six hundred German troops descended upon the hamlet, with tragic consequences.

On the eve of the Second World War, the market town of Sustary had around one thousand inhabitants, whose shops and other commercial enterprises attracted clientele from the rural, mountainous communities of Upper Xiberoa, including Urdos. Some five thousand people lived in Upper Xiberoa at that time. Unlike Maule and Ospitaleku, Sustary and the borderland commune of Urdos were continuously occupied by Germans from December 1942 until the Liberation in August 1944. In Sustary denunciations and collaboration with the Germans threatened to tear an already divided society further apart. The people of Urdos, by contrast, enjoyed considerable social and spiritual solidarity before the Germans arrived and combated the divisiveness of local denunciations through certain traditional, rural Basque practices.

Although these four communities lie within a twenty-mile radius, their people had widely differing experiences in their relations with one another, with the Vichy and German authorities, and with the numerous strangers who passed through their territory in search of food, shelter, and work during civil wars and world wars. In order to make sense of that web of human experience, I begin not with Vichy and the German Occupation, but with a more distant, still dynamic past that is not separated from the present. The lens needs to be widened by examining the historical and cultural roots of Xiberoan society as a Pyrenean borderland area.

1: Insiders, Outsiders, and Trans-Pyrenean Relations

In the late nineteenth and early twentieth centuries, the Basques were by no means unique among French citizens in their distrust of strangers and the caution with which they "treated not only the unfamiliar, but everyone who was not part of their community" (M. Weber 1976: 49). Like the people of many other regions in France, the Basques distinguished insiders (natives) from outsiders (strangers) in a variety of ways: in spatial and linguistic terms, in social and symbolic acts, in their customary laws and trans-Pyrenean treaties, and in forms of popular culture that clearly distinguished between "good" people (natives) and "bad" people (foreign charlatans and enemy-outsiders). When war and foreign occupation strike at the heart of what people cherish most in life, they force people to focus on essential matters and alter the ways in which they view themselves and others. How did Xiberoans define themselves and the Other during the first decades of the twentieth century? What perceptions, actions, and appreciations characterized their relations with other borderland citizens of France and Spain during the Great War and inter-war years?

No single, homogeneous moral community existed in Xiberoa, owing to long-standing traditions of trans-Pyrenean migration, immigration, and human displacement brought about by civil wars and world wars. Although Xiberoa was relatively isolated geographically, even its most secluded inhabitants had contacts with the world around them, fleetingly in the case of itinerant populations, and continuously in the case of neighboring Pyreneans in whose habitus Xiberoans saw both difference and similarity. A substantial number of Spanish and southern Basque neighbors settled in Xiberoa during the first decades of the twentieth century, and the process by means of which they tried to become insiders forms an important part of Xiberoan contemporary history, especially in relation to the Resistance.

The notion of the moral community developed in this book draws primarily upon departmental archives, fieldwork, and studies of some sixteenth-century Basque customs and norms that still had relevance in the 1940s (Bidart 1977; Desplats 1982; Heiberg 1989; Lauburu 1998). The moral community contains components of Pierre Bourdieu's concept of habitus as a system of durable, transposable tendencies that integrate past experiences and function as a matrix of perceptions, appreciations, and actions (Bourdieu 1977: 82–83). A habitus is a lived environment consisting of practices, rules, inherited expectations, norms, and sanctions imposed by both the law and neighborhood pressures (Thompson 1991: 102).[1] One key component of habitus is central to the notion of the moral community: habitus as social space, as a shared sense of one's own (and others') place and role in the lived environment (Hillier and Rooksby 2002: 3, 5).

Xiberoans had a strong sense of attachment to their place of origin, a specific sociophysical space (*xokhoa,* "the space where one is") that included not simply their dwellings and other property, but all the communal land, flora, and fauna that came within the geographical-administrative boundaries of their community.[2] Xiberoans defined their personhood through the house (*etxea*), the neighborhood (*aizoa*) and the community in which they were born (*herria*). Xiberoans shared a habitus, a common culture, and certain customary rights, values and expectations that guided their behavior and shaped their perceptions of what constituted right and wrong in human actions and desires. As happened elsewhere in the Basque Country, membership in a Xiberoan moral community required compliance with certain moral codes, values, and behavioral norms (Heiberg 1989: 146–47). Membership also required validation by public opinion, which served as a primary arbitrator and protector of the Xiberoan house and local norms, values, and morality in all spheres.

Basque-speaking Xiberoans made a fundamental distinction between two categories of people: those who belonged to a particular house (who were *etxeko,* literally "of the house") and those who were strangers (*arrotzak*) to it. An *arrotz* was someone whose practices and behavior seemed strange and socially unacceptable, whose culture and upbringing were contrary to those of a Xiberoan Basque (Peillen 1997: 453).[3] Strangers were perceived as *auher* (which denotes both "useless" and "lazy") and as a potential source of danger and harm to the two most powerful institutions in Xiberoan society: the house and the community of inhabitants. Xiberoans who belonged to a community by birth were also classified as "here people" (*hebenkuak*), an inclusive social category of insiders native to a particular village, commune, or town. A native Xiberoan who emigrated permanently to another place relinquished entitlement to the category of "here people," which required residency in the community or, in the case of military conscription, seasonal migratory labor or emigration, a widely accepted intention to return permanently to it. Xiberoans classified Basques who resided in a Xiberoan community but came from elsewhere in the province as *herriko* ("of the community") and as *kanpotarrak* ("people who come from the outside"). Such residents had civic rights and duties, but they could never become "here people" in a community that was not their birthplace.

Xiberoan Basques tended to regard their culture as distinct from those of adjacent borderland communities in France and Spain. In the first decades of the twentieth century, they had a reputation for ethnocentricity among people from neighboring *pays* on both sides of the Pyrenees. Basque-speaking Xiberoans contended that their dialect (*üska*) was more pure than the dialects spoken by all other Basques (classified as Manex, the Basque word for "Jean," which also denotes a particular race of black-faced sheep). French Basques from the province of Behe Nafarroa, west of Xiberoa, and the Béarnais, to the north and east, tended to regard Xiberoans as culturally arrogant; Xiberoans, in turn, disdained intermarriage with both groups. One Xiberoan proverb captures their ethnic prejudice against Behe Nafarroan Basques: "Only evil winds and evil wives come from Manex territory" (*Manexetik eztela aize tzar eta emazte tzar baizik jiten*). Xiberoans often branded Occitans and Gascons as braggarts and nicknamed them "crocodiles" owing to their "big mouths and little feet" (*aho handiak eta aztaparra txipiak*) (Peillen 1997: 455). In the face of opposition or criticism from the Béarnais and Gascons, however, Xiberoans and Behe Nafarroans united as culturally proud, mutually supportive Basques, especially when their non-Basque neighbors mocked the Basques' lack of fluency in the French language. Mutual support and camaraderie among Xiberoans and other northern Basques played a particularly important role during the First World War, a major turning point in Basques' perceptions of themselves in relation to the French state and their understanding of non-Basque French citizens.

In the first decades of the twentieth century, lowland Xiberoans often regarded people of Spanish origin and descent (Espaiñulak) as their racial and ethnic inferiors and as political troublemakers. In Lower Xiberoa, where the largest concentration of Espaiñulak lived, indigenous Basques commonly referred to them as "evil Spaniards" (*tzar* Espaiñulak) and as "Reds" or "red craws" (Gorriak or *papogorriak, les rouge-gorges* in French).[4] Although many of the Spanish workers and day laborers who settled in the industrial town of Maule were socialists and communists in the interwar years, northern Basques often applied the epithet "Red" without regard for the political ideology embraced by the Spaniards in their midst. Relations between Upper Xiberoans and their borderland neighbors in Nafarroa were, by contrast, rarely tinged with racial or ethnic prejudice. Borderland Xiberoans and the Nafarroans of the Erronkari (Roncal) Valley recognized similarities in their cultures, even as they constantly reaffirmed their separate identities and the customary rights attached to the adjacent spaces in which they lived.

In many parts of France, rural people had a long-standing dislike and fear of the laws and law enforcers external to their moral communities. Among the Basques, the concept of justice separated outsiders (police inspectors, gendarmes, and magistrates, among others, who came from elsewhere) from insiders, those who belonged to the *pays,* to local territory and local, familiar spaces: to the province of Xiberoa, to a particular valley, parish, or community. For the Basques, justice derived from what was good and morally right and was inextricably linked to Basque customary law as a protector and guarantor of the two primordial Basque (and Pyrenean) institutions: the house and the community. Among Xiberoan Basques, where "every community has its law, every house has its custom" (*Herriak beren legea, etxeak beren hastüra*), a community's desire to manage its own affairs and system of justice dates back to at least the sixteenth century, when the customary laws of the *pays* were first codified.

In Xiberoa the common good of the village or valley community took precedence over the interests of any individual, and citizens had a collective obligation to defend the community from both external and internal harm. In order to do so, people exercised a long-standing civic right to make moral judgments about their fellow citizens (insiders and outsiders) and, in certain contexts, to address wrongdoing that threatened to disrupt local society. The roots of legitimate, community-based judgment lay in Xiberoan customary law. Codified on the instructions of Francis I in 1520, this set of laws (la Coutume de la Soule) guaranteed the liberty of all individuals born or permanently resident in Xiberoa and granted them the rights to bear arms in self-defense, to hunt, to fish, to pasture their livestock, and to construct and use their own mills (Cordier 1859; Grosclaude 1993). A substantial part of the Coutume concerned Xiberoans' jural rights and obligations in relation to rules of succession and inheritance; matrimonial and family matters; free enjoyment (*libre jouissance*); and free passage (*libre passage*) in the mountain pastures, the right to use the herding huts there, and the right of *carnal,* which entitled a shepherding syndicate to confiscate outsiders' livestock that strayed into Xiberoan territory (Lefebvre 1933: 190; Nussy Saint-Saëns 1955: 66, 90). The Coutume also established legal frameworks for the local administration of justice in both civil and criminal law, granting ordinary citizens the right to vote on matters considered by the Xiberoan general assembly (the Silviet), a democratic institution through which Xiberoans administered their own affairs (Grosclaude 1993; Larrieu 1899: 466; Nussy Saint-Saëns 1955: 99).

The notion of a moral community appears in eighteenth-century judicial and notarial records for territory now within the department of the Pyrénées-Atlantiques and including Xiberoa (Desplats 1982: 59).[5] During the eighteenth century, a Xiberoan community had a right to intervene in the private lives of citizens and any resident outsiders who broke its moral codes. Citizens mediated relations between the moral community and the official judiciary (jurats and courts) responsible for administering legal justice. If villagers suspected an illegitimate pregnancy, they called upon jurats (insiders to the moral community) to confront the young woman about her alleged moral transgression and to ascertain the identity of the genitor. Such visitations also addressed accusations of adultery, concubinage, and prostitution and served as community-based constraints against improper social and sexual behavior. In the eighteenth century, illegitimate births gave rise to greater community-based concern than adultery, for an external judiciary dictated that a Xiberoan community had a moral responsibility to feed unwed mothers too poor to support themselves and their illegitimate offspring. Citizens were particularly disgruntled when such unwed mothers were outsiders to the community (*arrotzak,* non-Xiberoans, or *kanpotarrak,* women from elsewhere in Xiberoa).[6]

Until the French Revolution, every Xiberoan parish had a guardian (*sainho*), a hereditary position attached to a particular house. The guardian monitored the actions of his fellow citizens, organized parish assemblies, and acted as the local bailiff. According to the Coutume, he did not, however, have the power to administer justice as a judge (Grosclaude 1993: 14–15). Unwritten moral laws placed communal constraints upon citizens, whose private lives came under the scrutiny of the guardian. When public opinion found an individual guilty of immoral behavior, a citizen could legitimately denounce the wrongdoer to the community, for in the Basque Country and neighboring Béarn, the eighteenth-century charters of some valleys condoned and even institutionalized denunciation as a means of social control (Bidart 1977: 55–56). By reporting infractions against written and unwritten laws to the authorities, a citizen fulfilled his civic duty to the moral community.[7] As intermediaries between community and courts, the guardian could call upon the official judiciary to caution or penalize wrongdoers (Desplats 1982: 59), but according to Xiberoan custom, the community itself had a right to do so as well, in spite of opposition from the legal authorities.

The eighteenth century brought the decline of traditional Xiberoan institutions such as the Silviet (Régnier 1991: 245). In 1790 Xiberoa came under the jurisdiction of the newly created department of the Basses-Pyrénées, which included the Basque provinces of Lapurdi, Behe Nafarroa, Xiberoa, as well as Béarn. The department was further divided into districts (*arrondissements*), cantons, and communes, each of which corresponded to a village or a valley community of several villages (Gomez-Ibáñez 1975: 59–60). Following the tradition of the medieval Pyrenean valley community, Xiberoan communes were jural entities that could own and administer property. Although the state had in theory suppressed customary law, Xiberoans continued to regard the Coutume as their legal charter, particularly in relation to inheritance practices and communal resources such as the high mountain pastures along the Franco-Spanish border. In an attempt to reconstitute the province of Xiberoa as a corporate sociospatial entity and to regulate the exploitation of natural resources, the departmental prefect created the Syndicate of the *pays* of Xiberoa in 1836 (Nussy Saint-Saëns 1955: 154). The citizens of two Xiberoan borderland communes (including Urdos) refused to join the Syndicate, which, they argued, contravened the rights and privileges established in Xiberoan customary law. The two communes thus retained ownership of and controlled access to the physical space in which they lived and exploited for their livelihood.

Most of the democratic institutions through which Xiberoans had long administered their own affairs had ceased to exist by the nineteenth century, but with the connivance of local notaries, most citizens still protected the integrity of the house by practicing impartible inheritance, in accordance with Xiberoan customary law but deviating from standard republican practice, which required the equal division of property among all offspring. In Upper Xiberoa, households also continued to exercise four-hundred-year-old pastoral rights granted by customary law (Nussy Saint-Saëns 1955: 89; Ott 1993b: 131–50). These rights were particularly important to borderland communes such as Urdos, not only because their economy revolved around sheep and cheese making; borderland Basques also had a particularly acute sense of attachment to the mountains (F. and M. Eyheralt 2000: pers. comm.). These factors played a major role in shaping local attitudes toward the Germans who occupied the frontier zone from early December 1942 until August 1944. Borderland Xiberoans, in particular, deeply resented the Germans' presence on territory that was not simply a physical space, but also an inextricable part of their personhood and spirituality and of their community's identity. That close attachment to the mountains also explains, in part, the tensions that arose between borderland Basques when their livestock strayed across the Franco-Spanish frontier. If the territorial boundaries of Pyrenean Basque communities were mutually respected, trans-Pyrenean relations were characterized by cooperation, mutual aid, and complicity when authorities representing the French and Spanish states confronted borderland Basques.

Flanking the oldest and arguably most stable political boundary in Europe, Xiberoa has long been closely linked to Nafarroa and Aragón, its southern neighbors in Spain, through traditions of trans-Pyrenean socioeconomic exchange and cooperation (Sahlins 1989: 1). Military conscription, political oppression and persecution, opportunities in trade and commerce, and trans-Pyrenean kinship ties have all, at various stages in contemporary Xiberoan history, contributed to a constant two-directional movement of people, goods, and information across that border, which Basques on both sides of the Pyrenees have used to their advantage for centuries (Bray 2004; Douglass 1975; Sahlins 1989). Reaching elevations of more than six thousand feet along the Xiberoan-Navarrese frontier, the Pyrenees have long served as a channel of two-directional communication.

Local people, rather than diplomats, established the boundaries that eventually separated the nation-states of France and Spain (Lafourcade 1998: 340–41). From as early as 1171, but mainly from the fourteenth century, valley communities along what was to become the international boundary drew up pastoral treaties (*faceries* or *traités de lies et passeries*) that fixed and marked out the precise limits of communal pasturage on both sides of the Pyrenees.[8] The conventions regulated the use of water and wood as well as the passage of livestock and established zones of compascuity where livestock from either side of the mountains could graze together (Cavaillès 1986: 11–13; Gomez-Ibáñez 1975: 25, 45). Such valley communities enjoyed a large measure of autonomy as juridical, economic, and relatively isolated geographical entities. Their treaties sought to establish peaceful trans-Pyrenean relations and imposed sanctions upon those who threatened the well-being of people or their property. In order to enforce such sanctions, neighboring valleys appointed one or two local agents to prevent borderland conflict and to oversee the space about which most intervalley arguments arose: pasturage, livestock, and hunting rights.

The most celebrated of all the Pyrenean treaties, drawn up in 1375, obliged the valley of Baretous in Béarn (along the northern and eastern borders of Xiberoa) to pay annual tribute to the Navarrese valley of Erronkari (Roncal). On July 13 the seven mayors of Erronkari's valley communities met the seven mayors and notary from Baretous at the Rock of St. Martin on the border between Béarn, Nafarroa, and Xiberoa. In an elaborate ceremony, the Béarnais notary swore on a cross that the people of Baretous would uphold their pact with the people of Erronkari and thus ensure peaceful relations between the two Pyrenean valleys. The Baretous mayors presented their Erronkari counterparts with three heifers and then invited the people of Baretous and Erronkari to eat together (Cavaillès 1986: 42–43). Two other treaties linked the Xiberoan borderland communities of Larraiña and Urdos to the Navarrese valleys of Zaraitzu and Erronkari respectively (Gomez-Ibáñez 1975: 46). During the wars of succession in Spain, borderland valleys along the Pyrenees continued to communicate with each other, engage in economic exchange, and protect each other's interests against those of their sovereigns (Lafourcade 1998: 343).

Drawn up in 1659, the Treaty of the Pyrenees identified that mountain range as the official division between France and Spain and incorporated many trans-Pyrenean treaties (*faceries*) into the international agreement. In 1856 the Treaty of Bayonne officially recognized the *faceries,* but only two treaties retained all of their original features: the treaty between the northern Basque *pays de Cize* and the southern Basque valley of Aezcoa, and the treaty between the Béarnais valley of Baretous and Erronkari Valley in Nafarroa (Lafourcade 1998: 343). In 1868 commissioners in the northern Basque coastal city of Baiona (Bayonne) delimited the Franco-Spanish boundary by establishing an imaginary border between two national territories (Sahlins 1989: 6–7). That international boundary did not, however, interrupt trans-Pyrenean relations.

From at least as early as the mid-nineteenth century, the seasonal migrations of trans-Pyrenean workers strengthened socioeconomic ties between Xiberoa and Béarn and their southern neighbors in Spain, notably the Erronkari Valley in Nafarroa and the valleys of Fago, Hecho, and Ansó in Aragón. In Erronkari the local economy revolved around the lumber industry and transhumance. Erronkari men were renowned as lumberjacks and as rafters (*almadieros*), who transported logs down Navarrese rivers as far as Saragossa on the Ebro (Inchauspé 2001: 4). Many of the lumberjacks sought seasonal work in the forests of Xiberoa and further north in the Landes. From the 1870s until 1930, the Erronkari Valley and the Aragonese valleys of Fago, Hecho, and Ansó were the main source of seasonal manual labor in the sandal-making factories of Maule, the capital of Xiberoa (Ikherzaleak 1994: 13). Known as "the Swallows," the migrant workers were mainly young unmarried women. The Swallows regularly passed through the borderland commune of Urdos in their seasonal trans-Pyrenean journeys. During my fieldwork in the 1970s, elderly Urdos people still had vivid memories of the young Spanish and southern Basque migrants, who often sang as they made their way across the mountains and along the rough tracks that linked Urdos to the lowlands.

Urdos Basques knew some of the Navarrese families whose daughters became Swallows and whose sons became unskilled or semiskilled laborers in France (G. Harispe 1979: pers. comm.; B. Hondagneu 1979: pers. comm.), because the Urdos people had long-standing relations with northern Navarrese Basques through shepherding, cheese making, seasonal agricultural work, trade, and smuggling. Urdos and Navarrese shepherds came into regular, close contact during the period of summer transhumance from May to September, when flocks from the valleys of Erronkari, Zaraitzu, and Ansó moved north to the Xiberoan border. The largest flocks came from the Erronkari village of Izaba, where five caciques owned more than six thousand sheep in the first decades of the twentieth century. One of the wealthiest caciques was elected mayor of Izaba in 1931 (Altaffaylla 2003: 521). Like his wealthy counterparts, the mayor hired Urdos shepherds during the period of summer transhumance, for they were widely regarded as the region's best cheese makers (F. Eyheralt 2000: pers. comm.; J.-P. Jonnet 1978: pers. comm.; Peillen 1997: 470).

Contrary to Xiberoans' insistence upon their cultural uniqueness, rural Xiberoan social organization had much in common with that of neighboring Pyrenean territories. Xiberoans, the Béarnais, the northern Navarrese, and the people of Upper Aragón all derived their social identity from the house, an institution central to Pyrenean societies (Bourdieu 2002: 24; Violant i Simorra 1986: 318). The people of all four areas practiced impartible inheritance as a means of preserving the integrity of the house from one generation to the next. In all four borderland zones, institutionalized vicinal relations linked houses in a web of mutual rights and obligations.

In many respects the people of Erronkari had closer social, cultural, and commercial ties with Xiberoans than with their fellow Navarrese (Altaffaylla 2003: 521). Although the Erronkari people jokingly referred to Xiberoans as Frenchified Pyreneans (*gabachos*), people from the two provinces spoke similar dialects of Basque and shared many of the same values and customs (Estornés Lasa 1996: 38). Izaba and Urdos Basques classified each other as neighbor communities (*herri-aizoak*), a relationship based upon the rural Basque institution of first neighbors (*lehen aizoak*), which permanently linked two or more houses as givers and receivers of goods and services (Ott 1993b). Although feuds over pasturage sometimes strained relations between such borderland Basques, "neighbor communities" shared the dual obligation of providing mutual assistance in times of crisis and cooperating in matters affecting the management of borderland spaces and borderland affairs such as mutually beneficial trade (especially contraband), labor exchange, and the provision of shelter, food, and aid during civil wars and world wars.

Urdos men regularly attended dances and festivals in Izaba. They spoke Spanish, as well as the local patois that freely mixed Erronkari and Xiberoan Basque with Spanish (Estornés Lasa 1996: 69–74; F. Eyheralt 1979: pers. comm.; G. Harispe 1978: pers. comm.). Urdos women also traveled to Izaba on a regular basis for commercial reasons, making the twenty-mile return journey to Izaba to sell donkeys, piglets, wild agaric mushrooms, cheeses, peppers, and woolen cloth (G. Harriguileheguy 1979: pers. comm.). The women spoke the Izaba patois and were well known among Izaba merchants for their tenacity in haggling over prices and the terms of their bartering (D. Prebende 1979: pers. comm.). Although the people of Izaba and Urdos often bore close physical resemblances, few intermarriages took place between the two communities during the first half of the twentieth century. Both Izaba and Urdos Basques disapproved of village exogamy, which they regarded as "marriage with strangers" (Inchauspé 2001: 3). In both borderland places, the moral community expressed its disapproval of an exogamous marriage in a practice known as the *naharr* (literally, thorn or bramble). When a stranger tried to enter the community on his wedding day, local young men blocked his path with an arc of thorns and forced him to pay a fine before allowing him to proceed to the church. The money was then distributed among the community's eligible young women as an incentive for them to marry local men (G. Harriguileheguy 1979: pers. comm.; Violant y Simorra 1985: 286). *Naharra* was a form of popular justice that sought to protect the two primary Pyrenean institutions, the house and the community.

In Xiberoa the private sphere of the house and the public sphere of the community overlapped when citizens exercised their long-standing right to judge one another through the informal courts of public opinion and to address certain types of wrongdoing by means of popular justice. When attempts to hide domestic strife failed and neighbors became aware of it, Xiberoan moral codes required such neighbors to refrain from malicious gossip, which was widely regarded as the work of "bad tongues" (*mihigaixtoak* in Basque, *les mauvaises langues* or *les langues de vipère* in French). Such gossip included slander and injurious information about an individual or household that had not been widely accepted as truth by the community. In both town and countryside, people who engaged in harmful gossip could expect social ostracism, avoidance, or at least extreme wariness from fellow citizens keen to observe local rules about legitimate means of sharing information. "Bad tongues" focused on alleged immoral behavior by other members of their community, including sexual promiscuity, adultery, and other kinds of moral treachery. In public or semipublic settings, "bad tongues" also gossiped about alleged improper behavior, including domestic violence, excessive quarreling, inheritance disputes, and a range of incompetent behaviors, such as laziness, selfishness, lack of control in sexual matters, drunkenness, poor decision making, and inefficient management of privately owned property and resources.

Rule-abiding citizens also engaged in such gossip, but any exchange of detailed information and opinion about moral turpitude could only legitimately take place within the privacy of the house and in the presence of its adult members. Heads of household took considerable care to exclude their children and any visitors from such conversations. If a neighbor came to the door during a discussion about someone's misfortunes or immoral conduct, family members quickly fell silent or abruptly changed the topic. If the family enjoyed particularly amicable relations with a neighbor, local standards of conduct permitted male and female heads of household to test the visitor's knowledge of local scandal without openly interrogating him or her.

A similar set of rules applied to public places of sociability, such as taverns, markets, shops, the post office, communal fountains, and washhouses. In the public sphere of the community, people tried to avoid being the first person to divulge information about conflict within a house, moral treachery, or other scandals, but once accusatory rumors had begun to circulate that a certain house was disordered (*barreatu*) or a particular person had committed a serious moral offence, the Xiberoan moral community exercised its right to judge the sentiments and actions of that citizen by means of public rumor (*ots* or *aipü* in Basque; *la rumeur publique* in French). Public rumor consisted of information accepted as truth, whether or not it was official, by a majority of those who belonged to the town or village. It was not created by a homogeneous public at large, but by individuals who felt concerned about particular events and behaviors in their community, as well as their social and political consequences (Kapferer 1995: 108). Citizens received and circulated information about alleged wrongdoing through a range of social practices such as gossip, speculation, shared confidences, and accusatory rumors.

Xiberoans disliked uninvited attempts by outsiders to interfere in their affairs, especially in matters relating to the private sphere of the house. Households prided themselves on their ability to uphold local values and codes of conduct and cultivated a self-image of harmony and solidarity when facing the scrutiny of outsiders. In the first half of the twentieth century, Xiberoans still recognized the right of a community to address certain forms of moral treachery without interference from external authorities. A community had recourse to three closely related forms of popular justice that can be traced to sixteenth-century practice: bell noise (*tzintzarrotz,* a type of charivari), the donkey ride (*asto lasterka* or *la course à l'âne* in French), and strewing greenery (*berdürak* or *la jonchée*). Neither world wars nor the socioeconomic crises of the interwar years interrupted such traditions in the rural countryside and small towns of Xiberoa (Desplats 1982: 158). All three rituals of popular justice constituted informal tribunals in which local people condemned sexual and conjugal misconduct by their fellow citizens and, by extension, their houses. The agents of such community-based judgment were usually young men. The moral community strictly forbade children to take part and normally excluded women as well.

The *tzintzarrotz* generally focused on the remarriage of a widow or widower who was too old to procreate and whose second spouse still had reproductive capability (A. Carricart 1978: pers. comm.), for a sterile second union did not contribute to the continuity of the house. Often initiated by a brother-in-law of one of the victims, the noisy disturbance involved a varying number of protesters, who had to be "here people." (The community did not normally allow outsiders to take part.) The group assembled a short distance from their victims' house and kept the couple awake much of the night by ringing bells, banging pots, reciting lewd rhymes, and firing guns. Clashes between victims and victimizers sometimes occurred, but more often the victims appeased the *charivariseurs* by paying them a sum of money or providing an ample quantity of cider or wine (Bidart 1977: 150; G. Harispe 1978: pers. comm.). In some cases the *tzintzarrotz* recurred nightly for several weeks. The instigators of bell noise generally made their intentions known to the wider community and sometimes used public rumor to warn the local gendarmerie several days in advance. The police rarely intervened, for they understood that in certain circumstances, Xiberoans safeguarded their long-standing right to judge one another and to seek popular justice. Law enforcers only became involved with great reluctance, when violence occurred. On rare occasions the agents of a charivari themselves became the victims of reprisal, when the man whom they had ridiculed or his family took revenge by wounding or, in exceptional cases, killing a *charivariseur* (Desplats 1982: 176–79).

Although the often violent tradition of the donkey ride disappeared in most of southwestern France during the nineteenth century, Xiberoans still used it to sanction unacceptable conjugal behavior in the interwar years (Desplats 1982: 95; G. Harispe 1979: pers. comm.). This form of popular justice ridiculed spouses who quarreled, husbands who tolerated physical abuse by their wives, and the wives themselves. The instigators strapped the victims backward on donkeys and forced the animals to run through crowds of jeering onlookers. In 1932, with donkeys and victims in tow, one crowd traveled more than five miles from Urdos and ended up in the market town of Sustary. The local constable respected the right of Urdos citizens to exercise popular justice and watched the crowd at a distance without intervening (Desplats 1982: 95; G. Harispe 1978: pers. comm.). Both bell noise and the donkey ride used the public ridicule of wrongdoers and, by extension their houses, as a means of social control.

As elsewhere in the Pyrenees, a Xiberoan community also had a right to sanction immoral behavior by means of a nocturnal practice known as strewing greenery (*berdürak*) (Desplats 1982: 171–73; Fabre and Traimond 1981: 23–24). An exceptionally grave sanction, the practice usually targeted adulterers and parodied the customary spreading of greenery and flowers between the houses of a bride and groom on their wedding day. Unlike the participants in the charivari, the instigators (usually men) spread greenery between the houses of adulterers during the night with no noise or violence. The men sought to preserve anonymity, and the unwritten laws of the moral community guaranteed their impunity, because moral codes obliged anyone who knew their identity to remain silent. Although people could legitimately speculate about the instigators within the privacy of their houses, the moral community disapproved of public or semipublic discussion about the agents of *berdürak,* who thus rarely became the focus of extrahousehold gossip or public rumor (A. Carricart 1979: pers. comm.; K. Irigaray 1978: pers. comm.). In keeping with the rural Xiberoan ethos of egalitarianism, the sanction targeted all wrongdoers, regardless of their sex, age, or secular or spiritual authority in the community. The Xiberoan moral community did not grant impunity to its wealthiest citizens, its politicians, its municipal officeholders, or its parish priest. As law enforcers of the state, the police had no right to interfere in *la jonchée,* for this form of popular justice did not figure in any article of the French penal code (Desplats 1982: 172), and the police, in any case, recognized the power of public opinion and its ritualized public manifestations to correct wrongdoing by insiders to the moral community. The enforcers of France's legal justice also understood Xiberoans' deep-rooted desire to manage their own affairs when their community became disordered by local wrongdoing. During both world wars, that desire often frustrated the external authorities in their attempts to identify and punish those who violated French law. As regional authorities noted again and again, the Basques were notoriously reluctant to turn a fellow insider over to representatives of the French state, even when the moral community recognized that an individual had committed an offence. During the Great War and the German Occupation, local reluctance to denounce a "here person" as a civic duty to an external power led many Basques to remain silent about the transgressions of a fellow citizen. In the borderland community of Urdos, such reluctance was particularly pronounced.

2: Urdos, a Borderland Moral Community

The commune of Urdos stretches ten miles along the Franco-Spanish border separating Xiberoa from the southern Basque province of Nafarroa in the most mountainous part of the northern Basque Country. Although its terrain is steep and rugged, with deep gorges and peaks reaching elevations of six thousand feet, Urdos was a favored point of passage for civilian and political refugees in the civil wars and world wars of twentieth-century France and Spain. The topography of Urdos provided easier routes across the international boundary than the Hautes-Pyrénées to the east of Xiberoa. Urdos also offered better cover for clandestine trans-Pyrenean crossings than the less mountainous terrain of Behe Nafarroa to the west.

On the eve of the Great War, Urdos had 883 inhabitants.[1] Divided socially and geographically into an upper and a lower community, the commune had nine named, rural neighborhoods with widely scattered farms. At the southern end of the valley, an eleventh-century church, the adjacent cemetery, the priest's house, and a cluster of farmhouses constituted the *bourg*. A mile away, a modest hotel-restaurant served as a center for local sociability during religious festivals and rites of passage. The hotel also catered to travelers, the occasional tourist, and lowland Xiberoans who vacationed there annually (G. Althapignet 2004: pers. comm.). At the northern end of the valley, a French customs house also served as the town hall. A nearby chapel and several taverns provided other venues of sociability for Urdos people, whose local economy revolved around sheep, cheese making, subsistence-based farming, trans-Pyrenean trade, and smuggling.

Every house owned a share in one of the many shepherding huts scattered along the high mountains on the Franco-Spanish border. The huts belonged to named shepherding syndicates that had existed at least as early as the sixteenth century. Xiberoan customary law defined the pastoral syndicates (*olhak* in Basque; *cayolars* in Béarnais) as a group of shepherds whose houses jointly owned a particular hut and who had a right to graze their communal flock and to make cheese in the high mountain pastures (Nussy Saint-Saëns 1955: 89).[2] Summer transhumance on both sides of the Pyrenees regularly brought Urdos men into contact with shepherds from other Xiberoan communities and from Nafarroa and Aragón in Spain.

In the early decades of the twentieth century, Urdos people spoke the Xiberoan dialect of Basque and often had fluency in Spanish and the patois of neighboring Béarn. Although French law forbade the use of Basque in school, children did not always gain fluency in French, owing to poor school attendance rates and a deep-seated cultural attachment to their own particular version of Xiberoan Basque (J. Lascombes 1978: pers. comm.).[3] Children learned Béarnais on farms in the Baretous Valley, where they worked as live-in servants in order to support themselves and make a modest cash contribution to their natal households.

In Urdos as in other rural communities, the house and the community constituted two powerful entities that shaped an individual's personhood. Both the house and the community sought to control access to their resources, to exercise power and authority over the use of those resources, and to maintain a long-standing Pyrenean tradition of autonomy in the management of their own affairs. The members of a household shared certain fundamental responsibilities with fellow citizens who belonged to the community by birth (*herritarrak*) or who qualified for the status of *herriko* ("of the community") through residence in a local house, in conjunction with social acceptance by *herritarrak*. Such acceptance was conferred upon an individual through public opinion, a process of collective, community-based judgment. Basque and Pyrenean custom obliged such citizens to preserve the integrity of both house and community and to protect them from internal divisiveness and external harm. They did so through the vestiges of Xiberoan customary law, through the unwritten laws of the moral community, and by means of certain social conventions.

Like its Pyrenean counterparts, the rural Basque house was not simply a physical structure; it was also an indivisible social and moral entity that had characteristic qualities, rights, and obligations (Augustins 1986: 205; Fougères 1938: 89; Ott 1992: 195; 1993b: 41). The Urdos house had certain attributes that were independent of both its inhabitants and the property (*etxalte*) to which it belonged. Every house had a name, which was often the surname of the person who built it or which described its physical location. The house name established the social identity of both the house and its inhabitants, for an individual was known by house name rather than by surname. A person took the house's name from birth and acquired a new social identity when he or she changed residence at marriage or remarriage or as a result of adoption. House names remained unchanged through successive generations of inhabitants.

The house was also a spiritual entity, with certain attributes that its members had a right to use: a house tomb in the cemetery, where household members were buried; a particular space on the church floor, where the female head of household sat during Mass; and certain ritual goods, used by female heads of household when death occurred or when houses exchanged life-giving gifts of blessed bread (Ott 1993: 103–16). An immutable bond existed between the living and dead members of a house. By means of prayer and blessed candles, female heads of household preserved and perpetuated the spiritual bond linking a house, its inhabitants, the souls of its dead, its space in the church, and its tomb.

As a social entity, the house constituted a private domain for its inhabitants. Whether open or closed, the front door marked a social and symbolic boundary between the people of the house and those who belonged elsewhere. Spatially close neighbors constituted the most frequent and socially acceptable visitors in a rural Xiberoan house. Local etiquette required all visitors to remain on the threshold until a head of household invited them to enter the kitchen, the center of domestic sociability. Hospitality distinguished insiders from outsiders. Local custom obliged the female head of household (*etxeko-andrea,* literally "the woman of the house") to offer refreshments to anyone who entered the house, although a total stranger received limited hospitality or none at all. The woman of the house reserved the right to withdraw hospitality if a visitor failed to respect local codes of etiquette or offended the household in some other way.[4]

The ideal domestic group consisted of three generations: an elder couple, their successor and his or her spouse, and the unmarried children of both couples. Household members shared a moral obligation to work together for the common good of the house. Respect was a primary virtue, cultivated and cherished in the family, and an essential feature of being well brought up. Parents taught their children to respect their elders and to show special deference to their grandparents. Respect also figured prominently in correct gender relations. Men used the formal mode of address in Basque (*züka min-tzatü,* the equivalent of *vouvoyer* in French, rather than *hikatü,* or *tutoyer*) when speaking to women of any age. Husbands and wives also addressed each other formally and were expected to treat each other with courtesy. Public rumor branded a man who maltreated any female in his household as "badly brought up, disrespectful, and wicked" (*de mal élevé, d'irrespecteux, de méchant*) (Lauburu 1998: 94–95). The same principle applied to a woman who mistreated a man in her household.

In rural Xiberoa and notably in Urdos, a relative equality existed between the sexes, with its roots in sixteenth-century Basque customary law (Fougères 1938: 49–50; Grosclaude 1993; Nussy Saint-Saëns 1955). In contrast to stereotypes of gender inequality reported for other parts of France during the interwar years and 1940s, Xiberoan men did not regard women as the weaker sex, morally or socially, nor did they normally treat women as their inferiors

(Capdevila et al. 2005: 76–78; Diamond 1999; Fishman 1991: 130; Hawthorne and Golsan 1997). In the countryside and small towns, Xiberoan men and women regarded themselves as "equal-equal" (*bardin-bardiña*) in their personhood and in their power and authority as heads of household. Both men and women were eligible to inherit the natal house and its associated property, which passed intact from generation to generation in accordance with the rule of impartible inheritance in Xiberoan customary law.[5]

In Urdos as in other Xiberoan communities, customary law ruled that the eldest child, whether male or female, should inherit (Nussy Saint-Saëns 1955: 77). Parents did not, however, necessarily follow the tradition of primogeniture. When demographic circumstances permitted, parents gave more emphasis to moral, physical, and social qualities than to age or gender in selecting their successor. Parents assessed the suitability of their children for that role at an early age, seeking the qualities of respect, honesty, fidelity, a willingness and ability to work hard for long periods, a strong emotional attachment to the natal house and community, and an ability to get along well with other people and to exercise good judgment. Parents taught their children to take responsibility for their actions. A person gained responsibility (*ardüra*) during the process of socialization in the household, neighborhood, and community. Children learned about the role, rights, and responsibilities of the person who would inherit the house (the *etxenko zaiña,* "the guardian of the house") and the role nonheirs would play if they chose to remain in the house as unmarried adults.

Parents established a close rapport with their chosen successor at an early age, and that son or daughter understood the importance of finding a suitable spouse by the time the elder couple was ready to retire. When two households approved the marriage of a young inheritor and fiancé/fiancée, a complex set of rights and obligations had to be upheld. In order to satisfy the French rule of partible inheritance, the elder, retiring heads of household divided the property equally among their children in one contract. In a second contract, those siblings then granted full ownership of the property to the chosen successor. The successor compensated them with cash payments in order to "put in order" and to equalize (*bardintu*) their relationship. With the successful completion of an inheritance settlement, the successor partook of the house's spiritual essence (*indarra*) and acquired its good influence (*zuzena*). Rural Xiberoans believed that these qualities enabled an inheritor to preserve and perpetuate harmony within the moral community. Although only the inheritor had access to the *indarra* of the house, he or she shared power and authority in decision making with the in-marrying spouse. As the younger heads of household, husband and wife had complementary and at times overlapping spheres of influence (Grosclaude 1993: 98; Nussy Saint-Saëns 1955: 76–78; Ott 1993b: 52–53).

When any member of the household illegitimately retained or obtained jural power and authority, the house became "disordered" by conflict and the spiritual essence of the house was thought to be violated. Such violation occurred in three main circumstances: when the siblings of the designated inheritor refused to relinquish their claims to the property; when the elder couple refused to retire and relinquish ownership of the property to their successor; and when someone other than the inheritor (usually a disgruntled sibling) gained legal ownership of a room inside the house with the aid of the elder couple before they turned the rest of the property over to their chosen successor.

Xiberoans recognized the possibility of conflict between elder and younger heads of household in premarital and inheritance-settlement contracts. Prepared by the local notary, such documents established the moral and material rights of the two couples in the event of incompatibility. As a source of agency, the notary served as a key intermediary between the moral community and external agents of legal justice. Urdos Basques employed the services of the notary in Sustary, an outsider about whom they had ambiguous feelings. The notary's education, fluency in French, and knowledge of French laws relevant to Urdos interests earned the respect of most Urdos citizens. They needed the notary and, reluctantly, had to entrust him with extremely private information about decisions relating to inheritance and conflict over property. The same notary continuously served the Urdos Basques from 1939 until 1976. When conflict did occur in a house, its members tried to conceal their problems, especially from their neighbors, and to resolve such difficulties without recourse to the notary or other external agents. According to one Basque proverb, it was better for the domestic group to "cover the fire of the house with the ashes of the house" (*etxenko suia, etxenko hautsareki tapa*), that is, to manage domestic discord on its own.

In the Basque Country and elsewhere in the Pyrenees, the neighborhood was not simply a physical collection of dwellings whose inhabitants lived in close spatial proximity. Feudal in origin, the neighborhood (*aizoa* or *auzoa* in Basque) constituted a moral order within which houses were permanently linked.[6] Basque customary law used the neighborhood as the basis upon which to distinguish between neighbors (insiders) and strangers (outsiders) in much the same way that Basques traditionally used membership in a house to distinguish "those of the house" from "strangers" (Fougères 1938: 96n.). In rural communities such as Urdos, the status of neighbor conferred citizenship upon an individual and granted him or her certain rights and obligations: the rights to use communal pasturage and to cut wood, and the obligations to provide mutual assistance, to treat other neighbors with piety and courtesy, to act as their guarantor and protector in times of crisis, and to be their witness in matters pertaining to both legal and social justice (Echegaray 1932: 5–6; Fougères 1938: 92; Grosclaude 1993: 22n.).[7] Membership in a neighborhood created an immutable bond between inhabitants and a specific space within which people gave and received goods and services for the common good of the entire community (Douglass 1969, 1975; Echegaray 1932: 391–92). Throughout the Basque provinces, forms of traditional "neighbor work" (*auzolan*) included road building, clearing paths for religious processions, house building, and helping its members move into their new residence.

Outside the house, the second most important relationship in rural Xiberoan society linked houses as "first neighbors" (*lehen aizoak* or *premier voisins* in French). The relationship established a social bond between two or more houses that was, in principle, unbreakable. Households did not have a right to change first neighbors if the two domestic groups did not get along well or became embroiled in a dispute. The number of first neighbors related to a rural Xiberoan house ranged from one to as many as four, and the structure of these vicinal relationships varied across the province. In some communities the first neighbor was defined as the first house "toward the church" from one's own dwelling. In Urdos every house had three first neighbors: the "first first neighbor" was conceptually located to the right of one's own house, whereas the "second first" and "third first neighbors" were to the left.[8]

First neighbors had certain mutual responsibilities that promoted social cohesion. Their institutionalized relationship carried expectations of cooperation, trust, and amicability and obliged such neighbors to help each other reciprocally with the hay and maize harvests, fern cutting, wheat threshing, and pig killing. In Urdos and many other rural Xiberoan communities, first neighbors also took turns giving gifts of blessed bread to each other and to the entire community at Mass on Sunday. The obligation to give such bread rotated from house to house in a particular order around a community. The female heads of first-neighbor households fulfilled the obligation on behalf of their houses. In some rural Xiberoan communities, the ritual played a vital role in fostering and maintaining solidarity in the moral community during the German Occupation (Ott 1993b: 103–16).

As in other parts of the rural Basque Country and along the western Pyrenees, first neighbors in Urdos performed their most valuable services at times of life crisis, particularly during childbirth and when death occurred (Douglass 1969, 1975; Lagarde 2003; Ott 1993b). A female first neighbor typically served as the midwife and, in the event of miscarriage or stillbirth, baptized the infant. During the process of death, as surviving members of a household separated themselves from the deceased, their first neighbors played a vital role in assisting both the living and the dead. From the time of death until the funeral, first neighbors took charge of all domestic work, prepared the body of the deceased, and facilitated the passage of the soul to purgatory. When death disrupted the social and economic orderliness of a house, first neighbors restored it.

According to one Basque proverb, "It is better to have one good first neighbor than one hundred kin" (*Hobe da aizo hün bat eziez askazi ehun bat*). The saying reflects an expectation of conflict between extradomestic, close consanguineal kin (*askaziak*) that was particularly marked in rural Xiberoan society until recently. In the countryside, cooperation, trust, and amicability did not normally characterize relations between extradomestic kin, who rarely enjoyed the harmony and solidarity of first neighbors. Disputes over an unsettled inheritance agreement deeply divided families with conflicting loyalties to different houses, and unresolved arguments over property sometimes led to a total cessation of social relations between opposing sides.

In rural Xiberoa and notably in Urdos, people preferred to marry a "here person," someone from their own community.[9] They disdained marriage to a non-Xiberoan Basque (a Manex) and highly disapproved of marriage between a Xiberoan and a stranger.[10] The ideal marriage partner was a first neighbor, someone whose house was permanently linked to one's own house in a relationship characterized by mutual trust, mutual aid, and numerous other forms of reciprocal exchange. Such marriages allowed an in-marrying spouse to remain spatially and affectively close to his or her natal household. Urdos Basques particularly prized a marriage strategy known as "child exchange" (*haurr-ordarizka*), which linked two first-neighbor houses twice through marriage.[11] The true form of child exchange entailed the marriage of two brothers to two sisters in houses classified as first neighbors. People preferred the strategy, because it "equalized" the relationship between the two neighbors as givers and takers of marriage partners.

The survival of a Xiberoan house depended upon a successful marriage, among other factors. Under the surveillance of family members and neighbors, young people had opportunities to mingle at local dances, sporting events, fairs, and religious festivals. If amorous relations developed between a young man and woman, they tried to conceal their feelings and to meet secretly for as long as possible (A. Carricart 1977: pers. comm.; M. Idiart 1978: pers. comm.). When public rumor circulated about a couple's courtship, the girl's parents sought to confirm the young man's good intentions by inviting him to the house for an evening with the family. If such parents or public opinion judged a man to be a womanizer (an *emazteika* or *un coureur de femmes*), with no respect for the possible consequences of his actions, he severely reduced his marital chances. Such men were suspected of having uncontrolled sexual force (*indarra*).

The preservation of the Xiberoan house also depended upon the procreative union of the younger couple. In the countryside, premarital sexual relations did not usually give rise to scandal, as long as neither lover was married or widowed and the couple intended to marry. News of amorous relations quickly entered the domain of public rumor, which classified young, unmarried lovers as *eskontsiak,* those who enjoy the sexual benefits of marriage without actually being married. If the woman became pregnant and bore a child, the couple had proof of their fertility. In certain conditions, such births constituted no more than "a little disgrace" in rural communities (A. Carricart 1979: pers. comm.; Lauburu 1998: 97; Ott 1993b: 194, 202–3). A man did not damage his moral standing in the community if he married the woman and legitimized his relationship with their offspring through an official declaration of paternity in the local town hall. Among some rural Xiberoans, it was not uncommon for a couple to have two or more children out of wedlock. If the genitor refused to marry the mother, public rumor classified him as a womanizer and he became the target of intense public criticism that typically focused on two moral issues: his inability to control his sexual force (*indarra*) and his refusal to accept responsibility for the pregnancy he had caused (A. Carricart 1978: pers. comm.; G. Harriguileheguy 1979: pers. comm.).

If the mother refused to marry the genitor, she and her household typically defended her decision as a legitimate response to uncontrolled male sexual force, perceived to threaten the moral and social order of a house.[12] In Urdos at least, public opinion rarely censured an unwed mother for turning down her child's father if the moral community judged that man to be an unsuitable marriage partner (e.g., having uncontrolled sexual force, excessive drinking, a quarrelsome temperament, or laziness). The presence of an illegitimate child in the household did not necessarily reduce the mother's marital eligibility, especially if she was likely to inherit the farm. Public knowledge of an abortion did, however, bring shame to a woman's household; abortion violated both church law and the matrimonial duty to establish a successful procreative union. When an unwed woman had an abortion, she typically did so in another community to protect the integrity and privacy of her household (A. Carricart, G. Harriguileheguy 1977: pers. comms.).[13]

Although women bore less responsibility than men for agency in a pregnancy, an unmarried woman who behaved in a sexually provocative manner quickly earned a bad reputation as a "man-chaser" (*gizonkari* or *une coureuse d'homme*). Uncontrolled female sexual desire, like its male counterpart, constituted a threat to the moral community. In both towns and countryside, a sexually promiscuous, unmarried woman risked exclusion from her natal household if she did not change her ways. In cases of persistent sexual misbehavior, some parents opted for total exclusion from the moral community by arranging for an unruly daughter to live with a sibling in another part of the Basque Country, Bordeaux, or Paris. Unsurprisingly, the parish priest highly approved of the strategy (M. Idiart 1978: pers. comm.).

In Urdos people proudly regarded themselves as "mountain people" (*borthü jentiak*), who had a particularly close affective bond with the space in which they lived and which they collectively owned. People had a deep love of the land, of animals, of the earth, and of the mountains that surrounded their valley, regarding both the earth and the mountains as principal sources of knowledge.[14] They also believed that the earth and the mountains had *indarra,* an inherent natural power or force, which made them potentially dangerous places. In the time of "the old religion," people associated the mountains with spiritual, supernatural spheres, within which both good and evil operated. Until the 1950s many elderly people still believed in sorcery and evil spirits (A. Carricart 1977: pers. comm.; G. Harriguileheguy 1979: pers. comm.).[15] Although primarily Catholic in principle and practice, "the old religion" also contained pagan elements.

The mountains also served as the space (violated by German occupation) in which parishioners reaffirmed their belief in and adherence to the Catholic creed through an annual cycle of processions and pilgrimages that were central to "the old religion." The physical grandeur of the mountains constantly reminded parishioners of God's supreme power over humanity. "The old religion" constituted a set of strong Catholic beliefs, religious observances, and practices that exercised considerable control over the lives of most Xiberoans. People believed that "the old religion" itself had a unique, supernatural power (*indarra*) that compelled parishioners to fulfill their spiritual duties, to uphold their faith with fervor, to take part in religious activities, to practice fast and abstinence, to respect the priest and the holy sacraments and the blessed things (blessed bread, blessed candles, and holy water). In 1923 one priest noted that most Urdos people diligently attended Mass two or three times weekly, "even those (parishioners) whose houses were as much as twelve kilometers from the church" (Foix 1922: 573). Like the mountains, the eleventh-century church at the upper end of the commune was a physical focus of "the old religion." Local people maintained that it was no architectural accident that the contours of the church followed those of the mountains rising behind it to the southeast. This "projection of a building upon nature" served as a visual representation of the link between the mountains and the Catholic faith (Aytaberro 1983: 141).

In "the old religion" Urdos people closely associated their spiritual identity with a long-cherished symbol of their Catholic faith: the relic of their saint, which was the ring finger of her right hand. They believed that the relic had a supernatural power to prevent drought and storms.[16] On Corpus Christi Day in 1923, the people and their priest joined parishioners from the town of Sustary for an annual procession to a mountain sanctuary nearby. When the relic mysteriously disappeared, the Urdos people angrily accused the Sustary people of theft. According to the Urdos priest, his Sustary counterpart could neither walk properly nor say Mass when he returned from the procession. For the Urdos people, such sudden, peculiar disabilities unequivocally identified the Sustary priest as the thief. According to the local story, the Sustary priest's deep humiliation and guilt compelled him to return the relic to the Urdos priest, who declared that neither he nor his parishioners would ever again participate in the procession to the mountain shrine of Sustary. The Urdos priest decreed that his parish had its own special holy place in the mountains of Urdos. From 1923 until the German Occupation, Urdos Basque people went to that particular holy place on the days of St. Mark and Corpus Christi. The relic's theft gave rise to hostile feelings between Urdos and Sustary people and their respective priests. On several occasions during the 1920s and 1930s, fights between men from the two communities broke out on market days in Sustary (J.-P. Jonnet 1977: pers. comm.).

The proverb "He who is Basque is a believer" (*Eskualdun, fededun*) captures the long-standing, close relationship between Catholicism and Basque ethnic identity. Like Xiberoan customary law, the Catholic Church was a pillar of conservative Basque society, in which priests played a vital role as both secular and spiritual leaders, particularly before the separation of church and state in 1905–1906. At the start of the twentieth century, the Basque clergy mobilized local populations against France's Third Republic and strongly opposed the government's attempts to establish its authority in villages and communes that cherished their independence. As happened elsewhere in the northern Basque provinces, Xiberoan clergy were staunch defenders of the Basque language and Basque culture. With the crisis of church and state, the region's teaching orders closed their seminaries and the clergy members' power as local leaders was, to a great extent, neutralized (Jacob 1994: 49–54). In Urdos, however, the parish priest continued to play a prominent role in both the secular and spiritual life of his parishioners in the aftermath of the crisis.

Parish records show that the Urdos priest played a dual role as secular and spiritual leader at least as early as the mid-nineteenth century. Unusually, he served as town-hall secretary of the commune, a position normally held by the local schoolteacher in rural French society (Fauvet and Mendras 1958: 490–92). The priest protected the two primordial Xiberoan institutions: the house and the community. As town-hall secretary, in conjunction with the mayor, he regularly mediated relations between Urdos citizens and external authorities. Unlike many of his parishioners, the priest could read French and thus kept abreast of prefectoral circulars and other documents that contained information relevant to his parishioners' interests and welfare. The priest assisted the mayor and municipal council with financial matters concerning the commune; registered all births, deaths, and marriages; and often helped his parishioners resolve difficulties with external authorities such as the notary in Sustary. The parish priest also read and wrote in the Basque language, skills that his parishioners often utilized in wartime when they wished to conceal information from the French authorities.

As spiritual leader of the community, the priest mediated relations between parishioners and God, from whom he received spiritual power (*indarra*) at his ordination. People respected the priest's supernatural power, which enabled him both to bless and to curse. In the local form of Catholicism, responsibility for the punishment of sinners rested with the priest, who could decide for himself how and when to use his supernatural power to address wrongdoing against the church. The priest had the power to curse someone "in the name of God" and to inflict physical harm upon a parishioner who disobeyed the rules of the local clergy. He could also use his supernatural, God-given power to exorcise evil spirits. People thus regarded priests as potentially dangerous, to be feared and above all to be obeyed (Ott 1993b: 92–96).

Priests were often insiders, native Xiberoans, and sometimes belonged to the parish (and moral community) they served as a "here person." During the 1930s and until 1941, however, the Urdos priest was an outsider. Fr. Etxecopar was a Manex Basque from Behe Nafarroa and thus did not initially speak the Xiberoan dialect. Politically conservative citizens disapproved of the priest's "Red" sympathies, for he encouraged parishioners to help the hundreds of civilian and political refugees who passed through Urdos during the Spanish Civil War. Fr. Etxecopar was also on excellent terms with a militant socialist schoolteacher who had married an Urdos woman and who regularly visited her parents' house. Some politically conservative parishioners privately accused Fr. Etxecopar of communist sympathies (A. Carricart, M. Idiart 1978: pers. comms.). Although such parishioners strongly disapproved of Fr. Etxecopar's political views, they feared his extraordinary supernatural powers more than they fretted over his potential agency in politics.

In "the old religion" people believed that the extent to which a priest used his supernatural power depended upon his temperament. Fr. Etxecopar had a volatile, irascible temper and abundant energy, qualities that made him dangerous. Most parishioners took great care not to provoke him in either religious or secular matters. In 1937, however, one incautious man started talking to a friend at the back of the church during Mass and broke out laughing. Fr. Etxecopar stopped the service and admonished both men. When the man laughed a second time, the priest "cursed him in the name of God." The parishioner's face suddenly became disfigured and remained that way for the rest of his life. On another occasion, a parishioner decided to harvest his maize on the Sabbath and failed to gain the priest's permission, as "the old religion" required him to do. His disobedience enraged Fr. Etxecopar, who used his supernatural *indarra* to induce torrential rains that fell only on that parishioner's field and ruined his crops.

As both spiritual and secular leader, Fr. Etxecopar ruled over his parishioners with aggressive and sometimes vindictive determination. Although "the old religion" dictated that parishioners had no right to criticize the views or actions of the priest in his capacity as their spiritual leader, the moral community did have a right to judge the priest in his secular role as town-hall secretary. No one, however, dared to oppose him or his political views in face-to-face debate. When Fr. Etxecopar met a violent end in a road accident in 1941, more than one parishioner wondered whether supernatural powers from a higher source might have been involved (A. Carricart, G. Harriguileheguy, M. Idiart, K. Irigaray 1978: pers. comms.).

As happened elsewhere in Xiberoa, Urdos Basques fully recognized that all priests were emotionally and physically human and as susceptible to temptation, folly, and sin as any parishioner and that the moral community had the right to judge a priest as a man. If parishioners widely suspected their priest engaged in sexual misconduct, citizens had a right to ridicule and punish him in a ritual of popular justice known as "strewing the greenery" (*la jonchée*). Although Urdos Basques never had cause to exercise that right in relation to any of their priests, they did so on three occasions to chastise adulterers in the 1920s and 1930s (K. Irigaray, G. Harriguileheguy 1978: pers. comms.). On one occasion during the Great War, Urdos women took popular justice into their own hands and enacted the charivari in the absence of their husbands and adult sons. Their victims were two adulterers, a local man in his fifties and the wife of a soldier in the Eighteenth Infantry Regiment of Pau. Armed with pots and bells, the women alternated between the houses of the two culprits and kept them awake at night for several days with their "rough music" and lewd rhymes (G. Harriguileheguy 1978: pers. comm.). When the couple vowed to end their immoral liaison, the women suspended their nocturnal ritual of popular justice. Although such female emancipation in popular tribunals of public censure rarely occurred in Xiberoa, the incident demonstrates the adaptability of popular justice to the unusual circumstances of the Great War, a tragic phenomenon in which Xiberoan women played a prominent, varied role both as supporters of men at the front and abettors in the avoidance of military service for France.[17]

3: Basques in the Great War

In their mental, interior geography of the world around them, rural Xiberoans associated the spatial entity called Frantzia with military service (Lauburu 1998: 30). On the eve of the First World War, rural people had a vague notion of Frantzia as a space located somewhere beyond the Xiberoan lowlands, known simply as Pettarra ("the space below"), and of the two spaces adjacent to Xiberoa, Manex (non-Xiberoan Basque territory) and Biarno (Béarn). In the first decade of the twentieth century, rural Xiberoans relied upon donkeys, mule-drawn carts, and their own two feet for transportation in and around their own small social universe. In the mountain valleys of Upper Xiberoa, the first bicycle appeared shortly before the war. When a physician in Sustary bought the first automobile in Upper Xiberoa in 1914, rural people flocked to see it and felt amused when the machine struggled to cope with a steep stretch of road (A. Carricart 1976: pers. comm.). In the lowlands, a tramway (known as the *teuf-teuf* because of the noise it made) linked the Xiberoan capital of Maule to towns in Béarn and the *pays basque* from 1906 until the end of the war. Some Xiberoans used the tram to attend festivals and fairs in their province, and young men called up for military service rode the *teuf-teuf* to report for duty in Baiona or Pau.

Oral testimonies, wartime letter-writing, and local press reports indicate that most Xiberoan Basques backed France's war against the Germans. Basques were accustomed to the idea that they were French citizens, a lesson in French nationalism taught in both lay and Catholic schools from the 1880s. In Xiberoa as elsewhere in France, mobilization gave rise to contradictory emotions. Within the private domain of the house, families wept over the imminent departure of a loved one; yet in the public domain of the community, families sang together enthusiastically at the railway station where young recruits prepared for their departure. In Maule as in other regional towns linked by the railroad, mobilization triggered a collective spirit of patriotism; it also greatly enhanced a sense of belonging to that particular place as "here people" (R. Elissondo 2007: pers. comm.). In 1914 the local press, public opinion, and schoolteachers, in particular, urged Xiberoan men to do their duty for France (Ikherzaleak 2006: 45). In keeping with long-standing Basque traditions, decisions about military service, its evasion, or desertion typically involved an entire household, whose members shared a common, deep commitment to the well-being and continuity of the Basque house. A young man's decision to serve France was also highly influenced by the advice of other family members, his classmates, and the priest and by neighborhood pressures to conform to the expectations of the moral community. At the start of the war, the patriotism for France that Basques had learned in school was not the only motivating force behind a man's decision to fight. In 1914 men often regarded mobilization as an opportunity for camaraderie with other Basques in foreign territory, for adventure and participation in an extraordinary experience that was both frightening and exciting (Ikherzaleak 2006: 45).

Once mobilized, Basque soldiers began to reflect more deeply upon what it meant to be French, as well as Basque (F. Eyheralt 2003: pers. comm.). Xiberoan letters from the front gave rise to much emotion in the soldier's household and were often passed from house to house and discussed throughout the neighborhood.[1] Mainly written in French, the correspondence also typically included Basque phrases when the author wished to conceal something from the postal censors.[2] One young infantry soldier from Xiberoa wrote more than 379 letters and 103 postcards to his family during his five years of military service.[3] In his early correspondence, the Basque regarded himself as "a humble soldier defending a great cause" (*un petit soldat défendant la grande cause*) (Ikherzaleak 2006: 34). Before the soldier reached the front, his letters reflected patriotic propaganda about the honor attached to dying for the *patrie*. By December 1915 the young Basque felt disgust for a war that seemed unending, yet he still did not challenge its legitimacy. He was deeply angered when the authorities temporarily suspended leave for all soldiers from his borderland canton in Xiberoa as a means of reducing the number of desertions by Basques in the area (Ikherzaleak 2006: 25).

By 1914 the process of making French the common language of the *patrie* was well advanced owing to increased mobility, greater sociocultural interaction among people of different regions, and industrialization in the decade preceding the war (E. Weber 1976: 78). Military conscription forced millions of men to use French on a daily basis. Although Basques had been required to speak French in the public schools since the 1880s, many rural Xiberoan men lacked fluency in the language when the war began, for they mainly spoke Basque at home and either Basque, Spanish, or a Béarnais patois in their dealings with Pyrenean neighbors (F. Eyheralt 1980: pers. comm.; G. Harriguileheguy 1979: pers. comm.).[4] During the war, Xiberoan conscripts often felt culturally alienated and stressed when they had to live among soldiers from other regions in France, especially if their commanding officers did not speak Basque (Pourcher 1994: 438).

Affected to varying degrees by the different cultures they encountered and by the circumstances that brought them into contact with strangers, many

Xiberoans experienced an intensified sense of belonging to the sociogeograph-ical space in which they were born, their *xokhoa*, their *coin*, their localized *pays* (F. Eyheralt 2003: pers. comm.; A. Barbe-Labarthe 2004: pers. comm.). When fellow Basques met at the front, their happiest moments occurred when they shared the contents of food parcels sent by their families in Xiberoa (R. Elissondo 2007: pers. comm.). In their letters, soldiers often gave detailed descriptions of the food they enjoyed with a fellow Xiberoan. Cheeses, sau-sages, and other home-produced items provided physical and emotional nourishment, as well as a direct, psychological link to the *pays* from which the soldiers had come. Both the food and Basque commensality greatly en-hanced their sense of belonging to the same sociogeographical space.

Basques were not always fortunate enough to encounter their fellow coun-trymen at the front. One young shepherd knew virtually no French when he was called up for military service in 1914. Assigned to the French Navy, the shepherd had never before been on a boat and spent most of the war on the Mediterranean among sailors who spoke only French. Able to write little more than his own name, Johanne Bormape did not attempt to send more than a few postcards home. Soon after the war ended, a stranger sent his parents a letter from a hospital near Geneva. The soldier was a Manex Basque who, like Johanne Bormape, had been wounded. The letter described the joy shared by the two Basques when orderlies placed them in adjacent hospital beds, for neither man had seen a fellow Basque or spoken a word of his natal language in nearly four years of military service. On his return to Xiberoa, Johanne Bormape told his family that he had felt seasick and homesick for the dura-tion of the war. He told them how he had dreamed about the mountains and tasting the cheeses he and his father made every summer. Vivid memories of food from the farm provided the young Basque with a visceral link to his birthplace. On his return, he described those memories and his intense lone-liness, which fluency in French reduced but did not eradicate. Johanne Bor-mape reckoned that a certain part of him had become French as a result of the war, but he felt himself to be, more intensely than ever before, a "here person" who belonged in the valley and house of his birth (F. Bormape 2003: pers. comm.).

Basques on both sides of the Pyrenees have a long-standing reputation for resisting integration in the French and Spanish states and for evading mili-tary service (E. Weber 1976: 47, 99, 295).[5] Their propensity to be defaulting conscripts (*insoumis*) and deserters has its historical and cultural roots in Basque customary laws (the *foruak, fors, fueros*). The first article in sixteenth-century Xiberoan customary law decreed that no person had the right to con-script Xiberoans (Grosclaude: 1993: 9).[6] A Xiberoan's right not to perform military service remained integral to Basque culture across the centuries. In the nineteenth century, the possibility of conscription and a call to arms in French military service were among several primary motivating factors underlying male Basques' emigration to the Americas and to the southern Basque Country. Northern Basques' emigration to Argentina began in the 1820s. In 1840 one military report noted that "the Basques tend to desert to Spain to escape military service, which they dislike, just as they deserted the imperial armies."[7] By the 1850s almost half of France's evaders were Basques, even though they made up only a fraction of the nation's total population (Douglass and Bilbao 1975: 123). By the 1860s Basques from Xiberoa and, to a much greater extent, Behe Nafarroa had established themselves throughout California and in northern and western Nevada (ibid.: 335). By 1900, 120,000 northern Basques lived in California. They initially earned their livelihood as sheep herders before turning to dairy farming, a transition accelerated by the Great War (ibid.: 303). During 1914–18, families in the *pays basque* often had a greater awareness of day-to-day life in California, Buenos Aires, and Montevideo than in the towns and cities of France (Ikherzaleak 2006: 42; K. Irigaray 1977: pers. comm.). Although some Basque emigrants did return to France to do military service, many men remained abroad for a variety of social, economic, and personal reasons.

When the Great War broke out in August 1914, the prefect of the Basses-Pyrénées worried that Basques would once again seek refuge in Spain and the Americas. He recognized the fluidity and frequency with which borderland Basques crossed the Franco-Spanish border and how difficult it was to stop them. With only four inspectors responsible for the surveillance of 120 kilometers of frontier, Xiberoans moved freely into Nafarroa in search of work, to trade, to socialize, and to avoid military service for France. Shepherds too old or unwilling to go to the front continued to take seasonal jobs in the southern Basque provinces as cheese makers, hay makers, and herdsmen. Borderland Basque women, especially from Urdos, continued to trade in the markets and streets of Izaba, the main town in the Erronkari Valley. Urdos women played a particularly important role in the Izaba and Xiberoan economies throughout the Great War, for they bought or traded their wares for goods in Izaba that were unavailable or more expensive in France. The women then resold their purchases in Xiberoan market towns (Estornés Lasa 1996: 38; G. Harriguileheguy 1978: pers. comm.).

Soon after the war began, the French authorities opened the Franco-Spanish frontier to let a flood of foreign workers and their families out of the Basses-Pyrénées, for news of the war intensified local fears of the Other as a potential source of harm or danger to the moral community (Pourcher 1994:

47–49). In the Xiberoan capital of Maule, many people of Spanish and southern Basque origin refused to return to Spain, because they had established themselves in local jobs and had developed a sense of belonging to the Spanish neighborhoods in town, as well as having a growing sense of patriotism for France. By contrast, some established families from the other side of the Pyrenees worried about the well-being of their children in a climate of increased xenophobia among native Xiberoans and thus sent their offspring to stay with kin in Nafarroa and Aragón. From October 1914 until the autumn of 1915, the French authorities refused to let Navarrese and Aragonese seasonal laborers cross into France to work in Basque and Béarnais sandal factories (Inchauspé 2001: 66–67). Given that many of the workers came from borderland communities in Spain, the authorities feared that they would be inclined to help French and Basque men evade military service in France.[8]

During the first month of the war, the prefect's expectations about a high desertion rate in the Basses-Pyrénées were initially allayed as Basques across the three provinces joined infantry regiments in southwestern France during the first month of the war. Seventy percent of soldiers in the 49th Infantry Regiment (RI) of Baiona, the 18th RI of Pau, the 34th RI of Mont-de-Marsan, and the 12th RI of Tarbes came from the *pays basque,* the Landes, and Béarn (Rocafort 1997: 642).[9] Initially a reserve regiment, the 249th RI consisted mainly of Basques from the coastal arrondissement of Baiona but included some Xiberoans as well. By the end of August, approximately twelve thousand soldiers had assembled in Baiona, and a further four to five thousand recruits had gathered in Pau. The army sent an additional two thousand ill-equipped reserve soldiers back to their farms and businesses to await further orders (Pourcher 1994: 40). In the early months of the war, military service put many young rural Xiberoans into close, continual contact with other northern Basques for the first time (Lauburu 1998: 39). Until early 1916, the "Basque" infantry regiments of Baiona and Pau consisted almost entirely of men from the same province. They were often brothers, cousins, classmates, and neighbors from the same village, closely bound together by friendship and a shared habitus, until the death toll necessitated the recruitment of men from other parts of France and elsewhere.

Although the French Army did not wish to promote regionalism, commanding officers sometimes used the Basques' strong sense of ethnic identity and competitive nature as a means of reinforcing discipline and promoting combativeness among their men. A non-Basque officer at Verdun once observed that pitting the Basques against the Bretons and other regional groups was an effective means of increasing enthusiasm for combat. Basque soldiers tended to regard themselves as having greater physical stamina than comrades from elsewhere in France and perceived themselves to be more effective resisters against German aggression (Ikherzaleak 2006: 45). French military commanders recognized that Basque soldiers also wanted to fight together in order to lessen the effects of feeling culturally ill at ease and physically uprooted (*herritik elki,* literally "taken out of one's community"; *dépaysé,* in French). Conscription took men from the familiar sociophysical space and cultural setting in which they were born. Military service disrupted the habitus of men who had grown up together and had a shared understanding of their own small part of the world. Owing to cultural and linguistic differences, Basque soldiers typically feared and strongly opposed their dispersal among strangers.

Basques who were not assigned to one of the popularly known "Basque" regiments often evaded military service altogether rather than be forced into the company of strangers. Many evaders emigrated to the American West or sought refuge across the border in Gipuzkoa and Nafarroa, for Spain was a neutral nation, and its borderland citizens were long accustomed to helping their northern neighbors in wartime. The authorities often argued that emigration to the Americas offered Basques a convenient way of avoiding military service in France. In one rural valley west of Xiberoa, the mayor wrote to the regional recruitment officer on behalf of a young Basque who had not been assigned to the Baiona regiment, "where [the young man] had hoped to find himself among fellow Basques in the barracks as well as around town." The young recruit did not speak any French. He "dreaded going to a *pays* where his own language would not be understood" and "feared that he would become the laughing-stock of his comrades." The young man became a deserter and joined Basque-speaking friends and relatives in California (Rocafort 1997: 466).

As happened across France during the early stages of the war, the train stations in the Basses-Pyrénées became a central meeting place not only for young recruits reporting for duty in Baiona and Pau. Draft evaders met there as well (Pourcher 1994: 47, 49). At the end of July 1914, the subprefect in Maule prepared for an exodus of young men evading military conscription. Many evaders sought the assistance of Xiberoans, whose detailed knowledge of the mountains and trans-Pyrenean connections made them well placed to guide fugitives into Spain (Rocafort 1997: 642).[10]

In December 1914 the prefect of the Basses-Pyrénées in Pau reported his grave concerns about the desertion rate among Basques to the French minister of the Interior. The prefect attributed the desertions to "a special *mentalité*" among Basques that made them feel they had "no *patrie* other than the place in which they were born" (Pourcher 1994: 422).[11] The prefect recommended dealing with that *mentalité* by making use of the Basques' legendary endurance and obstinacy, qualities that (he reckoned) underpinned the success of Basque emigrants in the Americas. The prefect thus urged the minister of the Interior to send Basque battalions to Morocco in order to protect French interests and create a Basque colony there. The minister did not, however, approve of the scheme, which he claimed would favor the Basques and give too much recognition to regional differences among France's citizens.[12]

Three main factors privileged Basques who chose not to serve France in the Great War: their close spatial proximity to Spain; their long-standing trans-Pyrenean relations, characterized by traditions of cooperation and mutual aid; and the presence of Basque relatives in the Americas who had emigrated before 1914 and whose financial resources enabled the emigration of kin from the homeland to the New World. During the Great War, the highest rate of desertion in the department took place in the arrondissement of Maule, which included the borderland valley of Baigorri in Behe Nafarroa (Pourcher 1994: 433). According to the subprefect in Maule, borderland Basques tended to desert on a Sunday when they were home on leave.

In the spring of 1915, the prefect feared an increase in the regional desertion rate and asked military authorities to take preventive measures. The prefect urged the minister of War to withdraw leave entitlement from all Basque soldiers or at least to forbid their return to Xiberoa and Behe Nafarroa when they were on leave from the front. The minister rejected the proposal and argued, once again, that the Basques should not be treated any differently from other French citizens. He advised the prefect to increase surveillance along the frontier, but deserters and evaders of military service continued to cross the border. The gendarmes and territorial soldiers posted along the frontier rarely caught the fugitives, owing to local Basques' detailed knowledge of the terrain (Pourcher 1994: 425). In October 1915 the minister of War finally withdrew permission for active and convalescing soldiers to return to their natal communities along the frontier from the Basque coast as far as Laruns in Béarn. He reinstated leave privileges on April 26, 1916, but cautioned the prefect that such privileges would be suspended again if the desertion rate did not decrease.[13]

Public rumor and the regional press also claimed that desertion agencies operated in Gipuzkoa and Nafarroa (Rocafort 1997: 477–78). In a report from a security inspector to the subprefect in Maule (July 1917), a French policeman pretended to be a deserter when he met a Basque "desertion agent" in Pamplona. The agent promised him passage to Montevideo, through either Barcelona or Santander, and false identification papers for 565 pesetas (Pourcher 1994: 434).

During 1916–17, the French authorities charged thirty Gipuzkoan and Navarrese Basques with complicity in desertion. Sixteen of them came from the borderland town of Valcarlos-Luzaide and included the secretary of the town hall, who had falsified documents for deserters. French police identified two other southern Basques from a nearby hamlet on the Franco-Spanish border as anti-French and "big Germanophiles" who specialized in helping northern Basque soldiers on leave to join their kin in California and Argentina.[14] Basques on both sides of the Pyrenees continued to treat the borderlands as a zone they themselves regulated.

In a further attempt to stop desertions, the prefect monitored letters between Basque families and male kin who had deserted or defaulted on military conscription. Unlike their neighbors in Behe Nafarroa, Xiberoan families rarely corresponded in the Basque language (R. Elissondo 2007: pers. comm.).[15] A recent analysis of more than one thousand letters from the front received by Xiberoan families revealed very little patriotic discourse, especially among farmers and workers, and rarely mentioned the enemy (Ikherzaleak 2006: 47; R. Elissondo 2007: pers. comm.). The sons of notables and upper middle-class families were more prone to express feelings of patriotism, but their letters, like those of men less privileged, focused on material and mundane concerns rather than patriotic discourse (R. Elissondo 2007: pers. comm.). Whether abroad or in the *pays basque,* Xiberoans viewed what was going on around them in terms of their own interests, such as the cost of goods and the value of property.

In June 1917 a Spanish woman who had emigrated to Maule with her parents, husband, and five children wrote to her brother, Pedro B., in Los Angeles. Catalina B. complained to her brother about the high cost of living in Maule, the "very bad, very black bread" they had to eat, and the misery caused by the war that affected so many Maule families. Pedro B. had French citizenship and had done military service before 1914. His first neighbor had been a Navarrese sandal maker with relatives in Erronkari. In July 1916 Pedro B. and his neighbor had crossed into Nafarroa, and Pedro B. had made his way to California. Eighteen months later, the mayor of Pedro's village and its one policeman denounced Pedro's entire family and their Navarrese neighbor for complicity in Pedro's evasion of military service. The subprefect in Maule sanctioned the Navarrese neighbor by forcing his return to Spain. Pedro B.'s family denied all charges of complicity. None of them were arrested, although the authorities continued to intercept their mail.[16]

In the arrondissement of Maule, the desertion rate peaked during the last months of 1916 and early 1917, when the subprefect received daily reports of young men crossing the frontier into Nafarroa (Pourcher 1994: 433). In December 1916 a group of neighbors from the Xiberoan community of Ur-diñanbe decided to desert while they were home on leave. One of the men, Pierre E., had three brothers already established in the dairy industry in Buenos Aires. The deserters crossed into Nafarroa near Urdos and made their way to Argentina from a Spanish port. Pierre E. left a wife and young child on the farm Pierre had inherited from his father. Public rumor valued the property at ten thousand francs. The wife leased the farm to a local man and, with her two-year-old daughter, joined Pierre E. in Buenos Aires.[17]

A Maule soldier, Jean C., also deserted in December 1916 while home on leave. He crossed into Spain and worked in the mines near Elizondo, then as a mill hand. He and his family corresponded regularly and discussed his plans to join cousins already settled in California and Nevada who had them-selves either deserted or evaded military conscription. Jean C.'s uncle (his mother's brother) had emigrated to Winnemucca, Nevada, before the war began. The uncle wrote to Jean C.'s father about his nephew's plans to emi-grate and enclosed three hundred dollars for the young deserter's passage to America. The uncle promised to look after Jean C. and to find him employ-ment in Nevada. The French authorities continued to monitor the family's trans-Pyrenean and trans-Atlantic correspondence. In March 1917 French police interrogated Jean C.'s father, who denied any knowledge of his son's whereabouts or intentions. When police searched the house, they discovered a money order for fifteen hundred francs, arrested Jean C.'s father on charges of complicity in desertion, and sent him to prison for one year. An inspector went to Elizondo to persuade Jean C. to return to his regiment. The deserter proudly told the inspector that his father preferred to spend a year in prison rather than to see his son return to the trenches. With the assistance of shep-herds who regularly carried mail across the frontier, Jean C. continued to cor-respond with his sister in Maule. The authorities knew that she awaited her father's release from prison so the two of them could join Jean C. in Spain and make their way to Nevada.[18]

In March 1917 the authorities intercepted a letter from Jean A., a Xiberoan who had emigrated to Buenos Aires in 1898 after having done three years of military service in France. His elder brother was already established as a dairy farmer in Argentina. In 1917 one of their younger brothers was a machine gunner at the front. Another younger brother was a POW in Germany. Jean A. wrote regularly to his widowed seventy-three-year-old mother, Mme A., in a Xiberoan village near Maule. Mme A. and her husband had themselves emigrated to Argentina in the 1860s and returned to Xiberoa in the 1870s. During the Great War, she and her forty-two-year-old daughter ran a pros-perous farm with an estimated worth of fifteen thousand francs. The authorities feared that Mme A. would persuade her son at the front to desert and join his brothers in Buenos Aires. According to local police, the family had "a peculiar approach to patriotism, as a result of their experiences living abroad."[19]

By 1917 the authorities' postal interceptions and interrogations revealed a pattern of kin-based complicity in desertion in which women played a particularly prominent role. In one case the authorities' suspicions were aroused when a shepherd suddenly sold his entire flock of sheep. Public rumor maintained that he planned to emigrate to California. The shepherd did not want to go alone, however, and thus involved his wife, her sister, his sister-in-law, and her mother in a conspiracy to get the shepherd's brother, Pierre, back from the front. The shepherd's wife and her sister asked the mayor to send an urgent telegram to Pierre with the terrible news that his wife was dying. Suspicious about the veracity of the news, the mayor refused to do so. The shepherd's sister-in-law's mother then took charge of matters. She walked from her isolated farm in the mountains to ask the parish priest to send the urgent telegram to her son-in-law's commanding officer at the front. The priest doubted that the woman's daughter was in fact "dying," but—as he later told the police—he did not check the fact, since it took three hours to walk to the farmhouse. The shepherd and other family members had already written several letters to the soldier about their plans for his desertion and their collective emigration to California. The letters angered the soldier. When the telegram arrived, he turned the family correspondence over to his commander, accused the shepherd and the women of conspiring against him, and assured the officer that he had never had any intention or desire to desert. The soldier brought formal charges against only the shepherd and his wife (the soldier's sister-in-law), but the authorities gave each of the women a one-year prison sentence and jailed the shepherd for fifteen months for conspiracy to aid desertion.[20]

Although evasion of military service and, to a greater extent, desertion deeply divided Basque towns and villages, the Basques often frustrated the authorities by "refusing to take responsibility" as whistle-blowers. Local people usually knew about the "shirkers" (*les embusqués*) who belonged to their own moral community, but they rarely alerted the police. In December 1916 the subprefect complained to the prefect that rural Basques, in particular, did not "want to be the denouncer of a neighbor or friend who planned to distance himself from the front."[21]

At least two cases of betrayal did occur. In the early months of the war, a married couple from Uharte-Garazi in Behe Nafarroa strongly opposed their son's wish to desert and emigrate to America, as they feared that he would never return to the family farm to become its head of household. The young man approached a Xiberoan from Urdiñanbe who knew the borderland terrain well and who had several brothers in America. Desperate to prevent their son's departure, the couple asked a close relative to denounce their son to the authorities. The police promptly arrested the young man and his Urdiñanbe accomplice. The wife of the Urdiñanbe man then attempted to destroy the young soldier's uniform and other items issued by military authorities, but she was herself arrested when the gendarmes discovered remnants of military gear in the hearth of her farmhouse (R. Elissondo 2007: pers. comm.). The couple apparently did not appreciate the extreme danger their son faced at the front (Ikherzaleak 2006: 37). A second denunciation took place in January 1917, when a father denounced his son and two other young deserters to the police in Maule.[22] Many people highly disapproved of desertion and regarded it as an act that brought dishonor to a house, but Xiberoans did not—as the French authorities appreciated—condone the betrayal of one "here person" by another. A "here person" had a legitimate right to judge a fellow citizen who committed wrongdoing, but the moral treachery of denunciation of insiders by insiders both harmed and endangered the moral community.

By contrast, Xiberoans promptly did turn "shirkers" over to the authorities if they were outsiders. In December 1917 a deserter from the Tarn made his way by train to Sustary and continued on foot to a nearby village. A Basque deserter had given him the address of a farming family who would help him cross the Pyrenees. Two brothers in that family had deserted in 1916. The outsider-deserter knocked on the door of the mayor's house, by chance, and asked for directions to the farm. To the mayor's astonishment, the stranger announced that he was a soldier who wished to desert. "How long will it take to get to Spain?" the soldier asked. At first the mayor thought he was joking, but the local schoolteacher, who had joined them, whispered to the mayor, "It's true, what he says. He is a deserter!" The mayor asked for the man's papers and sent two neighbors to fetch the police. The teacher fed the stranger, who made no effort to resist arrest. As the mayor observed, the deserter was very discouraged and depressed (*il était très abbatu*).[23] Unlike the organized, premeditated desertions of so many Basques who had plans for America, the stranger's desertion was an act of despair (Ikherzaleak 2006: 37).

From January 1915 the regional press and public rumor attributed the high rate of desertion in the *pays basque,* in part, to German agents who operated on both sides of the Franco-Spanish border and encouraged Basques to desert from the French Army. In March 1915 the conservative Basque-language newspaper, *Eskualduna,* warned its readers:

> Don't deny it! It appears that there are many Germans in our neighborhoods, in the Basque Country on both sides of the mountains, who agitate our brothers to turn against France. The Germans have long wanted our men to deny their duty as soldiers. The Germans use flattery and lies on our poor men. They tell our men you are not a deserter if you cross over from this *pays basque* (in France) to the other *pays basque* (in Spain). The Germans tell our men that their time away from home will not last long, that at the war's end a total pardon will be forthcoming. . . . Those who deny their duty as devoted soldiers have permanently disowned their own house and natal *pays.* . . . All of these words and promises (made by the Germans) are lies. People know very well that there will not be a pardon for those who don't fulfill their duty. The punishments [for desertion] are outlined in articles 230a, 232a and 234 of the Military Code.[24]

Having read the article in *Eskualduna,* a special commissioner advised the prefect of the Basses-Pyrénées that the German consul in San Sebastián-Donosti did in fact solicit Basque deserters with the aid of German agents based in Gipuzkoa. The commissioner reported that although some deserters received monetary assistance from the German consul, "the majority refuse such shameful advances. Although I know the names of those men who have accepted German aid, I hesitate to tell you."[25]

By December 1916 an army commander for the company of the Basses-Pyrénées (including the Béarnais arrondissements of Pau, Oloron, and Orthez and the Basque arrondissements of Baiona and Maule) had recorded 536 deserters (with 220 arrested) and 6,630 defaulting recruits (with 154 arrested) (Pourcher 1994: 432; Rocafort 1997: 465). Of the 6,630 *insoumis,* 1,809 men were Xiberoans (Ikherzaleak 2006: 33). The commander noted that in some Xiberoan and Behe Nafarroan communes, every single eligible recruit had deserted and enjoyed impunity, owing to the connivance of their close kin and friends on both sides of the Pyrenees.[26] The subprefect in Maule called for reinforcements along the Xiberoan frontier and, controversially, for judicial enquiries involving these close kin and friends of deserters whom public rumor had accused of aiding and abetting desertion.[27] Desertions often strained relations within the same family, as well as between the families and friends of mobilized soldiers and those of deserters and defaulting conscripts (J.-B. Hondagneu 1982: pers. comm.; Rocafort 1997: 474–75).

During the Great War, Xiberoan society was largely rural, agrarian, staunchly Catholic, conservative, and controlled by political elites in Paris and notables from Maule. The members of such privileged groups traveled regularly to the two main cities in southwestern France (Baiona and Pau) and to Paris. They led comfortable lives, took holidays in resorts on the Basque coast, and moved in social circles that sometimes included Hollywood celebrities.[28] Closely associated with the Catholic Church, Xiberoan notables were industrialists, entrepreneurs, or military officers or worked in the professions. The Catholic Petit and Grand Séminaires on the Basque coast usually educated them, and the Great War often brought them together as officers in the same regiments. One of the most prominent, controversial figures in contemporary French Basque history was a product of those Catholic institutions and an officer in the 249th Infantry Regiment during the Great War: Jean Ybarnegaray.

Ybarnegaray was continuously elected to the Chamber of Deputies in Paris from 1914 until 1939, representing the Basses-Pyrénées and the constituency of Maule. Ybarnegaray, a Manex Basque from the village of Uharte-Garaze on the western edge of Xiberoa, had charisma and was extremely popular among rural Xiberoans. An eloquent and often fiery orator, Ybarnegaray had a deep understanding of rural Basque society and the *mentalité* of traditionally conservative Xiberoans (Jacob 1994: 87–88). A majority of his constituents regarded Ybarnegaray as a key defender of their moral community. They also admired Ybar (as he was known among friends) for his skill as a hunter and sportsman, especially in Basque handball (pelota).[29] Ybarnegaray's vision of Basque society was rooted in political conservatism, authoritarianism, and Catholicism. Adamantly anticommunist and anti–Spanish Basque, he strongly opposed Basque nationalist and regionalist movements. During his long political career, Jean Ybarnegaray was closely involved in several militant right-wing leagues. In 1908 he had joined the Action Française when it first recruited partisans in Donibane-Lohitzun, Baiona, and Biarritz on the Basque coast. The movement also attracted prominent members of the Catholic Church and students in the Basque seminaries. At the Grand Séminaire in Baiona, Monseigneur Mathieu (future bishop of Dax) initially regarded the Action Française as a guardian of Christianity (Moreau 1972: 183). In 1911 Ybarnegaray was among the estimated fifteen hundred people who attended an Action Française rally in Pau. Intensely xenophobic, anti-Semitic, and royalist, the movement opposed egalitarian individualism and democracy. On the eve of war in 1914, the Action Française was widely regarded as the chief exponent of nationalism in France (E. Weber 1962: 82). The movement spread its message through the writings of Charles Maurras, whose readership included many priests, army officers and members of the bourgeoisie, as well as those who rejected his ideology (Atkin 2001: 17).

During the Great War, Jean Ybarnegaray served as a second lieutenant in the 5th Battalion of the predominantly Basque 249th Infantry Regiment. Although he did not participate in the offensive at Le Chemin des Dames, Ybarnegaray gave a scathing account of errors made by the four French generals in command when he addressed the Chamber of Deputies in June 1917 in sessions closed to the public (Rocafort 1997: 440–45). A good friend of Ybarnegaray's, Dr. Henri Herbille, also served in the 249th Infantry Regiment as the deputy officer and physician of the 5th Batallion. Herbille, who belonged to a politically conservative, notable family in the Xiberoan capital of Maule, shared Ybarnegaray's abhorrence of communism and his belief in authoritarianism, discipline, and hierarchy.

In a letter written to his parents from the front in November 1914, Dr. Herbille described the strong sense of brotherhood shared by Basque soldiers, regardless of their province of origin. "We share everything we receive [from home]. Don't forget that packages are always greatly appreciated. Don't forget the matches. As a matter of urgency, please send a knife with multiple blades. I'm bound to lose mine in the trenches. Send some mouth wash, a little flask of rum, which will serve me well in tending to my wounded men, a tooth brush, and three or four metres of wick for a lighter" (Rocafort 1997: 152). In another letter, written on November 8, 1914, at Le Chemin des Dames, Herbille described the extreme difficulties faced by his stretcher bearers as they tried to rescue wounded comrades. During one eight-day period of combat in the trenches, Dr. Herbille tended to fifty-eight wounded soldiers, twelve of whom required amputations (ibid.: 163). Many years after the war ended, Herbille talked to his daughter about his experiences at the front. His memories often focused on soldiers who had resigned themselves to death in the moments preceding an attack, yet who could not bear the thought of being abandoned on the battlefield and denied the dignity of a grave.[30] For Henri Herbille and many other Xiberoans, the sacrifice of one's life on the battlefield for God and country constituted a good death (*une belle mort*) and brought honor to one's house and family; by contrast, desertion brought shame and dishonor, especially to a soldier's wife, mother, and sisters (ibid.: 493).

In August 1917 the minister of War and undersecretary of State for Health granted three months' leave to a Xiberoan army chaplain with the "Basque" 49th Infantry Regiment. Father Arnaud Etcheber had proposed a plan to the minister of the Interior for the return of Basque deserters living in the borderland villages of Gipuzkoa and Nafarroa. The chaplain had spent two years at the front, including Verdun and Craonne. Father Etcheber argued that as a Basque priest with military experience, he was well placed to "round up the lost sheep" who "lacked any sense of duty to France." The Basque chaplain planned to appeal to deserters' consciences as "heads of household and as believers" who had an obligation to return to their families, with whom Father Etcheber also planned to liaise closely. The prefect, a senator, the bishop of Bayonne, and the Basque deputy, Jean Ybarnegaray, had already made several unsuccessful attempts to entice deserters back to France and to gain the trust of their families.[31]

Using his "knowledge of the Basques' way of thinking and values," Father Etcheber persuaded a substantial number of deserters to return to their rural borderland communities. His success, however, caused great bitterness and discord in several borderland villages, as the families of men who had fought at the front faced jubilant deserters reunited with their kin who believed that amnesty would be granted. Consequently, the minister of the Interior ordered the prefect of the Basses-Pyrénées to terminate the Basque chaplain's mission among Basque deserters.[32]

The subprefect of Baiona blamed the socialists for advancing the idea of amnesty among the Basques and warned the prefect in Pau that the issue of amnesty deeply divided the Basques against themselves. The subprefect argued that soldiers who had done their duty for France, "the good French" (*les bons français*), firmly opposed the return of "the bad French" (*les mauvais français*) from the other side of the Pyrenees, for he regarded them as traitors to the *patrie.* He cautioned the prefect in Pau that the slightest confrontation between *les bons français* and *les mauvais français* could lead to violence.[33]

In the summer of 1917, the subprefect in Maule claimed that desertions had stopped entirely. He attributed the success of his campaign to the vigilance of the police, the zeal of numerous agents working for the authorities, the imprisonment of numerous Basque family members on charges of complicity, and, above all, the perspicacity of the magistrate presiding over a court in the market town of Donapaleu, located near the western edge of Xiberoa. According to the subprefect, the magistrate took only three months to solve a problem on which the police and gendarmes had been working for more than a year.[34]

Figures vary for the total number of deserters in the department of the Basses-Pyrénées, in part because the authorities often had difficulty differentiating between deserters and defaulting recruits (*insoumis*) and keeping track of Basques who had emigrated to the Americas. According to one report (November 30, 1918), 1,086 soldiers from the department had deserted. Between August 1914 and November 1918, nearly 17,000 men from the *pays basque*, Béarn, and the Landes evaded military conscription by taking refuge in other countries (Rocafort 1997: 495). No reliable figures are available for Xiberoa. One report indicates that by November 1916, only 17 Xiberoans had deserted, a much lower rate of desertion than that of neighboring Behe Nafarroa (with 164 deserters and a much higher rate of emigration to the Americas). A local historian in Xiberoa recently estimated that "no more than a few dozen" Xiberoans deserted during the Great War (Ikherzaleak 2006: 40).[35]

As the end of the war approached, the question of amnesty increasingly divided the Basques. After the armistice, regional authorities warned Basque citizens that the French government had no intention of granting amnesty to deserters and *insoumis* who had gone to Spain and the Americas rather than fight for their country. In the Chamber of Deputies and at political rallies in Maule, Jean Ybarnegaray strongly opposed amnesty for his fellow Basques but also felt that it was their moral responsibility to return to the *patrie* and face the consequences of their actions. In March 1918 Ybarnegaray went to a country inn on the Franco-Spanish border near Arnegi (Behe Nafarroa) to harangue a group of 20 Basque *insoumis* and deserters who had gathered there. When his efforts failed to return them to France, Ybarnegaray called the men "renegades" and criticized their unacceptable attitude toward France. He later admitted feeling that little could be done to make such men obedient French citizens.[36]

The Great War had a profound demographic impact on Basque society, as it did on all other French citizens. The war severely limited the reproductive capacity of the two primordial Basque institutions, the house and the community. Some villages lost 29 percent of their mobilized men (Rocafort 1997: 593). The war left one Upper Xiberoan village without a single young man in any of its fourteen households (Lauburu 1998: 99). Urdos lost forty-six of its men. The international conflict also had an impact on Basque culture. Many soldiers who returned from the war favored cultural assimilation into French society, particularly in relation to language use (Jacob 1994: 55). During the war, as happened elsewhere, Xiberoan soldiers and their families developed new perspectives on their own habitus and that of other French citizens. The extent to which the Great War turned Basques into Frenchmen was, however, tempered by the experiences of emigrants to the Americas and those who had deserted or evaded military service for France. Emigration to the Americas exposed Basques both at home and abroad to different cultures and altered their sense of self and sense of belonging, turning some Xiberoans into Basques (Eskualdunak) as they found themselves among Basques from other provinces and Basque unity took precedence over provincial loyalties. The self-imposed exile of Basque *insoumis* and deserters in the southern Basque Country also entailed a reshaping of identities and raised further questions about national identity and loyalty to any *patrie* other than the place in which a person was born.

The aftermath of the Great War deepened Xiberoans' perceptions of France as their *patrie* and enhanced their sense of multiple identities as Xiberoans, as Basques, and as French citizens. Many Xiberoans felt French out of loyalty to what had been accomplished during the war and, above all, loyalty to those who had perished (Ikherzaleak 2006: 52–53). The war did not, however, destroy local identities or long-standing customs in the Basque Country. The cult of the dead created by the French Republic, with its cycle of commemorations and war memorials, had a special resonance for the Basques. In traditional Basque society, the process of death entailed an elaborate set of mortuary rituals and vicinal obligations (Douglass 1969; Ott 1993b). Death had a profound impact upon the Basque house, its members, their first neighbors, and the entire community.

As happened elsewhere in France, the Basques engaged in a process of collective bereavement for the "lost generation" in the postwar years (Winter 1995). They remembered those who had died on the "field of honor" through war memorials and commemorative ceremonies. In rural Xiberoa, communities could not afford more than a simple marble plaque engraved with the names of the dead and placed in the cemetery or church porch. In June 1920 the people of Maule began to raise money for their monument. Two natives of Maule who had emigrated to Buenos Aires launched the fund-raising campaign with a donation of more than two thousand francs. In February 1921 a local committee was organized to determine the nature of the monument and its location and to appoint an architect. In the same month the municipal council of Maule granted space in the communal cemetery, in perpetuity and free of charge, to families without plots there so that they could mourn loved ones whose remains were never found (Régnier 2006: 195). By December 1922 the committee had raised more than twenty-six thousand francs. In October 1923 the Béarnais politician Léon Bérard inaugurated the monument, an obelisk and plaque that bore the names of eighty-seven Maule men (ibid.: 205, 207). Among the Basques, however, war memorials were not the only sites of memory and mourning. In keeping with long-standing Basque custom, the tombs of houses in Xiberoan cemeteries remained the primordial space in which Basque women preserved and perpetuated the bond between the living and the dead through prayer, even in the absence of mortal remains from the front.

4: The Roots of Divided Memories in Maule

During the first decades of the twentieth century, intracommunity divisiveness in Maule arose over matters relating to class, ethnicity, politics, and economic survival. The two main adversarial groups in the town consisted of wealthy, politically conservative Xiberoan factory owners and their poor, mainly left-wing workers of Spanish and Navarrese origin. When Germany declared war on France in August 1914, the Maule sandal factories abruptly closed down. The authorities ordered factory workers who did not have French citizenship to return to Spain and conscripted those of Spanish origin who had obtained it. When shipments of jute recommenced in late 1914, the factories reopened but faced labor shortages until the seasonal flow of female workers from Nafarroa and Aragón recommenced in the autumn of 1915 (M. Béguerie 2004: pers. comm.; V. Inchauspé 2001: 67). When southern Basque soldiers returned to Maule after the war, many of them, as well as their families, wanted to belong to French society as French citizens and also yearned to be accepted by Maule society as "Maule people" (Mauletarrak) rather than be looked down upon as the racial, ethnic inferiors of indigenous Basques. One-fifth of Maule men who died in the Great War traced their roots to Nafarroa or, to a lesser extent, Aragón.

Maule was created in the nineteenth century when regional authorities merged the two medieval *bourgs* of Mauléon and Licharre (Viers 1958: 1). Overlooked by a medieval citadel, the Upper Town (la Haute Ville) of Maule was built on a hillside in the twelfth or thirteenth century. In the early decades of the twentieth century, the Upper Town's thriving marketplace, large square, and tightly clustered houses were the heart of a subcommunity within Maule whose members were primarily of Spanish origin and descent. For that reason, the Haute Ville was popularly known as the Jota Villa ("town of the *jota*," the national folk dance of Aragón), a place of vibrant sociability owing to its seventeen taverns, lively fiestas, and dances and the gaiety of the young women who came from the poorest hamlets and villages of northern Nafarroa and Aragón to work in the town's numerous sandal factories.

Intersected by the Saison River, the Lower Town of Maule was the center of commerce, industry, and local government. A noble family from Upper Xiberoa, the Andureins, had inherited the magnificent Renaissance château of the Mayties in 1783. Linked by marriage, the Andureins and the Souhys remained two of the most influential and wealthy families in Xiberoa throughout the nineteenth century (Viers 1961: 92). The château of the Andureins, with its extensive gated gardens, stood next to an imposing eighteenth-century mansion built for the town's lord of the manor (*le capitaine-châtelain*). This manor house served as the subprefecture of Maule from 1790 until 1926 (Hastaran 1998: 73). The château and mansion dominated a broad, tree-lined boulevard with numerous nineteenth-century villas. The town's most prominent French Basque citizens lived on the boulevard and in villas nearby, while on an adjacent street, rows of shops, offices, artisans' workshops, and sandal factories formed the main commercial district. Factories and shops surrounded the town's cathedral and public school.

At the western end of the avenue and bordering the countryside, the adjacent *bourg* of Lextarre had a public fountain, a small square, a sandal factory, and modest houses that accommodated French Basque families as well as those of Spanish origin and descent. Located on the outskirts of town, the poorest neighborhood, the Ville-en-Bois, consisted of wooden houses built for Spanish factory workers at the height of Maule's prosperity in 1910, when the town claimed to be the sandal capital of France (Viers 1958: 1). From 1900 until 1940 the population of Maule remained stable at around four thousand inhabitants, even though it was highly mobile. During that period, the town lost around 4 percent of its native population every year, owing to war and to a steady exodus of Maule citizens to other parts of the Basses-Pyrénées and, in the interwar years, to Paris (ibid.: 114–15). From 1900 until 1930 that loss was largely made up by a regular influx of Spanish seasonal migrant workers, upon whose manual labor the sandal factories depended.

Maule society was hierarchical in structure, with the Andureins and Souhys as the only landed gentry. Other notables included the "big *patrons*," who owned the largest sandal factories, and a core of professionals related to them by marriage. The notables regarded themselves first and foremost as Mauléonais-Mauletarrak, native Maule citizens whose *mentalité* was both French and Xiberoan Basque. From the late nineteenth century until the liberation of France in 1944, they controlled the town hall. Adrien de Souhy served as general councilor of the Basses-Pyrénées from 1894 until 1940. His family and the Andureins were both close friends of the Basque deputy, Jean Ybarnegaray, who was the nephew of Souhy. Unlike the Andureins and Souhys, the wealthiest factory owners (*patrons*) were nouveau riche entrepreneurs who made their fortunes in the golden age of sandal making between 1890 and 1918. From 1900 until the end of the Great War, the three main Maule factories and their home-based artisans produced twelve thousand pairs of sandals a day, initially for South American markets and then for the miners of northern France (Ikherzaleak 1994: 10, 72). One of the industry's founders, Louis Béguerie, originally ran a small draper's shop and gradually expanded his business interests to a grocery, money lending, and sandal making (M. Béguerie 2004: pers. comm.; Viers 1961: 96). The Béguerie family owned an imposing manor house in the center of town and another substantial property in the nearby countryside, where Louis Béguerie had built an electricity generator on the Saison River in the late 1890s.

In the immediate aftermath of the Great War, royalists enjoyed unprecedented prestige in France for their patriotic, pro-Catholic brand of nationalism and their solid stance against threats of revolution and disorder. The ultranationalist movement Action Française prospered (E. Weber 1962: 124). In the towns and countryside, conservative Basques felt threatened by republicanism and were suspicious of change (Jacob 1994: 63, 65). In Xiberoa they relied upon politicians such as Jean Ybarnegaray to protect them and their moral community from Bolshevism, among other dangers, and to defend rural Basque traditions and Catholicism. Among Maule conservatives, Ybarnegaray and his friend, Dr. Henri Herbille, represented order and discipline in a society that right-wing sympathizers regarded as increasingly corrupt and immoral. For both Ybarnegaray and Herbille, order depended upon the hegemony of the landed gentry and *patrons* over the working class and the preservation of a hierarchical class structure. Both men firmly rejected republican egalitarianism and regarded militant Spanish "Reds" as a serious threat to social, political, and economic order in the Basque Country.

The Maule middle class included the "little *patrons*," who employed fewer than forty workers, as well as shopkeepers, merchants, artisans, tradesmen, teachers, and other professionals. The majority of middle-class citizens were native Xiberoans or Béarnais. They were largely self interested, Catholic, and politically conservative and tended to avoid involvement in the class conflict between *patrons* and the workers. The Maule middle class did, however, also include a few entrepreneurial socialist families of Navarrese origin and a core of socialist Xiberoans who played active roles in a Xiberoan resistance group during the German Occupation. The most influential socialist family of Navarrese origin, the Rodrigos, owned a prosperous bistro and sandal-making workshop in the heart of the mainly Spanish-speaking Upper Town. Francisco Rodrigo came from the Zaraitzu Valley of northern Nafarroa. He had married a woman from Aragón and emigrated to Maule in 1905. Francisco got a job in a sandal factory and, unusual among workers, gained promotion and eventually bought a bistro in the Upper Town. Francisco quickly attracted a regular local clientele, as well as the substantial number of rural Basque men who attended weekly livestock markets in the Upper Town. Francisco spoke Spanish, French, and Basque fluently. With proceeds from their bistro, he and his wife opened a sandal-making workshop in the 1920s. The Rodrigo family's socioeconomic mobility set them apart from most other families of southern Basque origin in Maule society. The Rodrigos were also one of the few families from the Jota Villa who had the respect of both elites and workers in a society deeply divided by politics, class, and racial tension (O. Huerta, M. Rodrigo Nicolau 2004: pers. comms.).

The vast majority of Navarrese and Aragonese in Maule belonged to the town's impoverished working class. The first workers had arrived in 1869, coming from two Aragonese villages, Fago and Salvatierra (Viers 1958: 107). By the end of the nineteenth century, a pattern of seasonal migration across the Pyrenees was well established by groups of young unmarried women known as the "Swallows" (Ainarak or Hirondelles).[1] The Swallows walked from their natal villages in Spain every autumn to work as sandal makers in the Basque towns of Maule, Hazparne, and Atharratze and in the nearby Béarnais town of Oloron. The young women retraced their steps every spring to help their families with seasonal agricultural tasks. They came from twenty-three villages scattered across northwestern Aragón and northern Nafarroa, a geographical area that stretched sixty miles south from Xiberoa's border with Spain and thirty-seven miles between the Gallego River and the Irati River (ibid.). The women ranged in age from twelve to twenty-five and were often accompanied by male kin who sought seasonal jobs in southwestern France. Toward the end of the golden age of sandal making in Maule (1900–18), six factories in Maule employed almost two thousand workers of Spanish origin (Ikherzaleak 1994: 12).

Although few Swallows worked more than three seasons in Maule, they were easily recognizable as a group. Their brightly colored native costumes and their distinctive songs and dances gave the *quartiers* in which they lived an atmosphere of gaiety despite their poverty and deplorable living conditions (M. Rodrigo Nicolau 2005: pers. comm.). The women worked sixteen hours a day for little pay or for tokens, with which they bought cloth and other items for their trousseaux (Inchauspé 2001: 120–24). Groups of young women from the same village usually lodged in the houses of established families of Spanish origin. In the Spanish quarters of the Jota Villa, Lextarre, and the "Village of Wood," it was not uncommon for two or three different domestic groups to share one dwelling. Such households often had as many twenty-five members, and cohabiting families took turns using rudimentary cooking facilities in highly limited space around the hearth (P. Amigo 2005: pers. comm.; M. Rodrigo Nicolau 2004: pers. comm.; Viers 1961: 58).

No single, homogeneous moral community existed in Xiberoa, owing to long-standing traditions of trans-Pyrenean migration, immigration, and human displacement brought about by civil and world wars. By 1930 two main moral communities existed in Maule: that of conservative, deeply religious Basques whose *mentalité* was both French and Xiberoan and who accepted the hegemony of the landed gentry and notables; and that of anticlerical, mainly socialist citizens of Aragonese and Navarrese descent whose *mentalité* drew from Basque, French, and Spanish cultures. During the interwar years, a process of cultural assimilation had begun to blur the social and spatial boundaries between those two moral communities as a result of intermarriage, military service, increasing fluency in the French language, and the acquisition of French citizenship. But their respective members did not yet share a habitus.

In Maule hierarchy, traditionalism, and authoritarianism, as the foundations of order and stability, shaped the habitus of notables and conservative, middle-class citizens. In their vision of society, the hegemony of political elites and notables promised security and well-being for all citizens who conducted themselves appropriately. Proper conduct entailed respect for, and submission to, the power and authority of men such as Souhy and Ybarnegaray and Xiberoan notables, many of whom were highly respected veterans of the Great War. Such individuals regarded themselves, and were seen as, the town's principal defenders and protectors of the family, property, the local economy, and the Catholic Church. From 1920 communism constituted a primary threat to their moral community. By contrast, secularism, anticlericalism, and egalitarianism featured prominently in the habitus of Spanish workers, who challenged the hegemony of French Basque political elites and notables. From 1917 until 1939, militant workers and their supporters repeatedly confronted powerful factory owners about workers' rights to better pay and better conditions at home and in the factories.

In spite of cultural similarities between rural Xiberoans and borderland people from Nafarroa and Aragón, lowland Xiberoans (especially in Maule) tended to regard people of Spanish origin and descent as strangers and foreigners whose habitus was different from their own and whose social habits sometimes offended local sensibilities. In the first three decades of the twentieth century, many Xiberoans regarded Navarrese and Aragonese as their racial and social inferiors and often described them as dirty (*zikin*) and despicable (*tzar* in Basque; *méprisable* in French) (R. Pérez 2004: pers. comm.). Indigenous citizens found the domestic arrangements of local "Spaniards" particularly repugnant, because their households often sheltered multiple domestic groups composed of migratory workers and, during 1936–39, civilian and political refugees from the Spanish Civil War. Tradition-bound Xiberoans decried such domestic promiscuity (and the promiscuous hospitality it entailed) as a violation of the Xiberoan house as a moral, social, and spiritual entity.

As the most culturally diverse and socially complex community in Xiberoa, Maule had unusual class-based and ethnic divisions. At the beginning of the twentieth century, the spatial organization of the town reflected such divisions. Navarrese and Aragonese workers lived in the poorest neighborhoods. Between 1906 and 1910 only 11 percent of the population in *les quartiers aisés* was of Spanish or southern Basque descent. By 1911 not a single person from Spain lived in those neighborhoods (Viers 1961: 59). In the predominantly French Basque *quartiers,* notables and middle-class households were bound together as first neighbors in relationships based upon mutual aid, trust, and cooperation. Every house had one first neighbor, classified as "the house nearest the church" from one's own dwelling. Although the institution was never as strong in Xiberoan towns as in the countryside, the first-neighbor bond gave Mauletarrak a social solidarity that events eroded in the interwar years.

Spatial segregation of "Spaniards" and Mauletarrak extended to venues of public sociability as well. Certain cafés and taverns catered only to Navarrese and Aragonese people, others served only Mauletarrak, and a few establishments catered to both groups by allocating each one a certain time of day (M. Rodrigo Nicolau 2004: pers. comm.). At the fountains and washhouses, another contested space, Navarrese and Aragonese women often clashed with Xiberoan women from the town and countryside. The two groups commonly exchanged insults (R. Pérez 2004: pers. comm.). When the local schools reached their capacity (or their *instituteurs* [teachers] claimed they had done so), the *instituteurs* often turned away children of Spanish origin. In the 1920s and 1930s Xiberoans often justified their contempt for and exclusion of "Spaniards" by pointing out that, with few exceptions, the immigrants "deliberately ignored the Church and Religion," behavior that conservative Xiberoans could not overlook or forgive (Viers 1961: 59). Allegations of anticlericalism ruined a Navarrese or Aragonese woman's chances of becoming a maid in the home of an elite or notable.

By the 1920s the "Spanish" community mainly consisted of people born in the Erronkari Valley of Nafarroa and in Upper Aragón, along with their Maule-born offspring. The community had its roots in rural Pyrenean cultures, where the first-neighbor relationship figured prominently (M. Rodrigo Nicolau 2005: pers. comm.). People of Navarrese and Aragonese origin responded to their new multiethnic, multicultural environment in ways that enhanced their solidarity. They celebrated their differences by retaining the native costumes of Erronkari and Aragón, their native languages, and their forms of popular culture (music and dance); they also used their cultural similarities and shared circumstances to promote cohesiveness. Navarrese and Aragonese immigrants shared aspects of the same Pyrenean habitus in their new lived environment; they understood the Pyrenean ethos of mutual coop- eration, trust, and amicability between neighbors, and they tried to uphold that ethos in their dealings with one another. Accounts of daily life in the "Spanish" quarters always emphasize the importance people attached to mu- tual aid (*entraide*), a Pyrenean practice that strengthened social bonds between Spanish workers and families. One Maule woman recently commented: "People who came from Erronkari and Aragón always helped each other. They helped each other find jobs and housing. When the factory workers went on strike, people shared their food with the families hardest hit by the walk-outs. I can remember three families sharing that house over there, across the square. They had twenty-three children among them, all needing food and clothes. My mother used to take them food from our bistro and clothes we'd outgrown. The custom of mutual aid was very important in those days" (M. Rodrigo Nicolau 2004: pers. comm.). As proprietors of a bistro and a sandal-making workshop, the Rodrigo family played an impor- tant charitable role in the "Spanish" quarters for several decades.

For many families of Navarrese origin, the Rodrigos embodied a goal that seemed unattainable: socioeconomic advancement in a class system that seemed, to many workers, impossible to break. The workers had much in common: poverty, illiteracy, poorly paid and physically unpleasant jobs. Edu- cational opportunities were extremely limited, and intermarriage between "Spaniards" and Xiberoans was still unthinkable. Between 1901 and 1910, only 5 of 215 marriages contracted by Spanish citizens involved a Spanish man and a French/Xiberoan woman. During that period, ten Spanish women married a French/Xiberoan man (Viers 1961: 59).

Conservative Xiberoans frowned upon intermarriage between Xiberoans and Spanish citizens and expressed uneasiness about the process of assimi- lation that began in the 1930s (Inchauspé 2001: 107–8; R. Pérez 2005: pers. comm.; Viers 1961: 59). The social construction of a hybrid "Spanish" Mauléonais identity drew upon their rural roots in Aragón and Nafarroa, but it also contained a developing sense of "being French," primarily as a result of military service in the Great War and the acquisition of the French lan- guage and citizenship. People of Navarrese and Aragonese origin often had contradictory, confusing feelings about patriotism, nationality, and cultural belonging. Some citizens from those provinces resolutely refused or never bothered to learn French or Basque, which many Maule people still spoke before the Second World War (Inchauspé 2001: 111). Many Xiberoans in Maule were fluent in Spanish, the main language of commerce, trade, and the shop floor, and such fluency reduced Spaniards' need to communicate in French (M. Etcheverry, M. Rodrigo Nicolau 2003: pers. comms.). Within the Navarrese/Aragonese community, different generations frequently spoke different languages. Parents from Erronkari often spoke Basque to each other but used Spanish with their children. In some households, siblings talked to each other interchangeably in Spanish and French. The linguistic hybridity of the Navarrese/Aragonese community was reflected in a grammatical mixture of French and Spanish that some elderly people still speak.

By the 1930s Maule lacked the institutionalized relationship between houses that gave rural Basque society such solidarity. Households no longer systematically recognized their first-neighbor relationships. Contrary to the rules of traditional, rural Basque society, individual households decided whether or not to activate a first-neighbor relationship. If two first-neighbor families enjoyed reasonably amicable relations, they upheld long-standing Basque traditions of mutual aid and cooperation. Amicable relations were not confined to households that had the same ethnic heritage, for some families of Spanish origin got along well with their French Basque neighbors. If political, ethnic, or socially driven animosities divided two first-neighbor households, however, their members simply ignored the vicinal bond that had once existed between their respective houses (M. Etcheverry, O. Huerta 2004: pers. comms.). The demise of the first-neighbor relationship derived in great measure from the political turmoil and class conflict of the interwar years in Maule, but personal animosities, commercial rivalries, and ethnic tensions also fragmented vicinal relations in the 1920s and 1930s. As one Maule woman recently observed, "People used to trust each other. Neighbors used to get along and help each other. But that all stopped. I don't know when, it stopped because so many people had differences" (M. Udoy 2004: pers. comm.). The breakdown of vicinal relations had a profound impact upon the moral community shared by indigenous Maule citizens. Inherited expectations and social rules began to change as native inhabitants found themselves increasingly surrounded by Spanish outsiders (*forasteros*) who had settled in their town.

Of the three "Spanish" neighborhoods in town, only the Ville-en-Bois remained an exclusively Navarrese and Aragonese enclave in the 1930s. In the Upper Town and Licharre, the houses of middle-class factory owners, shop-keepers, and merchants stood alongside the much less comfortable and less spacious houses occupied by Navarrese and Aragonese workers and their visiting relatives from Spain. Ethnic tensions often derived from differences in habitus. Navarrese and Aragonese families regularly socialized in the street rather than in their cramped and crowded dwellings, regarding the street as an acceptable space in which to exchange news and opinions in animated fashion. Although Xiberoans also socialized in the street, they had different rules of engagement from those of the "Spanish" community. Xiberoans limited their communications in public to polite enquiries about someone's well-being and brief exchanges of news. People refrained from asking too many personal questions and gave guarded answers. The rules of their Xiberoan moral community decreed that detailed social communications properly took place within the safe confines of one's own house or that of a trusted neighbor or relative, not on the street (M. Etcheverry 2003: pers. comm.; O. Huerta 2004: pers. comm.). Native Xiberoans often disapproved of (or felt uncomfortable with) the boisterous, public behavior of "Spaniards" and criticized the women, in particular, for "gadding about" in the streets (*kourritzen ari da,* in Xiberoan; *courir la prétantaine* in French). In the habitus of Xiberoan Basques, "gadding about" demonstrated a high level of irresponsibility, for it was thought that any woman who spent a lot of time visiting friends neglected her responsibilities in the house and thus deserved to become the focus of severe public criticism.

For some Xiberoan Basque children growing up in Maule in the 1930s, the "Spanish" neighborhoods constituted forbidden spaces, full of imagined dangers. As one woman recalled with great embarrassment in 2003: "As young children, we heard that all Spaniards were 'Reds,' that they were all communists, devils with tails! People always complained about the way they lived in the streets and kept their front doors wide open. Not like us! She found the Spaniards so noisy and rowdy in comparison to us. I never dared set foot in the neighborhoods where they lived" (M. Joanny 2003: pers. comm.). Not all Spanish citizens who passed through or settled in Xiberoa were left-wing sympathizers or "Red" activists. Many of them avoided involvement in political debate and tried, above all, to remain employed, to achieve a decent standard of living, and to gain acceptance in the Xiberoan moral community. All three objectives were difficult to achieve during the interwar years, as ethnic, socioeconomic, and political tensions deepened.

5: Class Conflict, Displacement, and Fear of the Other

By 1917 several factors deeply divided the citizens of Maule: animosities between the families of soldiers at the front and those of *insoumis* and deserters, factory strikes and class conflict, political and ethnic tensions. In an otherwise predominantly conservative region of France, Maule was widely known as a left-wing stronghold. In June 1917 the Maule police inspector reported that "a regrettable Spanish element" had rallied a militant group of Basque laborers to strike against their wealthy Maule *patrons.*[1] Of the 2,000, mainly Spanish and Navarrese workers in Maule, only 250 joined the strike, but their militancy, lack of respect, and open disdain for *patrons* infuriated Louis Béguerie, one of three most powerful Xiberoan factory owners between 1890 and 1920. When the militant workers flatly refused to do any work, Béguerie asked Maule's three gendarmes to arrest them. The police swiftly sent telegrams to the gendarmeries in Pau and Baiona requesting additional manpower. At the same time, the prefect in Pau told Béguerie to calm down and control his temper. Although most of the workers returned to their jobs, tensions between strike leaders and *patrons* remained high.[2]

In January 1918 the subprefect in Maule reported to the prefect that the conflict had deepened "owing to the violence of certain workers and to the intransigence of the *patrons.*" When violence involving both workers and foremen escalated, the prefect himself intervened and restored an uneasy order that lasted two months. The prefect convinced the factory owners to make some salary increases, but—as happened elsewhere in France at the time—the cost of living rose sharply and left many workers feeling as dissatisfied as ever. Militant workers organized demonstrations outside factory gates and launched an intense campaign to form a local chapter of the Syndicate of Sandal Workers (Syndicat des Ouvriers Sandaliers). A core of Xiberoan workers who were mainly First World War veterans led the campaign and recruited six hundred members. The *patron*-worker conflict reached a peak in August 1918, when a local magistrate attempted to negotiate a settlement between factory owners and militant workers. At that meeting Louis Béguerie and another *patron* angrily contested the mandate of the strike leaders. When the other *patron* became violent, the magistrate ended negotiations and sent everyone home.[3]

Factory owners and workers briefly put aside their differences when the armistice was declared. The church bells tolled, the factories closed, and citizens flocked to hear speeches by Mayor Jean-Baptiste Herbille (father of Henri) and members of the municipal council. On November 17 the church filled with people to honor the dead in a special ceremony (Régnier 2006: 190). Dr. Henri Herbille returned from the war with fellow Maule notables, including Pierre Béguerie, the only son of Louis Béguerie. During the Great War, Pierre Béguerie served in the Tenth Cavalry Regiment of the Hussars, based in Tarbes in the department of the Hautes-Pyrénées. In 1918 Pierre Béguerie was thirty-two years old and knew his future would be shaped by the Maule sandal industry. Although his father was sixty-two years old when the Great War ended, Pierre did not take charge of the family business until his father's death in 1920.

In 1919 the citizens of Maule reelected Dr. Jean-Baptiste Herbille as their mayor and two factory owners (including Louis Béguerie) as his deputies. In the following year, Henri Herbille assumed executive responsibilities in the Béguerie factory. Both Henri Herbille and his father became deeply involved in a *patron*-worker conflict that would continue to turn many Maule people against each other until the twenty-first century. As the mayor of Maule, the elder Dr. Herbille quickly got embroiled in a power struggle with the subprefect in Maule, M. Lepébie, who was not Basque and thus was an outsider to the Xiberoan and Maule moral communities. Although the Maule magistrate and local police were responsible for the management of local justice and law enforcement, subprefect Lepébie, as a representative of the external authorities, oversaw such matters. As an insider, the elder Herbille highly resented Lepébie's interventions and claimed that he, as mayor, had a right to manage both local justice and the local conflict between *patrons* and left-wing workers (M. Béguerie 2004: pers. comm.). To the fury of Herbille, Lepébie sided with the workers. According to Lepébie's reports to the prefect in Pau, Herbille openly favored the violent repression of troublemakers during the factory strike of August 1918. Commenting on the newly elected mayor's determination to repress strike leaders, the subprefect observed that "the workers are citizens who have the right to disagree with their employers and the civil authorities." The subprefect opposed "unjustifiable arrests" and blocked attempts by Herbille to detain militant workers. When the strike of August 1918 ended, Lepébie sought additional protection for the moral community from the external authorities, asking the prefect for an additional eight policemen on the Maule force "in order to ensure order and public tranquility" in the town.[4]

In other reports to the prefect in Pau, Lepébie expressed deep sympathy for the workers and felt that their complaints about low pay and poor conditions were justified. On March 10, 1920, a general assembly of striking workers met the subprefect on the handball court of the Upper Town, a space symbolically and socially associated with Maule's "Spanish" community. Workers advised Lepébie that they were willing to negotiate with him, but not if Mayor Herbille "continued to be both their judge and adversary." The subprefect called for calm and discipline and promised to exclude Herbille from their negotiations. The workers returned to the factories, but both the management and the workforce anticipated further trouble.[5]

In the French Chamber of Deputies, the majority of members were moving to the right, and serious labor disputes troubled the country. In the first months of 1920, railway workers and miners went on strike. Across France, citizens close to the Action Française organized civic unions to address the so-called Bolshevik threat (E. Weber 1962: 130). With the assistance of Deputy Jean Ybarnegaray, the Action Française recruited some of Maule's factory owners, who formed a Maule section for the movement, as well as a propaganda center in nearby Hazparne in Behe Nafarroa. Both developments gave rise to rise to vigorous protest among militant left-wing workers in those two industrialized Basque towns (Moreau 1972: 183). In the 1920s Ybarnegaray was also active in the Jeunesses Patriotes, a veterans' league founded by the Champagne magnate, Pierre Taittinger, and often seen as a fascist or protofascist movement (Soucy 1986: 60–62). Ybarnegaray later became a leader in the Croix de Feu, originally a First World War veterans' organization that came under the control of a fiercely nationalist soldier, Colonel de la Rocque, in 1931 (Atkin 2001: 21; Paxton 2001: 162).

In April 1920 nearly all of Maule's two thousand sandal workers went on strike for thirty-three days.[6] In July 1920 subprefect Lepébie organized a commission to discuss the possibility of pay increases, improved hours, and better working conditions. At that stage, he was prepared to let Mayor Herbille participate in negotiations. The commission consisted of three workers and three *patrons,* one of whom was the mayor's son, Dr. Henri Herbille, who represented the six major factories (including the Béguerie enterprise) involved in the strike. One worker, Jean Hegoburu, was a native Mauletarr whose parents had emigrated from Nafarroa. A committed socialist, Hegoburu was an officer in the local Syndicate of Sandal Workers. An outsider—Lepébie—external to the diverse moral communities of Maule, had given the two local, rival factions an opportunity to resolve a conflict that was constantly fueled by national and international events. The commission had little success, however, for the *patrons* refused to raise salaries to the level demanded by workers, and negotiations broke down. By the end of 1920, the prefect had a thick file on "the troubles" in Maule.[7]

In national elections of 1924, the moderate Left took power from the center Right, and conservatives grew increasingly anxious over social and economic reforms proposed by Radicals and Socialists in parliament (E. Weber 1962: 154). In Maule factory owners fretted over the possible enforcement of the eight-hour work law, but the chief concern of conservative Xiberoans was the French government's decision to recognize Soviet Russia. Across France, public fears of a communist takeover forced the government to act. Police raided Communist offices and arrested Communist leaders. The Action Française regained popular support for its long-standing anticommunist stance. In the Chamber of Deputies, Jean Ybarnegaray defended the royalists as "an important rampart against Communist revolt" (ibid.: 156). In Xiberoa the moral community of conservative, Catholic Basques felt threatened by communism, which was embraced by male and female factory workers of Navarrese and Aragonese origin (R. Pérez 2004: pers. comm.). In 1926 the French government relocated the subprefect to the town of Oloron, when it decreed that the two Xiberoan cantons of Maule and Atharratze should be attached to that Béarnais arrondissement (Hastaran 1998: 73). Although the move reduced the subprefect's opportunities to manage the *patron*-worker conflict himself, Lepébie kept closely informed about developments in Maule and continued to report them to the prefect. Without the intervention of regional authorities, some Maule citizens tried to improve relations between *patrons* and workers and to address certain critical needs in the Spanish community. In 1927 the Bégueries built a row of modest houses for some of his employees and their families.[8] In the same year, *patrons'* wives organized a crèche for the children of factory workers, who were still primarily women.

In November 1928, however, a special commission in Pau advised the prefect that "very serious differences" still divided the *patrons* and the sandal workers in Maule and warned that a massive strike would occur if the factory owners refused to increase pay levels. When one of the largest employers raised his pay rates, workers in all the other factories demanded the same treatment from their *patrons,* who flatly refused their demands. For three days, more than seven hundred sandal workers went on strike (R. Pérez 2004: pers. comm.). The conservative local press launched an attack on the workers: "Maule is in a state of agitation. The town is once again in crisis. The sandal workers are on strike. It's their right! They want pay increases. Each one of us does, too! All the screaming and yelling of the young workers in the street, their false laughter and forced gaiety make our hearts go cold. . . . We heard one shrew bawl out, with foam on her lips, 'The *patrons* must be killed! They get rich at the expense of their workers!'"[9] Strike leaders argued for a 20 percent pay increase. Factory owners offered between 10 and 12 percent. A special commissioner in Pau reported that, to end the conflict, *patrons* reluctantly agreed to pay increases of 16 to 18 percent.[10]

In August 1929 another strike closed the factories for fourteen days. The conservative press reported that a mood of relative calm prevailed in Maule when the strike ended:

> A few revolutionary songs were sung, not too ferociously, just as and when it suited the workers. No scuffles, lots of high spirits among the youth. A model strike, wasn't it! The workers got what they demanded. The *patrons* didn't pay close enough attention to what was going on, but it's OK to defend them a little. In the end, everyone seemed satisfied, and work in the factories started up again. Great! As always, someone has to have the last word, so for a laugh, here are some details of what happened at the last meeting (between *patrons* and workers): the most eloquent of the workers explained to those assembled that the *patrons* didn't want to give in any further to the workers. Matters had to go to arbitration. "We will accept arbitration," proclaimed the eloquent worker to the assembly, "on condition that you give us what we want!"[11]

Numerous other industrial disputes followed (Ikherzaleak 1994: 108–10).

Although the Swallows from Aragón and Nafarroa made their annual migration to Maule in the autumn of 1930, they stopped their trans-Pyrenean tradition the following year, when global depression finally affected the French and Maule economies. Roughly 11 percent of the town's Spaniards, primarily young women from Aragón, decided to return permanently to their natal villages (Viers 1961: 104). When some young women told *patrons* their intentions, the factory owners tried to change their minds. Some *patrons* promised to reserve all job openings for the Espagnoles "because they were the best workers." One young woman from Aragón told her *patron* that young Maule women should be offered all the jobs—that it would be better if the Aragonese girls went home rather than remain in Maule and "steal the jobs" from the local women (Inchauspé 2001: 90). In the sandal-making industry, production dropped dramatically, owing mainly to factory closures and reduced operating hours. Only one Maule factory continued to operate on an eighty-hour week. Many Maule workers of Spanish and Navarrese origin found themselves unemployed, and some sought jobs on the Basque coast, where they received twenty-seven francs an hour. In the Maule factories that remained open, workers earned the same amount in one week (ibid.: 87).

In Maule a major strike in 1931 led to the brief imprisonment of a Basque socialist sandal maker who was president of the local trade union, the CGT (Confédération Générale du Travail). On his release, St. Jean Lanouguère started up a sandal-making cooperative with other workers who had been fired during the strike. He initiated and led industrial disputes throughout the 1930s.[12] As the cooperative's spokesman, Lanouguère took part in business discussions alongside influential *patrons*. Although the trade unionist vigorously denied that he had thus acquired *patron* status, Lanouguère's communist critics mockingly referred to him as one and quarreled with him about local strike tactics (Zunzarren 2004: 12). Some *patrons* used such squabbling to dissuade workers from joining the union. As the husband of a Navarrese factory worker, Lanouguère belonged to a transitional generation of Maule French Basques closely linked to the town's Spanish community through kinship, friendship, and shared political sympathies with the Spanish Republican cause. Although Lanouguère had enemies on both the Right and the Left in all their varied forms, Lanouguère never became the target of denunciation.

The 1930s brought deep uncertainty in Maule, as the French confronted the rise of international fascism and the threat of Bolshevism. A global depression and a wave of scandals implicating members of the French parliament increased scorn for the Republic among nationalist and veteran leagues across France, and such factors empowered the leagues (Paxton 2001: 244). In early 1934 a financial scandal in the coastal Basque city of Baiona led to a political crisis in France. The Affaire Stavisky gave right-wing leagues an opportunity to demonstrate their power. A police spy, gambler, and confidence trickster of Jewish eastern European origin, Serge Alexandre Stavisky became involved in a series of fraudulent bond issues made by the town's municipal pawnshop with the approval of Baiona's Radical mayor and deputy in parliament (E. Weber 1996: 320). For the French Right, Stavisky embodied the corruption and immorality of the republican system. The national scandal that ensued led to the alleged suicide of Stavisky, the political ruin of Baiona's Radical mayor (in part through the efforts of Ybarnegaray), and a massive street demonstration in Paris on February 6, 1934. Some 40,000 members of nationalist and veterans' organizations (including the Action Française and the Croix de Feu) marched on the Chamber of Deputies. Firing into the crowd, the police killed 16 demonstrators and injured 655 others. Édouard Daladier's government resigned the next day. The demonstration and its repression "began the virtual French civil war of the mid-1930s" (Paxton 2001: 244–45).

In the wake of the demonstration in 1934, Jean Ybarnegaray called for a "French revival in work, order, authority, and honor" and for an answer to that "appeal of the race" that had been heard in Italy and Germany but not yet in France (ibid.: 162). In the same year, Pierre Béguerie joined La Rocque's extreme right-wing group, the Croix de Feu, because he "believed it was an association of elite veterans" (Béguerie n.d.: 15). When antileague legislation by France's Popular Front forced La Rocque to turn the Croix de Feu into a political party (the Parti Social Français, or PSF) in 1936, Ybarnegaray became La Rocque's most prominent deputy in the PSF. Ybarnegary pressed his friend Béguerie to join, but the factory owner declined. In his memoirs, Pierre Béguerie later reflected that "before 1939, I was considered by the Maule Left to belong to the extreme Right. In their eyes, I qualified as a fascist" (ibid.: 15).

In the legislative elections of 1936, Ybarnegaray achieved an overwhelming victory in the Basses-Pyrénées, largely owing to his robust defense of conservative Basque values and traditions. According to the census of 1936, only 26 percent of Maule's inhabitants were Xiberoans native to the town. A further 40 percent came from other Xiberoan communities. To the consternation of Ybarnegaray, 34 percent of his constituency was of Spanish/Navarrese origin or descent (Viers 1961: 48). Many of those who traced their roots to villages of the Erronkari Valley (Izaba, Burgi, Uztarroz, Urzainki, Erronkari, Vidangoz, and Garde) were left-wing activists or sympathizers. Although Nafarroa was a Carlist stronghold, the Erronkari Valley had an important core of republicans, anarchists, socialists, and communists, especially in the villages of Izaba, Burgi, and Garde (Altaffaylla 2003: 521).

Soon after the Second Spanish Republic began in 1931, Izaba socialists created a branch of the socialist General Workers' Union (Unión General de Trabajadores, or UGT) and an Autonomous Republican Party, which distanced itself from the Basque nationalist group in Izaba and vociferously opposed the Carlist Right, formed by Izaba's wealthy landowners and headed by the cacique Dositeo Ochoa (García-Sanz Marcotegui 2001: 322). Izaba republicans and socialists repeatedly challenged the hegemony of Ochoa and his fellow *patrons* and clashed with them over communal matters such as road building and the repair of village mills. When the Spanish Civil War began in the summer of 1936, most of the Erronkari Valley's left-wing sympathizers and militants crossed the frontier at Urdos and made their way to Maule and to Béarnais towns where they had numerous friends and relatives. In 1936 sixtynine people from Izaba alone sought refuge in France, mainly in Maule (Altaffaylla 2003: 524).

The Popular Front in France and the outbreak of civil war in Spain increased anxiety among Maule's conservative citizens, many of them fearing that Spain's conflict might spread to their side of the Pyrenees. As the most prominent deputy in La Rocque's Parti Social Français, Ybarnegaray called for the repression of Jews, communists, and Freemasons. He railed against the "Reds" in his constituency, as well as the Spanish Republicans who flooded into the region seeking aid, shelter, and work (Laharie 1993: 24).[13] The moral community of culturally and politically conservative Xiberoans feared communism and anticlericalism. They disliked disorder intensely and deeply resented the presence of so many strangers in their *pays* who required food, shelter, and work. The large-scale displacement of Spanish refugees into the region severely challenged the ability of Xiberoans to manage their own affairs and territory. The massive influx of strangers also fueled xenophobic tendencies.

Unrest in Maule deepened in 1937, when Ybarnegaray invited the renowned French agitator Henry Dorgères to speak at a rally in Maule.[14] Dorgères' radical right-wing farmers' movement promoted itself as France's best defense against rural communism and the trade union (CGT) responsible for massive strikes that year (Paxton 1997: 65–66, 85). When Dorgères' men paraded down the boulevard to "confront the soviets," the socialist Lanouguère stood alongside militant communists and left-wing farmers from Upper Xiberoa to taunt the "fascists" (P.-P. Dalgalarrondo 2004: pers. comm.; Ikherzaleak 1994: 109). Armed with bicycle pumps, the crowd challenged Dorgères' "Green Shirts" to fight and advanced on their adversaries. The fray left many men on both sides injured and bloody. From the safety of his château, Adrien de Souhy, general councilor of the Basses-Pyrénées, asked the police inspector to bring in horse-mounted troops. Ybarnegaray watched the violent confrontation through a window of the château (L. Blasquiz 2005: pers. comm.). Two of the communists who fought against the Green Shirts on that day, Lambert Blasquiz and Eustaquio Pérez, embodied the "Red threat" that conservative Basques regarded as an endangerment to property, Catholic values, and socioeconomic order.

Influenced by national and international events in the 1930s, the relationship between the departmental authorities and the mayor of Maule had begun to change, for the elder Dr. Herbille increasingly needed the state and its representatives (including Ybarnegaray) to deal with the communist threat, led mainly by men of Spanish and Navarrese descent, which had become far too complex for Xiberoans and the local police to manage on their own. From 1918 until the 1930s, Herbille had often clashed with the departmental prefect of the Basses-Pyrénées and the subprefect responsible for the arrondissement of Maule. Their antagonistic relationship was rooted, in part, in the long-standing tradition among Xiberoan Basques to manage their own affairs without interference from outsiders to their moral community. From 1936 to 1939, local authorities such as Dr. Henri Herbille and his departmental superiors also faced the turmoil caused by thousands of exiled Spanish Republicans on Xiberoan territory.

A two-directional trans-Pyrenean movement of people, goods, and services had long been in place when the first Spanish and Basque political and civilian refugees arrived in Xiberoa in 1936. Following the bombing of Irun on the Spanish Basque coast in September 1936, an influx of Republican refugees ended up in Pau, Orthez, and Maule (Arnould 1999: 339). Many Republican soldiers quickly moved on to rejoin the cause in Barcelona. A few were persuaded by French officials to move away from the politically sensitive Franco-Spanish border. In September 1936 a conservative newspaper with a wide readership in Maule decried the presence of so many Spanish Republicans who "salute, Moscow-style, and sing the International" in public (Arnould 1999: 340, quoting from *Le Patriote des Pyrénées*). In the spring of 1937 the Basque government in exile sought refuge in France and began to create colonies for Basque refugees in Behe Nafarroa and elsewhere (Arnould 1999: 341). In June 1937 a new wave of Spanish refugees flooded into the Basses-Pyrénées after the fall of Bilbo (Bilbao) to Franco's Nationalists. The prefect in Pau formed a committee to aid civilian refugees and asked the mayors of every commune in the department to provide much needed food, clothing, and medicine.[15] France had long served as a refuge for Spaniards in exile, but by 1939 their massive presence in the south posed serious problems for French politicians, particularly anxious to retain neutrality with Franco in case war broke out between France and Germany. Before the Spanish Civil War was over in 1939, the French minister of foreign affairs sent the Béarnais senator, Léon Bérard, to Burgos to negotiate with Franco's foreign minister (Thomas 2001: 860, 872). Following their secret talks, Daladier's government officially established diplomatic relations with Franco and agreed, among other things, to maintain friendly relations with its neighbor.

With the fall of Catalonia in January 1939, the final Retreat (La Retirada) of Republicans and frightened civilians fleeing Franco's forces sent an estimated 500,000 more Spanish exiles into southern France (Dreyfus-Armand 1999: 41–55). The French Chamber of Deputies debated "the refugee problem" at length and often violently. As left-wing parliamentarians continued to defend the refugees' right of asylum in France, the extreme right-wing voice of Jean Ybarnegaray railed against the arrival of another "405,000 Spaniards who added to the burden imposed upon France by the three and a half million foreigners already installed" there (ibid. 1999: 46; Marrus and Paxton 1995: 64). He heralded Spain's decision to reopen its frontier as "one of the fortunate consequences of France's recognition of Franco's government," for it enabled repatriation (Rubio 1977: 830). His socialist opponents, by contrast, expressed concern over the repression of Republicans who returned to Spain; Franco had not extended forgiveness to those who were "open to criminal prosecution for criminal offences" there (Stein 1979: 83).

When the massive exodus of Spanish Republicans into France took place in January 1939, the French government persuaded itself that the cataclysm would be short lived. The authorities initially had no intention of integrating "Red" refugees into the economy, which had not yet recovered from the recession. On February 5, 1939, the first convoys of exiled Spanish Republicans to arrive in Pau carried 1,700 refugees, mainly women, children, and the elderly. The prefect dispersed them in towns across the Basses-Pyrénées. On the following day, an additional 700 exiled Republicans reached Pau and were likewise sent into Béarnais and Basque towns, including Maule.[16] On February 9 a third convoy carried 700 more Republican refugees to Pau, whom the authorities sent to various communes in Béarn. In July 1939 border patrols reported an influx of male refugees through the Pyrenean valleys of Ossau and Aspe in Béarn and the borderland commune of Urdos. Military authorities instructed patrols to allow the "strangers" into France, request their identity papers, and disarm them. By the end of July the authorities had accounted for 20 male Spanish refugees in Maule, where they lodged with friends and relatives (Arnould 1999: 338).

In Xiberoan and Béarnais communities, citizens mainly responded to the arrival of exiled Spaniards in one of two ways: rejection or solidarity (ibid.: 342). The Béarnais press called upon French citizens to protect their own interests and cautioned readers to be particularly wary of female refugees, who were "even more undesirable than their male companions" and who, the press warned, would be "prowling around our territory" posing a serious moral and physical threat to the well-being of local people.[17]

Villagers from one Béarnais community near Urdos wrote a petition protesting the presence of so many female Spanish refugees in their commune. The community complained that the refugees' "deplorable morality" had attracted the attention of vulnerable young men between the ages of fourteen and twenty.[18] Not all Xiberoans and Béarnais, however, supported the approach taken by that Basque community, the right-wing press, and the parliamentarian Jean Ybarnegaray. When the "great exodus" of Catalan refugees reached their region in 1939, many local volunteers in Maule and Oloron received the exhausted, hungry refugees with great sympathy and generosity. Although most volunteers were of Spanish origin and descent, indigenous Basques and Béarnais people extended aid as well (M. Rodrigo Nicolau 2005: pers. comm.). In Oloron the subprefect, mayor, deputy mayor, and a large crowd of local people greeted 757 Catalan refugees on February 9 in a public demonstration of support. The radical socialist mayor, Léon Mendiondou, led the town's welcome committee, which provided a substantial meal and vaccinations for the refugees, some of whom, in turn, warmly thanked the townspeople of Oloron in the local press. A convoy took 78 of the refugees to Maule on February 10 (AMCB 1995: 89–91).

In the spring of 1939, the French state responded to the refugee problem by creating so-called "welcome centers" in southern France, with one reserved for anti-Franco Basques (Laharie 1993: 23). Their squalid, overcrowded conditions, the misery of the refugees, and the cost of their upkeep further divided parliamentarians. One of the "welcome centers" was at Gurs, eleven miles northeast of Maule. According to the right-wing regional press of 1939, few Xiberoans or Béarnais were eager to have a camp for Spanish and Basque Republicans in or near their own communities. Rumors about the refugees were plentiful: they were all communists who ate cats, had tails like the devil, and killed priests. Local anticommunist sentiment was fuelled by pro-Franco propaganda and vigorously promoted by Ybarnegaray. He argued that the presence of unruly Spanish and Basque "Reds" in his constituency would severely threaten the social order of "normally peaceful French Basque society" (ibid.: 24). Ybarnegaray lobbied the departmental prefect and his former fellow deputy, Léon Bérard, who was by then a senator in Paris, president of the General Council for the Basses-Pyrénées, and a key player in Franco-Spanish relations.

Yielding to pressure from Ybarnegaray, the prefect suggested several alternative locations in neighboring Béarn. Intense wrangling followed. When the tiny Béarnais commune of Ogeu-les-Bains was proposed, public outcry ensued. How could such a small community possibly provide enough food to support a refugee population thirty times larger than itself? How could it defend itself if the "Reds" became agitated and broke out of the camp? Only one local politician favored the proposal. Mendiondou, mayor of Oloron, argued that building the camp in Ogeu would bring prosperity to the region by providing work for local artisans and stimulating agricultural production. Mendiondou was the only Popular Front mayor in the department at that time. A few weeks later the prefect announced that the camp would be located at Gurs in Béarn, on the eastern border of Xiberoa.

The Béarnais press decried the creation of "a concentration camp for Spanish militia" in its territory. The development scandalized the young right-wing deputy from Orthez, Jean-Louis Tixier-Vignancour, supported by notables such as Léon Bérard, who regarded Tixier as his "dauphin." The left-wing press railed against Bérard as a "fascist" and suspected Tixier of having similar tendencies (Arette Lendresse 1988: 63, 183). In 1937 Tixier had organized and presided over anticommunist Republican committees in the region. When he learned about the camp at Gurs, Tixier argued that the refugees constituted "not only an army of anarchists but also of international criminals" (ibid.: 64; Laharie 1993: 25).[19]

In the Xiberoan hamlet of Ospitaleku, only a mile from Gurs, Basques expressed their own apprehensions about the camp. Without a telephone, they argued, how could they alert the police fast enough if the "Reds" escaped? Although rivalry had long divided conservative Béarnais and Xiberoan Basques, the creation of an internment camp on their borders had a singular effect in 1939: their collective hostility to it united them (M. Etcheverry 2003: pers. comm.; Laharie 1993: 25–26).

Under the direction of the French authorities, southern Basque Republicans built the camp at Gurs in forty-two days and were among its first one thousand internees (AMCB 1995: 118–24). People fully expected that the camp would be closed as soon as the government solved its "Spanish refugee problem" (E. Vallés 2004: pers. comm.). Its huts and double rows of barbed wire were laid out across eighty hectares of land and flanked a national highway. Once cleared of briars, ferns, and heather, the land was frequently flooded, its clay soil often a quagmire. Gurs was an inhospitable place. Within days, nearly three thousand more refugees arrived. By May of 1939 nineteen thousand Spanish and Basque Republicans and International Brigades crowded the huts. From some sixty different countries, the International Brigades were committed communists and anarchists and thus were deemed to be the most dangerous of France's enemies at the time. Clandestine communist tracts made their way in and out of Gurs with the help of Communist Party supporters from Maule and Oloron (R. Pérez 2004: pers. comm.).

In May 1939 the French authorities permitted one of Franco's loyal officers, General José Solchaga Zala, to promote the repatriation of Republicans to Spain during a visit to Gurs (Stein 1979: 81). Although a substantial number of internees did return to their homeland, word soon spread of the violent reception many Republicans received there. The rate of repatriation decreased markedly, especially among southern Basques. Telesforo de Monzón, minister of the Interior in the exiled Basque government, visited Gurs frequently and urged his fellow Basques to remain in France. When the inspector of special police in Maule complained about Monzón's activities, the camp's director suspended his visiting privileges and gave internees an ultimatum: repatriate or be forced to join the French foreign legion. As that failed to yield desired results, the prefect of the Basses-Pyrénées sought the direct intervention of the Spanish consul in Pau and the Spanish vice-consuls in Maule and Oloron (Laharie 1993: 114n., 115).

In March 1939 the French government decided that foreign refugees could contribute to France's economic recovery and created the first brigades of foreign workers (*compagnies de travailleurs étrangers*), which included an estimated fifty-five thousand exiled Spanish Republicans. The minister of the Interior instructed departmental prefects to identify appropriate work for such political "undesirables" that would not take jobs away from French citizens. The prefects sent the Spanish labor groups to build embankments, demolish derelict property, construct fortifications, and clean ditches (Dreyfus-Armand 1999: 104). The prefects provided the unpaid foreign workers with food and lodgings in local communities, for which their hosts received compensation from the departmental authorities (M. Rodrigo Nicolau 2004: pers. comm.).

Gurs held almost nineteen thousand Spanish and southern Basque refugees, as well as members of the International Brigades (Laharie 1993: 76). In 1939 the prefect responsible for Gurs, Angelo Chiappe, announced that the internees could be integrated into French society if the French public accepted them.[20] According to the French Home Office, the second generation of Spanish and southern Basques living in the region had already become good French citizens. When local employers got permission to hire "militant Spaniards," some two thousand internees left Gurs to work in nearby Basque and Béarnais communities. Although by no means all of the internees who remained at Gurs were militant communists in September 1939, public opinion maintained that everyone held in the camp belonged to the "third column" in one way or another. Organized by an association of First World War veterans, a campaign to rid the region of the "Red enemy" began (ibid.: 123).

Facing another war with Germany in July 1939, the Home Office ordered the registration of all foreigners living in France who were eligible for military service (Dreyfus-Armand 1999: 120–21). When Hitler and Stalin signed the Non-Aggression Pact in August, the Daladier government branded communists as Hitler's political allies, banned the French Communist Party's publications, and, in late September, banned the party itself. On the following day, Maule police arrested the militant communist of Navarrese origin Eustaquio Pérez for his "intense political activity" and his involvement in a local Federation for Spanish Emigrants (Fédération des Emigrés Espagnols). Both Pérez and his wife, Vitorina Olaverri, came from villages in the Erronkari Valley. Born in Uztarroze in 1897, Pérez emigrated to France in 1921 and initially worked as a lumberjack in the pine forests of the Landes. He joined the

Maule community of Erronkari Basques in 1927 and soon thereafter married Vitorina, an equally committed communist. Pérez took part in all of the Maule strikes from 1927 until 1938, when he left Xiberoa to fight against Franco with the Republicans. When he returned to Maule in 1939, the authorities assigned Pérez to a "work company for foreigners" in Cravant (Yonne). During leave in Maule, Pérez organized charitable events for exiled Spanish Republicans, many of whom had kin and friends in the town. His outspoken support for the Communist Party soon made Pérez a "suspect individual" under police surveillance (R. Pérez 2004: pers. comm.).

The militant communism and anticlericalism of Maule Spaniards and Basques alienated a core of workers fearful of change, committed to tradition and Catholicism, and increasingly attached to the habitus of conservative French Basques. Largely resigned to their socioeconomic situation, such workers simply wanted to keep their jobs and knew that loyalty to an influential factory owner brought mutually beneficial, albeit unequal, rewards in economically and politically difficult times (Ikherzaleak 1994: 108). Their close relations with wealthy *patrons* and the favors they received gave rise to jealousies and rivalry among the workers (R. Pérez 2004: pers. comm.). By 1939 many factory owners feared a communist takeover and gratefully received information from loyal workers about the politically dangerous sentiments and behavior of militant colleagues.

In Maule conservative Basques applauded Prime Minister Daladier's decision to launch a major anticommunist campaign (M. Etcheverry 2005: pers. comm.), and Henri Herbille soon became involved in the state's national pursuit of communists at a local level. Aware of Herbille's anticommunist sentiments and detailed knowledge of Maule's working class, Prefect Chiappe sought his advice on the communists who lived in the town. With information from factory managers and anticommunist shopkeepers who paid close attention to conversations on their premises, Dr. Herbille compiled a report on the thirty suspected communists of Spanish origin who lived in Maule, but it was not until December 1939 that the Maule police finally required all foreigners to report to the town hall with their identity papers. The gendarmes arrested six local communists, an anarchist, and a dozen Spanish Republicans who were staying with relatives. The authorities sent them to the internment camp at Rivesaltes on the Mediterranean coast. Following denunciations, the police arrested four other Maule communists of Spanish and Navarrese origin. One of them, Eustaquio Pérez, went to prison in Bordeaux. The Spanish Republicans went to Rivesaltes and the other "Reds" were interned at Argelès. A week later, the police commissioner of Maule proudly told a local tavern owner that he and his men had "sent the terrorists away" (Ayerdi 1999: 27).

Prior to his arrest, Pérez had regularly distributed Communist Party tracts and openly urged workers to take action against the "ruling class." Herbille and other *patrons* refused to hire him when Pérez returned from prison in December 1940—in their view he embodied strife and disorder. The police arrested Pérez again in January 1941, one hour after his former employer (a factory owner) saw him reading an underground communist newspaper in the middle of the square.[21] The factory owner, who hated communists and looked down upon Spaniards as his racial and social inferiors, allegedly remarked that he "ought to go back to Spain where he belonged, among other Red Devils." Following a denunciation, the police arrested Pérez, who returned to prison.[22] The *patrons* once again blacklisted Pérez when he returned from prison. Owing to political and personal disagreements, the trade-union leader, Lanouguère, blocked the communist's attempts to work in the cooperative as well and thus won some bargaining power with influential factory owners (R. Pérez 2004: pers. comm.).

In spite of her communist militancy, Pérez's wife, Vitorina Olaverri, was never arrested by the Maule police. Her name never appeared on Herbille's lists. Fearful of losing her job, Vitorina did not cause trouble in the factories, but she contributed to the class struggle by helping exiled Spanish Republican women and children. Vitorina gained the sympathy and support of Maule's Red Cross, whose local president was a female notable. As the wife of a former mayor-*patron,* Mme Bidegain knew Henri Herbille well. Dr. Herbille, in turn, had influence with the police commissioner in Pau, who ensured that the gendarmes did not arrest Vitorina Olaverri during their raids on "Reds" in the town (R. Pérez 2004: pers. comm.).

In 1939 the solidarity of Maule's "Spanish" community was threatened by collusion between one extreme right-wing factory manager and his young mistress, a worker of Spanish descent whose brother belonged to the Communist Party. Both brother and sister were naturalized French citizens. The manager solicited information from her about communists sheltering in the town, and soon thereafter the police arrested several Spanish "Reds." Although conservative Basque citizens regarded the manager's *dénonciations* as legitimate revelations of wrongdoing and acts of civic duty, the betrayals deepened the hostility of many workers toward the *patrons,* and a number of them ostracized the manager's young mistress for her suspected complicity in the arrests. When the manager negotiated the release of her communist brother from a German stalag in July 1943, some members of the "Spanish" community congratulated the young woman for her persuasive part in the process. Other, more militant communists, however, continued to regard her as a traitor to their moral community.[23] As one man observed in 2004, "there were a few *mouchards* [informers] in the factories who caused a lot of divisiveness, especially after the first big roundup of communists in 1939. Their families and friends had to search deeply for forgiveness" (P.-P. Dalgalarrondo 2004: pers. comm.).

On September 3, 1939, France declared war on Germany. In Maule many young men felt deeply disconcerted not only by the call to serve their *patrie*; they also felt anguished about leaving their wives, children, and homes to enter a war about which few young men had given much thought (Barbe-Labarthe n.d.: 1). The local strikes, political discord, denunciations, and ethnic tensions in Maule had distracted many of them and had strained numerous local relationships. The possibility of another war with Germany in a distant part of France was, however, clearly appreciated by veterans of the Great War, who responded to France's call to arms with sincere patriotism. As happened in 1914–18, Xiberoan men assigned to the Forty-Ninth Infantry Regiment felt grateful to be among fellow Basques (ibid.: 3). On September 4, 1939, crowds milled around the town as conscripts prepared for their journey to Baiona. Few men evaded military service for France. War with Germany, on this occasion, united Xiberoan men and women as French citizens whose local and regional identity remained profoundly Basque but whose national identity became more clearly French. Men tried to remain in good spirits as their parents sang out to them and onlookers gave them flowers, but inwardly the soldiers felt deeply distressed by the need to abandon their *foyers*. One recalled that "we left with confusion in our souls, without the dynamism essential to an Army's victory" (ibid.: 4). The *patron,* Pierre Béguerie, rejoined the Second Cavalry Regiment of the Hussars and became a squadron captain. Aged fifty-two, Dr. Henri Herbille took charge of the Béguerie factory. A few days after general mobilization had taken place, the mayor of Maule announced the distribution of fifteen thousand francs among the families of men who had been mobilized and who had insufficient means with which to survive. Nearly all of the sandal factories had been closed for several months, and the mayor called for solidarity in the town (Régnier 2006: 285).

Assigned to foreign-worker companies (*compagnies de travailleurs étrangers*) in September 1939, most of the nine thousand Spanish Republicans still held at Gurs went to work for the *patrie* (Laharie 1993: 128–29). In spite of intense local propaganda against "Reds," relations between employers and refugees were sometimes marked by mutual respect and appreciation (AMCB 1995: 127–29). Uneasy about the Spanish "Reds" in Maule and their links with the

International Brigades still held at Gurs, the prefect of the Basses-Pyrénées took many measures to isolate the camp during France's "phony war" (*drôle de guerre*). On September 26, 1939, the French government dissolved the French Communist Party. As happened elsewhere in France, many conservative Xiberoans remained obsessed with the enemy within (the communists), whom they initially regarded as a greater evil than Nazi Germany (Zaretsky 1995: 38). Fear of the Other, especially Spanish and Basque Republicans exiled in southwestern France, had not diminished during the interwar years. Another, even more massive displacement of people into southern France was about to begin in May and June 1940: the exodus of French civilians who fled Hitler's advancing army.

6: Xiberoans Under Vichy

Between 1930 and 1936, France spent substantial portions of its defense budget on the Maginot Line, a series of underground fortifications constructed mainly along the Franco-German-Luxembourg borders but not along the Franco-Belgian frontier, an omission for which France would pay dearly. The French believed that the Maginot Line would maximize their army's ability to mobilize and provide an effective line of defense against the Germans. French military commanders also incorrectly believed that a substantial German invasion through the rugged terrain of the Belgian Ardennes would be difficult to achieve. In addition the French High Command was shortsighted and failed to prepare for Germany's use of tanks and aircraft in a new, modern form of warfare (Price 2001: 247). The French themselves were not particularly enthusiastic about another world war with Germany. Many citizens lacked any strong determination to defend the Republic, especially in rural communities devastated by the high mortality rates of the Great War (Atkin 2001: 30).

A lengthy period of relative inaction followed France's declaration of war in September 1939 (Price 2001: 246). The German offensive in Belgium, Holland, and Luxembourg began on May 10, 1940. The French High Command misjudged the main thrust of the German invasion, which went through the Ardennes, and the aging reservists who guarded the area were ill equipped to deal with the massive assault of German tanks (Atkin 2001: 34; Jackson 2001: 118). Within five days German forces had advanced well into French territory; within five weeks, the Germans had taken 1,850,000 prisoners of war. By early June between six and seven million French civilians had fled the advancing German troops in panic as they sought to escape the expanding war zone (Price 2001: 248). The exodus clogged the roads with people and their belongings as refugees headed south for the Loire and then plunged deeper into rural southern France (Jackson 2001: 120). France's so-called "phony war" with Germany lasted less than ten months. When France surrendered on June 22, 1940, the French people responded to the news with relief, disbelief, disillusionment, and bitter resignation. Strategic errors, more than any other factors, brought about France's "strange defeat."

The terms of the armistice broadly divided France into an Occupied Zone and an Unoccupied Zone. The Occupied Zone comprised three-fifths of the country, including northern France and the Atlantic coastline; it also included an Annexed Zone (essentially Alsace-Lorraine) and various prohibited zones. The Unoccupied or Free Zone covered most of southern France and came under the jurisdiction of Vichy, headed by Marshal Philippe Pétain, a First World War hero whom many Basques deeply admired in the first months of his regime. The armistice also decreed that French armed forces would be demobilized and disarmed, except for a French Armistice Army of one hundred thousand soldiers responsible for maintaining internal order; the French government would fund German troops on French territory; and French POWs would remain in captivity (Jackson 2001: 127). The terms of the armistice also required French officials and public services "to conform to the decisions of the German authorities and collaborate faithfully with them." Marshal Pétain won fervent gratitude as the leader who saved France "from the abyss" (Paxton 2001: 14, 19). He warned that further disorder would ensue if the war continued, and the French, as well as many Basques, looked to Pétain to prevent further chaos, to restore tranquility and order (Paxton 2001: 15).

Rigorously patrolled by both the French and the Germans, the line of demarcation separating the Occupied and Unoccupied Zones in western France divided the northern Basque Country into two parts. Xiberoa lay in the Unoccupied Zone and thus came under Vichy's administration. The other two Basque provinces (Lapurdi and Behe Nafarroa) fell within the Occupied Zone. The prefect of the Basses-Pyrénées, Angelo Chiappe, welcomed the creation of the Vichy regime as an opportunity to take revenge against leftists who, he claimed, had mistreated him during the interwar years. In his previous post as prefect in the Aisne, Chiappe had clashed bitterly with socialists and communists and had played a key role in repressing two major strikes there. He fervently believed in active collaboration with Germany.

During Chiappe's tenure as prefect in Pau (1939–40), he had oversight of the internment camp at Gurs, which held 2,293 "undesirables" in May 1940. The internees were primarily members of the International Brigades (Laharie 1993: 125–26). That summer, a new category of "undesirables" began to arrive at the camp: Jewish women and children, three-quarters of whom came from Germany. Among the first of those female "enemy aliens," Hannah Arendt spent five weeks at Gurs before "liberation papers" enabled her to leave it (Arendt 1962). During the summer of 1940, Arthur Koestler also came into contact with female internees at Gurs as the disorderly process of demobilization began. Posing as a soldier in the foreign legion, he was in the Basque coastal city of Baiona when the Germans arrived:

I saw them at 200 yards—the dark green tanks, rattling slowly and solemnly over the roadway like a funeral procession, and the black-clad figures standing in the open turrets with wooden faces, and the puffing black motor bikes with men in black leather and black goggles on their eyes behind them, and the burning red flags with the white circle and the black spider in the middle, flapping lazily in the heat. The shutters of the windows were closed; the streets were empty, the sun blazing. I leant against a doorway and was sick and looked at them, and thought that in passing they all looked at me. For they had hunted me all across the Continent, and whenever I had paused and stopped, thinking there was safety, they had come after me, with their slow, rattling, thundering funeral procession and the lazy black spider on their flag. (Koestler 1948: 216–17)

Koestler made his way into the Unoccupied Zone just before the Germans established themselves along the demarcation line on the western edge of Xiberoa. He wandered into Maule and spent several weeks in Xiberoa and neighboring Béarn, sleeping in barns and fields. "These day-long, dawdling wanderings along the road with the distant screen of the white Pyrenees before my eyes, while the limpid air seemed to boil around me and the asphalt to melt under my heels, had a curiously calming effect; I had no luggage, not even a comb or piece of soap" (ibid.: 225–26). On July 8, 1940, he read a decree by Prefect Chiappe that was pinned on the notice board of a Béarnais town hall: all former alien internees at Gurs were ordered to leave the department of the Basses-Pyrénées within twenty-four hours or else be interned again; no alien would be allowed to travel or move from his or her place of residence (ibid.: 233). On the previous day, Koestler had met several German women in a café near Gurs; they had just been released from the camp and did not know where to go or what to do. One woman planned to contact all internment camps in the Unoccupied Zone in a desperate attempt to find her husband (ibid.: 231).

Soon after the armistice, Chiappe received a German officer at Gurs who, according to the prefect, "took pleasure in acknowledging the humanitarian regime that I had extended to the German internees, as well as to the 2,000 German citizens (women and children) driven from Paris in May 1940." The internees in question faced an uncertain future, and Chiappe's comments reveal his remarkable insensitivity (Zaretsky 1995: 137).

In September 1940 Chiappe requested a transfer from Pau to take on a "more difficult assignment" in the Gard, where he sought "to make the principles of the National Revolution prevail" in a more hostile and politically forbidding environment (ibid.: 137–39). Émile Ducommun succeeded him as prefect of the Basses-Pyrénées and served until December 1942. The "Jewish phase" of internment at Gurs began under Ducommun's administration. The first convoy of 7,500 German Jews from Bade, Palatinat, and Sarre arrived on the same day that Pétain met Hitler at Montoire (Laharie 1993: 201). During Ducommun's tenure at Gurs, the administration sent 2,212 Jewish men and women to Drancy and on to Auschwitz (ibid.: 236). Three Basques and four Béarnais officials served on Ducommun's advisory board. One of them was Jean Ybarnegaray, who served as Pétain's first minister of Family and Veterans and then as his minister of Youth and Family.[1] Prefect Ducommun appointed a new subprefect, who soon established a particularly close working relationship with Dr. Henri Herbille, president of the Légion Française des Combattants in Maule. Prefect Ducommun reappointed the incumbent mayor of Maule, a local factory owner, Jean-Pierre Bidegain, and his incumbent deputy mayor, Arnaud Aguer. Both Bidegain and Aguer had been elected to office in 1936 as representatives of the Third Republic (Béguerie n.d.: 4–5).

In June 1940 their friend and fellow factory owner, Pierre Béguerie, served as a squadron captain in the cavalry regiment of Hussars. During the process of demobilization, he and his soldiers were based in a small Béarnais town north of Maule through which Arthur Koestler passed on several occasions that summer. On receiving news of the defeat, Béguerie gathered his men in front of the local First World War monument. In his brief speech, the Basque captain "tried to bolster their morale but merely left them feeling deeply discouraged." Like his men, Béguerie felt "humiliated and bitter about the defeat" (ibid.: 1–2). In Xiberoa rumors spread that an armored German division had formed on the other side of the Pyrenees and was prepared "to flood across the frontier into Xiberoa and Béarn" (ibid.: 3). Citizens once again feared an invasion of dangerous strangers on territory they still hoped to be able to control under Vichy. Many Maule men, both Basque and of Spanish descent, remained in Germany as prisoners of war, their families anxiously awaiting their release (A. Labarthe 2004: pers. comm.).

Initially, the town's conservative core believed that Pétain's policy of collaboration with the Germans would hasten economic and social recovery (Peillen 1997: 189; Poullenot 1995: 42). During the first two years of Vichy, communism worried them much more than France's policy of collaboration with Germany. In the first summer of the Vichy regime, the special police inspector in Maule, Robert Bats, regularly communicated with his superiors, the special commissioner of police in Pau and the subprefect in Oloron, about political refugees in Maule. On his list of Spanish and Navarrese Republicans who did not have official permission to be on French territory, Bats provided the authorities with detailed information about ten men, six of whom came from the Erronkari Valley in Nafarroa. The others came mainly from Asturias. All ten men had a friend or relatives in Maule who "reclaimed" the refugees from one of the special companies for foreign workers.

In July 1940 the subprefect in Oloron detected a worrying trend among Maule employers who required manual laborers: they were hiring Spanish political refugees rather than French or Basque citizens. The practice gave rise to considerable discontent among unemployed war veterans, who complained to Dr. Herbille about the unfair competition caused by the "Red" refugees (M. Rodrigo Nicolau 2004: pers. comm.). The subprefect consulted Henri Herbille, who appreciated the contradictory needs of the patrons for order and labor. Herbille argued that Maule's sandal factories depended upon Spanish labor to remain operational. The prefect nevertheless ordered all Maule industrialists, entrepreneurs, and farmers to hire French citizens and decreed that "every position occupied by a foreigner had to be considered available to a French worker." He sent all unemployed foreigners to the internment camp at Gurs.[2]

The subprefect also instructed the inspector to draw up a list of Spanish political refugees "in irregular situations." It included one of the "terrorists" sent to an internment camp after the roundup of September 1939, Porfirio Ayerdi. When Ayerdi returned from the camp in August 1940, the Vichy authorities required his brother-in-law, Leon O., to vouch for him.[3] Leon O. owned a thriving fish business and crossed the demarcation line regularly to buy sardines from a relative on the coast. In 1941 a Maule mechanic denounced the fish merchant for illegally transporting lambs into the Occupied Zone. The inspector knew about the illicit trade but chose not to arrest the Spaniard. Widely known as an adulterer, the mechanic had once had an affair with Leon O.'s sister-in-law. When Leon found out about the affair, he "avenged his family's honor" by assaulting the mechanic.[4] Consequently, the mechanic took revenge against Leon O. at every opportunity. The inspector let the fish merchant continue his illegal trade and ignored the mechanic's letter, which was not, he concluded, written for patriotic reasons but to settle a personal score.[5]

A few months later, the prefect received an anonymous letter from Maule that also denounced Leon O.:

> We would like to ask why it is that so many people, cars and motor-bikes can regularly be seen coming and going at No. 20 rue Victor Hugo, when gasoline—that precious liquid—ought to be reserved for public services and only indispensable private use. We have also seen

ducks and chickens there that most certainly did not get there by any legal route! While the true French, those who are totally loyal to the Marshal and the Admiral, go without such things! Do not think that this is a mean-spirited denunciation. We merely wish to help the Marshal and the Admiral rejuvenate the Nation. It is thus a matter of conscience for us Good French to bring such matters to your attention, so that surveillance can be effectively carried out. VIVE PÉTAIN, VIVE DARLAN! Keep watching No. 20 rue Victor Hugo.[6]

Leon O. lived on the second floor of that address and owned the motorbike in question. One car often seen in front of the house belonged to a French commissioner responsible for a military checkpoint on the demarcation line. The fish merchant happily supplied him with the foods he liked. The prefect ignored the denunciation, which used a discourse commonly employed by the self-proclaimed "Good French." The anonymous denouncer exalted his "duty to the state" but also revealed personal grievances and jealousy over a fellow citizen's access to scarce resources.

In August 1940 Pétain created the veterans' association the Légion Française des Combattants to inculcate and enforce the policies of the Vichy regime.[7] Its leaders were intensely loyal to the marshal but also typically anti-German (Vinen 2006: 67). As president of the Maule Legion, Dr. Henri Herbille was ideally suited to the role, for he firmly believed that the association could bring an end to the long-standing class conflict between patrons and workers by suppressing agitation and reestablishing the hegemony of the notables. His plan mirrored many aspects of Pétain's vision for a rejuvenated France under Vichy rule, with hierarchy and authoritarianism prominently featured in both. Vichy's leaders intended the Legion to link the regime with citizens at a grassroots level. Veterans, they emphasized, had a moral and social obligation to be vigilant in watching for antinational behavior without undermining the authority of departmental prefects (Paxton 2001: 190). In some parts of France, *légionnaires* sometimes became directly involved in the denunciations of Jews, communists, Gaullists, and socialists (Sweets 1986: 73; Zaretsky 1995: 127). In Maule, Dr. Herbille focused his attention on communists.

As happened elsewhere in France, the Maule Legion drew its membership almost exclusively from the notables. The workers and other supporters of the Left widely regarded the association with suspicion and hostility (Sweets 1986: 66). One socialist schoolteacher bitterly asserted in his memoirs that "the *Mauléonais* revealed their true disposition as intolerant bigots" when they elected Henri Herbille to lead their Legion. Herbille was, the socialist asserted, "feared by most people because he was authoritarian and vindictive" (Lassus 2004: 6).

At the end of 1940, the town received forty non-Jewish families from Chicourt, a village in Alsace-Lorraine.[8] The first Gauleiter of Austria appointed after the Anschluss, Joseph Bürckel, coordinated the operation that expelled the Chicourt families from their homeland and sent them to the Vichy internment camp at Gurs, together with 6,500 German Jews (Laharie 1993: 170). The Nazis classified the Chicourt people as "undesirables" because they were "Aryans" who regarded themselves as French. In the summer of 1941, Vichy authorities released the Chicourt refugees, who made their way to Maule. The mayor found lodgings for them in the town hall, local hotels, and numerous private homes. Close relations developed between the Alsatian refugees and their Basque hosts during their four and a half years of exile in the town. After the people of Chicourt returned to their homeland in May 1945, many of them remained in regular contact with their Maule friends. To commemorate the vital aid and friendship they had received from Maule citizens, the Alsatians later named a street after their wartime place of refuge (J. Lougarot 2003: pers. comm.). Conservative Basques felt an affinity with the Chicourt people as French and Catholic citizens unjustly displaced by war. Particularly sensitive to the plight of refugees generally, the "Spanish" community sympathized with the Alsatians but felt a greater affinity with the Jewish refugees who passed through their town. As one man of Navarrese descent noted: "We sympathized more with the Jews because of the racial prejudice we experienced here. We knew what it was like to be treated as pariahs" (R. Pérez 2004: pers. comm.).

In 1940–41 Pétain's advisors and the Vichy media cultivated his public image as a father figure and hero of Verdun. In order to bolster public support for himself, the marshal visited several cities in southern, unoccupied France (Vinen 2006: 54). Accompanied by Admiral Darlan, Pétain stopped briefly in Pau on April 20, 1941, before continuing on to Lourdes and Tarbes. Elaborate planning and preparations preceded his visit. Closely observed by the German Censorship Services, the regional press extolled the marshal's military successes and the generous "gift of his person to France." Newspapers exhorted the Basques and Béarnais to extend a warm, enthusiastic welcome to their distinguished guests. Pétainism extolled the virtues of "tradition," and his image makers used Pétain's own rural roots extensively in their promotion of Vichy values, even though the marshal himself remained unsentimental about most things, including his origins (ibid.: 57). In preparation for the marshal's visit to Pau in 1941, Vichy authorities arranged for trains to transport rural citizens to the city from the mountainous borderlands, and the

Legion hired buses to bring other supporters of Pétain to Pau. Schools closed so that teachers and pupils could demonstrate their support for the marshal and participate in the ceremonies. Prefect Ducommun welcomed the entourage at the train station and led the group to the Monument to the Dead, where numerous dignitaries, including Jean Ybarnegaray, awaited Pétain and Admiral Darlan. One local newspaper reported that ninety thousand citizens attended the festivities, of which twenty thousand were said to be *légionnaires* (Poullenot 1995: 42–46). The departmental president of the Légion Française des Combattants, Henri Saüt, exhorted the crowd to follow the marshal's orders to ensure the creation of a New France, "a better France, more worthy of the sacrifices made by the best of her sons" in the Great War (ibid.: 45). That vision of a New France did not include communists.

In July 1941 the communist Eustaquio Pérez once again attracted the attention of the Vichy authorities in Maule when the politician Jean Ybarnegaray ordered another roundup of "Red agitators."[9] The prefect and subprefect had already had several conversations with Herbille about "undesirable Spaniards" in the town. Herbille consulted the Vichy police inspector, who recommended that Pérez and two other militant "Reds" should be interned or deported.[10] Rumors circulated that another purge was about to take place. In the same month, the prefect's brother-in-law denounced Henri Herbille to Pétain's most influential minister at the time, Admiral Darlan, for not taking a strong enough stance against local "Gaullists and anglophiles" or appreciating the importance of collaborationism with Germany. The Maule police inspector assured Herbille that no one took the denunciation seriously, given Herbille's loyalty to Pétain and the brother-in-law's reputation as a nuisance and a malicious busybody.[11] The denunciation and the national importance of its recipient nevertheless unsettled Herbille, who was by then seeking solutions to two local problems. His continuing pursuit of local communists had deepened tensions between factory owners and left-wing workers, and the Maule Legion had thus far failed to resolve the class conflict or to foster unity in his divided community.

By the summer of 1941, the boundaries of Maule's disparate moral communities had become blurred by the constant presence of strangers, as citizens were once again forced to reflect deeply on issues of patriotism, their attachment to Xiberoan territory, and what it meant to be both French and Xiberoan Basque. As happened elsewhere in France, the ongoing imprisonment of French POWs in Germany, rationing, high prices, and the Germans' continued presence on French soil diminished Xiberoans' enthusiasm for Vichy, although many notables and rural Basques retained an admiration for Pétain (Vinen 2006: 92). Vichy's popularity decreased further in August 1941, when approximately 2,500 German soldiers arrived in the Béarnais town of Orthez, some twenty miles north of Maule, to control the flow of illegal goods and unauthorized persons across the demarcation line (Poullenot 1995: 24). When the Maule industrialist Pierre Béguerie traveled to Paris for a national committee of sandal makers in August 1941, he encountered his first Germans in Orthez and watched them

> with some curiosity. They were young men who carried themselves well and were impeccably dressed. In Paris, I stayed at the Hotel Moderne, which was partly requisitioned. Two ss guards stood at its entrance. On Sunday, towards midday, I went into the Champs Élysées, which was nearly deserted. An infantry company filed along the pavement with their drums and pipes. Their captain was mounted on a horse. Not a single civilian stopped to watch them. Some twenty young Germans lined up along the sidewalk and saluted them with one arm raised. What utter humiliation, what a disgrace! I felt nauseated and for a long time afterwards, that vision obsessed me.

When Pierre Béguerie returned to Maule, he felt he "was in France again" (Béguerie n.d.: 16). When the Maule mayor, Jean-Pierre Bidegain, resigned from office owing to ill health, Béguerie's good friend, Arnaud Aguer, agreed to become mayor on condition that Béguerie become his first deputy. Having already served as a municipal councilor for twelve years, Béguerie accepted because he "understood that managing a city of such importance as Maule was a complicated matter" (ibid.: 17).

In August 1941, the subprefect commented on the remarkably diverse nature of his constituency and the extent to which the geographical configuration of his *arrondissement* corresponded to differences in custom and ways of thinking. The valleys of Aspe, Ossau, the *pays* of Xiberoa, and Cize were not, he noted, simply geographical place-names. The people who belonged to each space had different preoccupations and different ways of viewing the world around them. They responded differently to Vichy and to international events. The rural population objected to the regime's intrusive agricultural policies and attempts to control agricultural production and distribution. In one report the subprefect noted that "many farmers simply cannot fathom why they are not allowed to do what they want with their crops. Farmers regard their crops as their own property. . . . Rural people also complain about the lack of wine and gripe when its delivery to the wine merchants is delayed by the (Vichy) administration." In Maule and Oloron, the subprefect found that the workers followed developments in the German-Russian conflict closely and with much excitement.[12]

In such a politically volatile environment, the subprefect observed, Vichy's Legion had an important role to play in the maintenance of public order but needed to avoid involvement in the local quarrels that divided Maule. In August 1941 one of Maule's most distinguished citizens, Commander Andurein, started to recruit members to a Basque Legion (la Légion Basque) that venerated Marshal Pétain. Andurein's Legion sought "to rise above certain rivalries" that divided elites and notables in Maule, but its creation had the opposite effect on the "Ultras" in town and certain right-wing priests in Atharratze and Sustary, who vehemently opposed Andurein's initiative as a threat to the Légion Française des Combattants and to French unity. Rather than uniting rival factions in Maule society, Andurein's Basque Legion merely deepened existing divisions.[13]

In August 1941 the prefect, subprefect, and Dr. Herbille were equally concerned about the negative effects of denunciations, arrests, and deportations on working-class citizens of Spanish and Navarrese origin. They decided to counter the divisiveness caused by such actions by carefully choosing one Maule man of Spanish origin for "rehabilitation." As "a rising communist star in the Spanish colony," Manuel Serrano had been interned since 1939. His father had unsuccessfully sought Manuel's release through the patronage of the mayor (a *patron* and Manuel's former employer). The Maule mayor observed that the younger Spaniard had been a good worker but refused to comment on his moral character.[14] In the summer of 1941, the authorities sent Manuel Serrano to an internment camp in Algeria. Through Vichy authorities in North Africa, the prefect and Herbille learned that the young man regretted his earlier commitment to communism. Herbille felt confident that, if released, Serrano would help the Legion resolve the class conflict between *patrons* and workers. Clemency, Herbille believed, would demonstrate the ability of a beleaguered Legion to reunite Maule society. Nothing happened immediately.

By September 1941 the Maule police inspector had identified all communists living in the area, as well as *réfractaires* who belonged to the socialist party Section Française de l'Internationale Ouvrière (SFIO), which opposed Vichy but also continued to disapprove of the communists. The town's working-class community remained extremely hostile to Vichy. Their discontent with the socioeconomic situation deepened when certain merchants obtained cases of Algerian wine for local notables. As one socialist worker asked, "How is it that only the rich who don't work can afford to buy wine?" In rural Xiberoa, shepherds and farmers were outraged when Vichy authorities introduced a tax on the migratory pigeons that Basques had long hunted in Pyrenean mountain passes. In the same report, the inspector also noted that the Béguerie factory had received an order from the Germans for three hundred thousand pairs of cloth sandals.[15]

Maule workers became increasingly bitter about their pay, food shortages, reduced hours, and high prices. Noting their worried mood, the subprefect felt certain that liberating the reformed communist worker, Manuel Serrano, would have an "excellent effect" upon them. Clemency would, he claimed, make it easier to "purge the foreigners who constitute a cell of dangerous agitators" and would show the working class that Vichy kept its promises. The simultaneous internment of militant communists would demonstrate Vichy's power to take repressive action against "undesirable" citizens.[16] In November 1941 the Vichy minister of the Interior finally ordered the liberation of Manuel Serrano. On receiving the good news, the internee affirmed his loyalty to Pétain. Bureaucratic complications, however, delayed his release for several months. According to Herbille, left-wing workers in Maule used the delay "to create an atmosphere of bitterness and contempt vis-à-vis the local *patrons* and authorities" and thus set back Herbille's hopes for better interclass relations and some glory for the local Legion. When Herbille also negotiated the release of Manuel's brother, Severin, from another internment camp, politically moderate workers expressed their appreciation but refused to join or help the Legion.[17]

Police Inspector Carbou arrived in Maule during negotiations for the release of Manuel Serrano. Carbou, an outsider to the Xiberoan moral community, quickly developed a keen interest in the forces that united and divided Maule society, as well as in local perceptions of Vichy. Given the complexity of public opinion of Vichy, Inspector Carbou had difficulty assessing the ebb and flow of the regime's popularity. He carried out his duties with great attention to detail and with the curiosity of an ethnographer. In his voluminous correspondence with Vichy authorities, Inspector Carbou confirmed that several different kinds of Pétainism had evolved in Xiberoa. As happened elsewhere in France, there was no simple, linear shift from Pétainism to resistance (Vinen 2006: 77, 80, 81, 87).

Through Dr. Henri Herbille, Carbou quickly learned about the internal disagreements that divided members of the local Legion. Carbou noted that politics and the long-standing class conflict between *patrons* and workers also deeply divided Xiberoan clergy. The inspector traced such divisiveness to an article published in the parish bulletin in December 1941, written by the Maule vicar, Abbé Laxalt. The vicar lamented the contempt so many local people showed toward the workers and accused the *patrons* of treating their employees like human animals (*comme de bétail humain*). Laxalt also remarked upon the fierce hatred felt by workers for the men who exploited them. He railed against the factories for employing children as young as six years old, whom Laxalt described as "the damned of the earth." When the prefect belatedly saw a copy of the article in January 1942, he was outraged that departmental censors had failed to prevent the publication, which intensified the *patron*-worker conflict in a town long plagued by the class struggle.[18] When Herbille urged the vicar to help unite *patrons* and workers rather than rekindle animosities between them, the left-wing priest refused to modify his views or to publish an apology.[19]

In November 1941 Inspector Carbou found that most citizens took "a narrow, close interest in their own immediate well-being." No doubt aware of the inspector's regular presence in places of public sociability, former supporters of the Popular Front and communists adopted "a prudent reserve" in their conversations with fellow citizens. Less cautious and increasing in number, local anglophiles openly expressed sympathy for the British and de Gaulle, listened to Radio London, and, according to Carbou, tended "to forget that, above all, it [was] most important to think and act like Frenchmen." By the end of 1941, Carbou reckoned that only a minority of citizens openly supported Vichy. Most Maule citizens carefully avoided any discussion of politics "because they didn't care or didn't know what position to take." The inspector regarded such citizens "as the most dangerous elements of all, because their inertia [was] so difficult to break down." By the end of December 1941, Carbou detected growing hostility toward Vichy's policy of collaboration with Germany, especially among the increasingly numerous "clan of anglophiles and Gaullists." Local discontent with rationing and food shortages decreased somewhat when regional authorities lifted restrictions on pig killing. When pork reappeared in time for the town's annual fair and wine appeared in the cafés, citizens "were happy."[20]

By January 1942 Carbou noted that townspeople had begun to understand the mission of Vichy's national charity (the Secours National), which sponsored fairs (*tombolas*), lotteries, and *patronal* festivals for worthy causes such as helping POWs (Gildea 2002: 95), but rural Xiberoans remained largely unenthusiastic about the organization "owing to their *égoïsme*." Between September 1941 and January 1942, the Basque Group of the Secours National, based in the Maule town hall, sent 3,800 food parcels to prisoners of war. The local economy suffered as supply and market shortages forced the twelve main sandal factories to reduce working hours and employee numbers to a new minimum. But the black market continued to thrive, especially along the demarcation line, owing to complicities between Basques and the authorities and to a paucity of denunciations about wrongdoing.[21]

In early 1942 the Maule Legion faced more internal divisiveness when some of its members joined Joseph Darnand's anti-Semitic paramilitary arm of the Legion, the Service d'Ordre Légionnaire (SOL). Inspector Carbou noted that the initial veneration of Pétain, anticommunist stance, and authoritarianism of the SOL appealed to many *patrons,* including Herbille. In March a rival collaborationist movement, the fascist Parti Populaire Français (PPF), formed by Jacques Doriot, also sought the support of Maule people. Inspector Carbou eavesdropped on conversations between the PPF recruiter and Herbille, among other *patrons.* It pleased Carbou to hear the notables rebuff the recruiter, for the inspector opposed the party's violent tactics and fascist ideology. When the recruiter met with factory workers, he preached that the Legion had only the interests of the bourgeoisie at heart and promised the rehabilitated, ex-communist Severin Serrano an "advantageous position" in his party. Severin refused the offer. According to Carbou, who had overheard their exchange, "the Spaniard knew well the high cost of getting involved in politics and remained extremely grateful to the Legion" for its part in securing his brother's liberation and his own.[22]

Following the bombing of Paris by British forces in March 1942, local Gaullists "deplored the loss of life but treated the incident as an ineluctable consequence of war." Citizens anticipated a spring offensive, and Carbou detected "a widespread feeling of inquietude about the world's situation." In a sermon aimed specifically at rural Xiberoans, the Maule priest sternly reminded parishioners that they had a long-standing duty to promote the well-being of their community and vigorously attacked an increasingly common *égoïsme* that contradicted traditional Basque values. The sermon gave rise to much public debate, especially about the reluctance of some rural farmers to contribute their fair share to Vichy's food distribution scheme (*le ravitaillement*).[23]

By April 1942 Carbou estimated that 95 percent of Maule citizens firmly opposed collaboration with Hitler. Local Gaullists deeply lamented Pétain's decision to reinstate Pierre Laval as prime minister and to resume negotiations with Germany. They openly accused Laval of betrayal and launched their first propaganda campaign among factory workers. The few people who remained loyal to Pétain, but not necessarily loyal to his regime, staunchly maintained that the marshal had made a judicious decision in returning Laval to power and insisted that Laval "would obtain considerable concessions from Hitler without compromising the honor of France" (Vinen 2006: 53). In the countryside, Inspector Carbou noted, discontent focused more on bread than international politics. When their bread rations were reduced, Xiberoan farmers complained vociferously to Vichy authorities and argued that "rural people ought to get priority in such matters because *we are the source of bread.*" As Carbou observed, rural farmers knew that they were in dispensable and that townspeople greatly depend upon them for food.[24]

In June 1942 rumors circulated in Maule that the sandal factories would soon be forcibly closed so that their workers could go to Germany, for Laval had just introduced the relief scheme (Relève), which promised the release of one French POW for every three skilled French workers who volunteered to work in German factories. Highly unpopular and ineffectual throughout France, the Relève exacerbated class-based and ethnic tensions between factory owners and workers in Maule, for the notables pressed manual laborers of Spanish and Navarrese descent to volunteer, even though only skilled workers were meant to participate in the scheme.[25]

The first roundup of Jews in the Unoccupied Zone took place in late August 1942. According to Inspector Carbou, some Maule citizens regarded Vichy's treatment of Jews as "timely," but most people, he observed, found the anti-Jewish legislation excessive or inhumane.[26] Although anti-Semitism did exist in Xiberoa, many citizens regularly helped French and foreign Jews who passed through the province or sought temporary shelter there. Many Jews took refuge in the private Catholic Collège de Saint-François in Maule after having sheltered in the Benedictine Abbey of Belloc in Lapurdi (A. Gachitegui 2004: pers. comm.). An ardent Gaullist and director of the Maule Catholic college, Canon Ithurbide operated an escape network for Jewish refugees, among others, in collaboration with both Belloc and the local monastery of Christian Brothers on the other side of Maule. Canon Ithurbide often took in Jewish boys as his pupils and hid as many as thirty adult fugitives at a time. In the middle of the night he led refugees along the river, through the town, and into the hills, where Christian Brothers awaited them. The Brothers then arranged for their passage to Nafarroa with Xiberoan shepherds living in borderland communities (F. Meyer 2004: pers. comm.).

Before the occupation, several Jewish families owned houses and land in the Maule area. One Polish Jew married a local Basque woman from a remote hamlet. The couple spent the duration of the occupation quietly working their farm and avoiding contact with the occupiers. No one ever denounced the Jewish "Basque" to the authorities (M. Etcheverry 2003: pers. comm.). Two wealthy Jewish property owners in Maule and nearby Sohüta made their fortunes primarily in the textile business and had close, amicable relations with several local families, including the owners of Hotel Bidegain in Maule. During the early years of Vichy, the Hotel Bidegain had a loyal clientele of well-to-do Jewish professionals and businessmen. In a letter dated July 25, 1940, one Jewish lawyer wrote to the owners of the Hotel Bidegain from Nice to thank them for their kindness during a recent visit: "We will never forget your warm welcome in such difficult times," she wrote.[27] A second, undated letter from the same lawyer thanked the Basque couple for having forwarded her mail to Nice and sought their assistance "in a most worrying matter." The lawyer had received a letter from her eighty-three-year-old aunt, who had been interned at Gurs with her sixty-five-year-old sister-in-law in October 1940. The women had been forced to leave their homes in Karlsruhe without any money or belongings and were "living in complete destitution." The lawyer asked her Basque friends to give the women parcels of clothing and food she had sent to Maule from Nice and enclosed three hundred francs to cover any expenses the Basques might incur. "Dear Madam," the lawyer continued, "you can surely imagine our desperation and understand our reasons for asking these favors of you. It is heart-breaking to write such a letter to you, dear Mme. Etcheverry. The extraordinary circumstances in which we find ourselves force me to proceed in this fashion. I thank you in advance for anything you might do for me and my poor family, so badly stricken with misfortune." The lawyer's aunt died at Gurs in December 1940 and is buried in the camp's cemetery. The elderly aunt was among the first three and a half thousand Jews sent to Gurs by Vichy. The Vichy authorities interned nearly twenty-two thousand Jews at Gurs between October 1940 and November 1943.

In February 1943, a few days before the Germans first arrived in Maule, Inspector Carbou reported the presence of an affluent Jewish family in the Maule area. He identified Kaleb Salomon Castro as a Sephardic French Jew, born in Baiona in 1890 and married to a Sephardic Jew from a prominent Baiona family. Before the Occupation, M. Castro had worked as a leather and wool merchant. During the First World War, he served in the Eighteenth Infantry Regiment of Pau and fought at the Somme, Verdun, and the Marne before he was demobilized in 1918 as a decorated sergeant major. Inspector Carbou noted that M. Castro also fought in the war of 1939–40. The Castro family had moved to Maule on August 3, 1942 (soon after the Germans occupied Baiona), and spent a few days in the Hotel Bidegain. In late August the family moved to a Xiberoan village nearby. In February 1943 Inspector Carbou asked the prefect to give the Castro family "favorable review and consideration." The prefect at that time, P. E. Grimaud, granted permission for the Castros to remain in Xiberoa. Several other Jewish families remained in the province as well with the permission of local Vichy authorities.[28]

At the end of August 1942, Inspector Carbou made a detailed report to the subprefect on the concerns and views of workers, shopkeepers, and farmers in Xiberoa. Most workers were still of Spanish and Navarrese origin and, with few exceptions, prudently kept quiet about their political views, for they feared internment in Vichy or German camps, expulsion from France, and the withdrawal of French citizenship. Native Xiberoan workers likewise refrained from political discussions and avoided "nationalistic and patriotic events, because they [wanted] nothing to do with Pétain's National Revolution." Both northern Basque and Navarrese workers refused to join the Legion or the Secours National, both of which remained almost exclusively the preserve of the *patrons* and their wives. Workers remained hostile to Vichy and hoped, above all, for the victory of the world's democracies over Hitler. "Democracy," Carbou noted, was "far from being a myth among working class citizens." For them, it was "one of the only means by which they could achieve individual freedom." By contrast, Carbou found middle-class townspeople "entirely preoccupied with their own affairs." The *population commerçante* in Maule were "a privileged class who rarely suffered, thanks to the local system of *troc* [bartering] with rural Xiberoans." Carbou found such citizens "politically opportunistic" and, with few exceptions, extremely hostile to the Popular Front and supportive of Great Britain. Only the factory owners remained "in harmony with the [Vichy] government, in control of municipal matters, of the Legion and the Secours National." Although the town's industrial leaders "tried to apply a policy of appeasement and understanding to their relations with the working class," they had little success. According to Inspector Carbou: "The principle of the class struggle, divergent political opinions, and living conditions that were much more difficult for the workers than for the *patrons* all posed serious obstacles to any reconciliation or unification of the two classes. Two castes have long existed in Maule, separated by their aspirations and, above all, by their living conditions. Long-standing rancor between them never dissipated. Prejudices rooted in former times remain intact and form the basis of their mutual misunderstanding."[29]

In the summer of 1942, the Spanish and Navarrese community in Maule still included militant communists and anarchists. They did not escape the attention of the Legion's president, Dr. Herbille, or Inspector Carbou, who led a selective pursuit of communists in Xiberoa that mirrored a trend across France. The trend peaked in 1942, with widespread repression of communists and roundups, often triggered by the discovery of clandestine communist tracts (Dreyfus-Armand 1999: 149). In August 1942 Vichy authorities permitted members of the Navarrese community in Maule to attend a festival on the Xiberoan-Navarrese border. One anarchist from the Erronkari Valley, Joseph Seisdedos, took a sack of illegal tracts to the event. Someone denounced him to the police, who contacted Henri Herbille; accompanied by Inspector Carbou and his men, Herbille set off for the festival to investigate the matter. The police arrested Seisdedos and two other Maule communists from Erronkari. Following a separate denunciation, Maule police arrested Eustaquio Pérez at home that same night. With the approval of Herbille, the external authorities sent the four "undesirables" to internment camps and prisons for "hardcore communists."[30] The denunciations, arrests, and incarcerations gave rise to further turmoil among left-wing citizens in the town. To counter the negative effects of such actions, Herbille negotiated the release of another Maule communist-internee on the grounds of "good behavior and morals," which entailed submission to the hegemony of the elites and notables, rejection of anticlericalism and communist ideals, and acceptance of class-based hierarchy. Workers praised the wealthy patron and the local trade unionist (St. Jean Lanouguère), who first proposed the communist-internee's release to Herbille, but remained hostile to Herbille himself.[31]

Following the Vichy roundup and deportation of fourteen thousand Jews at the Vél d'Hiv in Paris during July 1942, an increasing number of French and foreign Jews left the Occupied Zone and sought clandestine passage into Spain through Xiberoa.[32] In the fall of that year, more and more Maule citizens listened to Radio London. Although no organized, fully formed resistance group yet existed in Xiberoa, a "culture of the outlaw" had begun to develop as rural and urban Basques grew increasingly hostile to Vichy and worked together to oppose its policies (See Kedward 1985: 56–57). Local opposition focused on the STO (Service du Travail Obligatoire) and French authorities' attempts to intercept "undesirables" and their guides as they crossed the Pyrenees. In Sustary posters appeared in the public lavatory and on post-office walls: "Vive de Gaulle and liberty! Down with collaborators!" As happened elsewhere in southern France, previously law-abiding Xiberoans (including numerous gendarmes and local Vichy officials) found themselves forming an "outlaw culture," in which people no longer trusted the legal justice (*légalité*) of the Vichy regime or believed in its legitimacy. By contrast, as a principal holder of civic and moral authority in Maule, Dr. Henri Herbille needed the assistance of external, Vichy authorities and access to Vichy's legal justice in order to protect his community from communism, primarily through the agency of local denunciations and purges. In his attempts to reduce class tensions in Maule through acts of clemency, Herbille had to collaborate with Vichy authorities at departmental and national levels. The total occupation of France by Germany dramatically shifted the balance of power away from Vichy. Holders of civic and moral authority in Xiberoa such as Dr. Herbille recognized that they had new, much more difficult and potentially dangerous roles to play as mediators between the local population and the external authorities.

On November 11, 1942, German forces moved into the Vichy Zone. Hitler dissolved the Armistice Army, although its officers remained obliged to obey Pétain's orders not to act against the occupiers (Paxton 2001: 281). With the total occupation of France, German surveillance operations turned their attention to the Franco-Spanish border and the growing number of French and foreign people who were trying to escape the tyranny of Hitler, Vichy's increasingly anti-Semitic legislation, and increasingly unpopular regulations about forced labor in Germany. The Germans had already established a presence in Béarn in the summer of 1940 through its surveillance troops based in Orthez and German members of the Armistice Control Commission in Pau, whose resident officers monitored the region's economic contribution to Germany's war effort (Sweets 1986: 171).[33] Although the Germans' presence in the region had not gone unnoticed before November 1942, the arrival of German occupying troops in Xiberoan territory violated Xiberoans' fundamental right, rooted in sixteenth-century customary law, to manage their own affairs and their own space. A new enemy threatened the Xiberoan moral community—its values, institutions, and traditions. Xiberoans faced new choices as they learned how to cope with the occupiers, and with one another, in a war that had begun to affect their lives directly in their own territory.

7: The German Occupation and Resistance in Xiberoa

Seven months before the Germans arrived in Xiberoa, Inspector Carbou had predicted that only a serious assault on French territory would force citizens out of their deep-seated complacency.[1] When Germany occupied the Vichy Zone in November 1942, Carbou realized that some Xiberoans would not be jolted out of their indifference to world events until the Germans invaded Xiberoan space. The inspector appreciated the Basques' attachment to their own sociophysical territory, their *xokhoa,* their *coin,* their localized *pays,* a fundamental component of their habitus. At the end of November, German customs officers requisitioned houses and herding huts in Xiberoan borderland communes, including Urdos. A fortnight later, the German authorities created a forbidden frontier zone (*une zone frontière interdite*) in Xiberoa and neighboring Béarn, which extended ten miles north of the Franco-Spanish border. Although both German and Vichy officials agreed that the international frontier required surveillance, they disputed each other's authority over the French police in such matters.[2] The departmental prefect and subprefect objected when German officers ordered French gendarmes to establish patrols along the Béarnais-Xiberoan border with Spain. In January 1943 the authorities reclassified the twenty French Basque borderland communes as a reserved zone, accessible only to those with an appropriate pass (Poullenot 1995: 27). The reserved zone included the market town of Sustary and Urdos.

In December 1942 the German security service (SD, Sicherheitsdienst) established a commissariat in the Béarnais city of Pau and a garrison of fifty-eight soldiers and customs officers in Sustary.[3] Their mission was to intercept Jews in the reserved zone; to gather information about the organization of resistance activities; to uncover and to destroy enemy intelligence and escape networks; and to remove resisters and communists from Urdos and adjacent borderland communities (ibid.: 103). Soon thereafter, the Germans replaced the gendarmes on the frontier with German customs officers.[4] As happened elsewhere in France, the Germans did not trust the French police to do what was required (Gildea 2002: 18).

In spite of overtures made by Hitler to Franco, Spain remained neutral.[5] Long-standing trans-Pyrenean relations between borderland Basques made them well placed to help fugitives trying to escape Vichy and German oppression: Jewish refugees, Allied pilots, and the numerous young people who chose to evade Vichy's compulsory labor scheme in Germany.[6] Assisted by French police and local citizens, the Germans sought information about the numerous intelligence and evasion networks that operated across the Pyrenees.

In January 1943 Vichy created the Milice, a paramilitary movement set up to crush dissent and pursue Jews, resisters, and STO evaders. A few weeks later, some Maule factory owners informed Inspector Carbou that they strongly opposed the Milice "because it embraced doctrines that were fundamentally anti-French." They expressed their hatred of the Germans and their uneasiness about the open commitment of the Milice to collaboration with Hitler.[7] In February 1943 the introduction of Vichy laws on obligatory work service (STO) in Germany coincided with the arrival of German troops in the Xiberoan capital, Maule. Both factors greatly increased opposition to the Vichy regime and aided locally formed resistance groups (Kedward 1994: 38–40). The STO laws sharpened class-based tensions and jealousies in the town. Since the law required all men born between 1920 and 1922 to register for compulsory labor service, the workers expected that all classes would be made to participate, only to discover that it was very easy for the sons of *patrons* to obtain dispensations.[8] It was also easy for wealthier families to hide an eligible son on a farm as an alternative to the uncertainties and dangers entailed by clandestine passage to Spain (M. Béguerie 2004: pers. comm.). Of the 200 Maule men sent to Germany in the spring of 1943, nearly all were factory workers of Spanish or Navarrese origin. As Inspector Carbou observed, many workers felt that compulsory work service was part of "some grand scheme aimed at neutralizing their class and seeking to punish them for political beliefs they held before the war began."[9]

On February 25, 1943, some five hundred German soldiers and SS from the Das Reich division entered Maule. According to Inspector Carbou, citizens responded to their arrival with a mixture of resentment and resignation but "did not react to the German troops. They had been prepared for such an eventuality ever since the occupation of Pau, Oloron and the borderland communes." A number of citizens, primarily children, watched the impeccably dressed, disciplined soldiers with great interest, especially when they unloaded military equipment from their trucks. Carbou observed that such curiosity was "perhaps unhealthy, but understandable, given that such a sensational display seemed like the arrival of a circus to people with little experience of the world."[10] The soldiers also inspired some teenage youths to play dangerous pranks, such as flashing postcard images of de Gaulle at the Germans as they marched past (J. de Jaureguiberry 2005: pers. comm.). Carbou also noted the presence of Russian soldiers, who "were said to have been volunteers in the German Army but who, it seems, had been recruited by force." The soldiers dispersed throughout the town, occupying the private Catholic

school (the Collège Saint-François), the two public schools, the Hotel Sau-
bidet, the Hotel Bidegain, a café, and a mechanic's workshop. During the
first few months of the town's occupation, Mayor Aguer and his assistants in
the town hall established nonconfrontational relations with the German
commander. Aguer and the German exchanged polite correspondence about
the need for German soldiers to treat civilians and their property with respect
(Aguer 1964: 3).

According to Inspector Carbou, Maule citizens worried as much about
the STO as they did about the presence of so many Germans in their town.
"The deportation of so many young Frenchmen to Germany sows anguish
in parents' hearts," Carbou wrote, "and many young men are thinking about
fleeing towards the Spanish frontier, that is to say, towards the unknown."[11]
In keeping with their long-standing reputation for evading service of any
kind in a foreign country, the Basques once again used their trans-Pyrenean
connections to escape duties they did not wish to perform for outsiders and
strangers. Their initial destinations were not, however, "unknown." The borderland villages of Nafarroa once again provided Xiberoans with a safe haven.
People quickly realized, however, that the Occupation greatly increased the
risk of denunciation, arrest, and deportation for a burgeoning number of
people seeking passage to Nafarroa and more distant destinations, as well as
the local guides who helped them. The STO evaders flooded into the region
and used Maule as a principal point of contact with clandestine escape networks and independent operators (Eychenne 1987: 158–62; Lougarot 2004).

Although survivors of the Occupation now insist that they never dared
discuss France's policy of collaboration with Germany or their support for
the British, the Americans, or the Free French, Inspector Carbou's detailed
reports indicate that citizens did indeed talk about such issues in local cafés.
In January 1943 most people predicted an American-led victory but disagreed
about which of France's own generals ought to lead the Free French effort in
North Africa to aid the Allies.[12] Most politically conservative citizens initially
favored General Giraud, the arch rival of de Gaulle, while the town's substantial working-class and socialist population mainly supported de Gaulle. The
two factions eventually contributed to the formation of Xiberoa's two main
rival resistance groups, the Giraudist Corps Franc Pommiès and the Gaullist
Secret Army.

In January 1943 those communists who remained in Maule once again
began to distribute illegal tracts, plaster walls with propaganda posters, and
foment anti-German sentiment in the factories. Inspector Carbou kept them
under surveillance but reasoned that the majority of workers, who were
socialists, would keep matters under control by ignoring their militant col-

leagues.[13] At that stage neither Carbou nor Herbille took any actions against the communists in their midst. Both men realized that the Germans were creating their own lists of "suspect individuals": communists, resisters, their helpers, and STO evaders. In the town hall, Vichy's representatives soon engaged in their own resistance activities. The secretary of the town hall was a former POW who had escaped from Germany in 1940. Aguer's first deputy was the father of an STO evader arrested by German police in April 1943 and deported to the Nazi camp at Dora. The two Vichy administrators were responsible for providing the Gestapo with information about local citizens. With Mayor Aguer's knowledge and approval, however, the town-hall secretary and deputy often alerted the "undesirables" on the Gestapo's list before the Germans made a nocturnal raid on suspects' homes (Aguer 1964: 3). The town-hall officials were, however, selective in administering their preventive measures, for local communists had to depend upon other means by which to escape arrest.

One particular communist family at once attracted the interest of Hitler's security services. The Vichy authorities had already revoked the citizenship of François Blasquiz, a native of Salvatierra, Aragón, for his communist militancy. In July 1942 his son, Lambert, also lost his citizenship, and soon thereafter Lambert became a clandestine guide for fugitives escaping the tyranny of Vichy and Hitler. By the fall of 1942, with several intelligence and escape networks operating in Xiberoa, Lambert had more clients than he could handle alone. His father and brother became involved as well. Between the autumn of 1942 and his arrest by the Germans in March 1943, Lambert Blasquiz took some three hundred people into Nafarroa (L. Blasquiz 2005: pers. comm.; Lougarot 2004: 229). His clients usually waited for him at the Lopés' hotel beside the railway station, where a railway worker and his wife briefed them on the next part of their journey to Spain. Depending upon the physical fitness of Lambert's clients, the nighttime journey on foot from Maule to the frontier took twelve to thirteen hours. "From November to March, the snow in the mountains made it terribly hard for the people to walk. Their feet froze and they often held hands in a chain to keep everyone moving forward. We always had to be on the lookout for the German patrols. The young lads I passed never said much. Who were they? Where did they come from? I knew nothing about them, and that made me think hard about who brought down our network. I know who denounced us" (ibid.: 232).

A twenty-two-year-old man, Roger D., denounced the Blasquiz men and their Maule network. Born on the Basque coast, Roger D. worked for the Gestapo and specialized in the infiltration of escape and intelligence networks. One day he asked a railway worker in Blasquiz's network to arrange his passage to Spain. The railway worker and his wife became suspicious when, three days later, Roger D. asked Blasquiz the same thing. On the following day, Roger D. turned up at the Blasquiz home with a revolver in hand and fifteen German police, who arrested Lambert, his brother, and his father. The Germans confiscated more than one hundred thousand francs in cash and helped themselves to bed linens, tablecloths, clothing, forty boxes of sardines, and forty jars of pâté de foie gras.[14] Once inside the commandant's headquarters in Maule, the three Blasquiz men decided that the two young men would escape, which they did. Lambert and his brother made their way across the Pyrenees into Nafarroa, where local Basques helped them evade the Gestapo on several occasions. The Blasquiz brothers did not escape the attention of the Spanish police, however, and spent a year in various Spanish prisons, as well as in the notorious Camp Miranda de Ebro.[15] From there, they made their way to Malaga and on to Casablanca, where they joined the Allies (L. Blasquiz 2005: pers. comm.; Lougarot 2004: 233–34).

The other members of the Blasquiz's network had quite different experiences. Fifteen Gestapo and French *miliciens* arrested the Maule hoteliers (the Lopés), interrogated them in Biarritz, and eventually released them. The Gestapo never caught the railway worker, who went into hiding following a tip that he had been denounced. The Germans did arrest his wife, a Maule factory worker, who went to jail. Her fate is unknown.

Shortly after the Maule raids, the Germans arrested Roger D. for buying black-market coffee and released him only on condition that he would work solely for them. An unknown citizen then denounced Roger D. to the Germans for warning a Basque resister about plans to ambush him. The Gestapo arrested Roger D. a second time. On his release a few weeks later, the young opportunist denounced several communist railway workers on the Basque coast, but he realized that the Gestapo no longer trusted him. Roger D. then fled to Spain with one of his mistresses and ended up in a Casablanca jail after Allied intelligence networks identified and arrested him. As Allied police took Roger D. to his cell, they passed a group of Basques who awaited their debriefing. The Blasquiz brothers immediately recognized their denouncer. In 2005 Lambert Blasquiz still vividly recalled the two occasions on which he faced his denouncer: "In Casablanca that day, my brother and I would have given Roger D. some rough justice, if we'd had the chance! The next time I saw Roger D. it was after the Liberation. He was on trial in Pau, and I testified against him. I was still wearing my uniform, because I hadn't yet been demobilized. He was condemned to forced labor for life, but he was freed after only ten years" (L. Blasquiz pers. comm.: 2005; Lougarot 2004: 233,

239–40).[16] Lambert Blasquiz also clearly remembered attempts by the Milice to foment anticommunist sentiment in Xiberoa.

On March 1, 1943, the departmental head of the Milice organized a rally in Maule to recruit anticommunist Xiberoans. Fifty *miliciens* and around a hundred local people attended the event. The deputy head of the Milice spoke at length about the "communist threat" and the urgent need to restore faith in Pétain and Laval. In his monthly report to the subprefect, Inspector Carbou observed that "no one defaced any of the numerous posters advertising the Milice's meeting."[17] Most *légionnaires,* including Dr. Herbille, boycotted the event, as they held *miliciens* responsible for the arrest and torture of their association's departmental leader. Factory workers regarded the Milice as a kind of French Gestapo.[18] Maule's most influential *patrons* knew the departmental head of the Milice through their business and social networks in Pau, for he was an industrialist from Pau who had belonged to the extreme right-wing movement, the Croix de Feu, and the Parti Social Français before the war. In 1943 he became departmental head of the Service d'Ordre Légionnaire (SOL), from which Vichy created the Milice as a paramilitary organization to crush dissent. The industrialist was a good friend of the head of the Gestapo in Oloron and was responsible for the arrest and murder of numerous resisters in the Béarnais maquis based in Bielle, Luc de Béarn, Morlaas, and Laborde.[19]

By the spring of 1943, the much respected Maule clergyman Canon Ithurbide had long been engaged in acts of resistance against both Vichy and the Germans. His escape network for Jewish and other fugitives continued to use the Collège de Saint-François as its base, despite the presence of several hundred German soldiers on the premises. He and another priest, who taught chemistry, belonged to the Gaullist resistance movement the Secret Army. The chemistry teacher regularly made incendiary devices for Secret Army *maquisards* (J. Haristoy, J. Larroque 2004: pers. comms.). In April 1943 several priests and their pupils at the Collège carried out their own acts of resistance against the Germans in their midst. On two occasions, a priest led a large group of boys around the premises singing patriotic songs. Soon thereafter, pupils set fires in the middle of the night directly beneath the Germans' sleeping quarters. Soldiers quickly extinguished the flames and confronted Canon Ithurbide. The Basque priest concealed from them the letter he had found, scrawled on the school's headed paper:

Monsieur le Supérieur, It is truly regrettable that this establishment has been occupied. You know that everywhere the enemy is there will be resistance. Wherever the enemy is, we will sabotage them. We have given you the first and last warning. By starting the fires we made you all sense danger. In the best interests of your colleagues, your pupils, and yourself, evacuate this school before Palm Sunday. That action will spare French blood and let German blood flow. I ask that you carry out this order, Monsieur le Supérieur, and moreover that you do not reconvene classes after the Easter holiday. You will find asylum elsewhere.[20]

Canon Ithurbide promised both German and French police that no further anti-German acts would occur in the school, but he continued to run his highly popular escape network for fugitives fleeing Vichy and Nazi persecution. Former pupils who remember the fires knew about the letter and regard the incidents as a reflection of their youthful tomfoolery and deep yearning to get involved in the organized Resistance (J. de Jaureguiberry 2005: pers. comm.).

A few weeks later, in May 1943, German military police arrested three Xiberoan teenagers (one of whom attended the college) and took them to an abandoned house on the outskirts of Maule. The Germans handcuffed the youths, blinded them with pepper, beat and insulted them, and shaved their heads. On the previous night, the teenagers had ambushed a local female acquaintance as she walked home on a country road. They had cut off her hair as punishment for having had sexual relations with a German soldier and, at considerable risk, the youths erected a large placard beside the war memorial in Maule. Beneath the girl's locks of hair, the placard warned Xiberoan women to "beware!"[21] The fourth youth involved in the incident managed to escape when someone warned his father, Pierre Béguerie (M. Béguerie 2004: pers. comm.). The Germans' brutality against the three other youths triggered a fundamental shift in notables' perceptions of the Germans, for until that time the town's privileged families had not been directly affected by German violence.

Mayor Aguer wrote at once to the German commander to express his indignation about the soldiers' brutal acts "while under military orders." Aguer called for the soldiers to be identified and brought to legal justice. The German promised to investigate the matter, which Aguer regarded as "evasive behavior." Aguer thus wrote a second, more strongly worded letter to the German officer demanding that the guilty soldiers "should be the focus of an official investigation and should be held accountable to French Justice." Mayor Aguer went on to complain about the frequency with which Maule citizens "received nocturnal visits from members of the German military" and appealed to the German's "spirit of justice and equity" in ensuring that the soldiers responsible for the youths' torture and head shaving would be appropriately punished. Aguer received the German's reply straightaway. The commander appreciated receipt of information about the soldiers from the French police and agreed with Aguer that the culprits needed to be punished. He assured Aguer that he would do everything in his power "to prevent repetition of such a deplorable incident" and reaffirmed his commitment to maintaining "correct relations between Maule citizens and German troops" under his command.

A few days later, Aguer received a visit from German police based in Artix in Béarn, who informed the mayor that "detachment commanders had no authority to resolve conflicts between civilian populations and occupying troops." Aguer once again demanded punishment of the soldiers responsible for the youth's torture and head shaving, and the German police replied that "appropriate sanctions would be made, but according to German laws." In June 1943 Mayor Aguer received confirmation that "the guilty soldiers" had been "held responsible for their actions," though their precise fate remained unknown (Aguer 1964: 3).

How did Maule citizens respond to the female hair-cutting incident that had provoked the German soldiers' revenge against the young men? Some people regarded the incident as a mildly amusing prank. Pierre Béguerie applauded the girl's haircut as a legitimate act of popular justice against a "virago." In his view, the youths' actions constituted "a just judgment of the Germans by the local population that reflected the brutality and savagery of the so-called defenders of European civilization" (Béguerie n.d.: 12).

The female hair cutting by Basque youths and male head shaving by German soldiers, as well as Béguerie's assessment of them, deserve comment for a number of reasons. Between 1943 and the beginning of 1946, some twenty thousand French women had their heads shaved as punishment for collaboration with the Germans (Virgili 2002: 1). Nearly 94 percent of reported cases occurred during the process of liberation throughout France. Only forty-two cases (6.6 percent) took place during the Occupation. The first and only reported incident in 1943 happened in Pau, thirty-five miles from Maule (ibid.: 62, 64). An underground newspaper, *Populaire du Midi,* reported the head shaving, which happened in June: "A group of young people sickened by the way in which certain women—new style procurers—behaved with the German army rabble, they shaved their hair off. They will be more discrete from now on and especially so if they are aware that what they have done is going to be made widely known" (ibid.: 66). The Maule incident took place in May and thus preceded the first publicly reported case.

The practice of hair cutting or head shaving as a means of punishing women for sexual wrongdoing was not unprecedented; it may have started as early as the thirteenth century in France. In 1918 the French had also used this form of popular justice to punish women who had consorted with Germans during the Great War (Diamond 1999: 136). When the French occupied the Rhineland in the 1920s, Germans shaved the heads of German women who had slept with French soldiers (Fraenkel 1944: 143), and from 1940, some sections of the Nazi Party used the same form of punishment on German women who had slept with foreign workers (Burrin 1995: 212). Thus, the German soldiers who shaved the heads of male Xiberoans in 1943 used a practice applied to female sexual wrongdoing in their own culture, but which the French had not yet begun to use in response to female sexual collaboration during the Occupation. How can the Germans' actions in May 1943 be interpreted?

The high incidence of female head shaving during the process of liberation across France has variously been attributed to a widespread need among the French for scapegoats who would take the blame for collaborationists (Novick 1985); a need for revenge against female denunciators and sexual collaborators (Cobb 1983); a need to cleanse the country of collaboration symbolically (Virgili 2002); a need to exorcise feelings of sexual insecurity (Kelly 1995: 117–19); and a need to reestablish a patriarchal order in France (Diamond 1999: 141). The Germans humiliated the three young Basque men by performing an act normally applied to women and may thus have tried to make their victims feel emasculated. Male head shaving also enabled the Germans to assert symbolically their dominance and control over an occupied people, as well as their physical dominance over young Basques eager to join the Resistance.

How did Xiberoans react to the hair cutting of the young woman? As happened at the liberation of Xiberoa, some men (including Pierre Béguerie) applauded the act as a just punishment of a woman who had slept with the enemy. For many men and women, however, both hair cutting and head shaving (*la tonte*) violated Xiberoan moral codes relating to men's respect for women and were thus condemned as inappropriate and offensive behavior. It is thus of interest that Béguerie treated the young woman as a symbol of German brutality and savagery in wartime, rather than as a female Xiberoan citizen who deserved male respect.

Although most Xiberoans shared Béguerie's hatred of the German occupiers, a few citizens belonged to, or at least sympathized with, France's largest collaborationist movement, the Groupe Collaboration (GC). Founded in September 1940 by the essayist Alphonse de Châteaubriant, the movement promoted Franco-German collaboration in cultural matters. Its members typically belonged to one of the collaborationist political parties, such as the PPF (Parti Populaire Français) (Gordon 1980: 230, 233). Colonel George B. formed a branch of the GC in Pau during May 1942.[22] He wrote pro-German editorials and worked closely with the heads of the Gestapo, the PPF, and the Milice in Pau, as well as with Jacques Schweizer in Paris. Schweizer had attended several Nuremberg party congresses before the war and became leader of the Groupe's youth movement (JEN, Jeunesse de l'Europe Nouvelle) (Gordon 1980: 236). Through the president of Groupe Collaboration in Pau, Schweizer became aware of local support for the movement in Maule, where a factory manager used his connections with the GC to promote both business and personal concerns. In the summer of 1943, the factory manager secretly negotiated with the president of the GC in Pau to secure the release of a Maule communist of Navarrese origins from a German stalag. The communist was the brother of the factory manager's young mistress. The president of the GC in Pau used his connections with the local Gestapo and Jacques Schweizer to bring the communist safely back to Maule (ibid.: 234).[23]

In June 1943 Inspector Carbou noted that Maule citizens "awaited important events." The first meeting of the National Council of the Resistance (Conseil National de la Résistance, or CNR) had taken place on May 27. The CNR represented the "crowning achievement of Jean Moulin's efforts to unite the Resistance within France under de Gaulle" (Kedward 1994: 291). Following a meeting in Algiers on June 3, the rival generals, de Gaulle and Giraud, in theory became joint heads of the National Committee of French Liberation (Comité Français de Libération Nationale).[24] At the time, Giraud enjoyed greater popularity than de Gaulle and had the support of the Americans, while de Gaulle risked losing Britain's backing. Giraud wanted to secure American arms so that the French Army in North Africa could reenter the war, whereas de Gaulle's primary concern was to establish a single political authority to represent France in negotiations with the Allies (Jackson 2001: 457). Six months later, de Gaulle assumed single leadership of the CFLN. American military commanders had by then recognized General Giraud's inadequacies (ibid.: 459).

According to Inspector Carbou, Maule citizens followed the struggle for power between de Gaulle and Giraud "with a certain curiosity," for two substantial dissident groups existed in the town by then. Gaullist partisans greatly outnumbered Giraudists.[25] By September 1943 Carbou had developed a network of informers who eavesdropped on conversations in the town's various bars. Carbou noted that the Gaullists in Maule included "all the former parties of the Left and, primarily, the working class," whereas the Giraudists were old-guard conservatives and partisans of the Right. At that stage Carbou detected "no apparent antagonism between the two dissident groups" but reported that a split was already in the making.[26]

In September 1943 someone denounced Maule's long-standing political representative in the French Chamber of Deputies, Jean Ybarnegaray. German police arrested him, his wife, his chauffeur, and two others for having helped some fugitives escape to Spain. News of the arrest shocked Maule elites and notables. On September 23, 1943, the former general councilor for the Basses-Pyrénées (and elite member of Maule society) wrote a letter to the prefect in Pau:[27]

> The chauffeur of our nephew, M. Ybarnegaray, came to see us today. Full of emotion, he told us of the arrest, yesterday afternoon, of M. and Mme Ybarnegaray, whom the Germans took to a prison, though we do not know which one. M. Ybarnegaray has not been feeling well of late, and these events will do nothing to improve his health. These are the terrible circumstances in which M. Ybarnegaray and his courageous wife find themselves. One can only hope that their friend, M. Laval, will quickly intercede and return them to their home. One hopes, M. Prefect, that the great leader of our government and M. Laval will not abandon their friends. I do not know if there is anything you can do, in their favor, but let us count on you as always.[28]

Ignoring the prefect's plea for clemency, the Germans sent Ybarnegaray to a concentration camp in the Tyrol (Paxton 2001: 162n.). A month later the Germans deported Eustaquio Pérez, the militant communist never earmarked by local authorities as a candidate for clemency. Pérez died in Mauthausen in 1944 (Altaffaylla 2003: 83; R. Pérez 2004: pers. comm.).

In the months preceding the deportations of Ybarnegaray and Pérez, German violence against Xiberoan citizens deepened hatred of the occupiers. At daybreak one morning in March 1943, German police surrounded the Xiberoan hamlet of Mendikota, near Maule, and forced its inhabitants into the square. The police suspected villagers of hiding two Russian deserters from the German Army. After extensive interrogations and a search of all houses and farms, the Germans released the citizens but then raided the homes of other Xiberoans nearby whom they suspected of passing STO evaders to Spain.[29]

In June 1943 an experienced clandestine guide (*passeur*) led thirty-seven STO evaders to a farmhouse in the Xiberoan commune of Barkoxe, ten miles north of Maule. The household often sheltered fugitives and trusted their local *passeur,* Michel Olazabal. While Olazabal returned to Pau to collect a second group of evaders, a French Waffen ss/Milice patrol based in nearby Moumour raided the Barkoxe farm.[30] The *miliciens* held the fugitives and farmers hostage while they waited for Olazabal to return. A day passed, with no sign of him. In the middle of the night, the farmers' teenage son crept out of the house into the courtyard and was shot in the back by a *milicien*. The guide heard about the tragedy on his return to Barkoxe the next day. The murder provoked intense emotional reactions among the villagers, who were bitterly divided over the identity of the informer. For several decades, one faction accused Olazabal of "selling" the Barkoxe family to the Waffen ss and Milice. Others suspected two Barkoxe citizens, a brother and sister who had regular dealings with the German police. One of the fugitives captured that day also came under local suspicion, because he had been allowed by the *miliciens* to "come and go freely" while they lay in wait for the guide and his second group.

The Germans deported the fugitives and their helpers but did not find Olazabal until July 1944, when they arrested him and ten young Xiberoans suspected of helping the Resistance. The Germans sent Olazabal to prison in Toulouse, where resisters freed him at the Liberation. Two of the young Xiberoans became victims of Nazi barbarity. One week before the Liberation, German police took them and fifty-four other prisoners to a remote field in the Haute-Garonne. They forced the men and women to lie facedown in the grass, machine-gunned them, poured gasoline over the dead and the living, set fire to their victims, and threw incendiary grenades at them.[31]

In Olazabal's diary, discovered shortly after his death in 1973, the guide wrote at length about his profound sense of guilt over "the Barkoxe affair." For thirty years he had mulled over events during those tragic days. He finally concluded that the denunciation had come from some French undercover agents posing as resisters who knew about the guide's extensive activities in the region. "It wasn't those fugitives they really wanted to get, it was me," he wrote.[32] On the eve of the Liberation, the brother and sister from Barkoxe, suspected of denunciations and collaboration, discretely left Xiberoa. In December 1945 French authorities arrested the brother when he tried to cross the Franco-Spanish border on the Basque coast. He had belonged to the fascist group Légion des Voluntaires Français contre le Bolchévisme (LVF), whose members wore Nazi uniforms with Hitler's permission.

In October 1943 another German raid occurred in Maule that left many people emotionally shaken. In the middle of the night, Marie and Raymond Hoquigaray heard someone pounding on their neighbor's door. Knowing that the neighbor was deaf and suspecting a raid, their friend, Laurent Aphesbero, jumped out his bedroom window in the Hoquigarays' house and escaped.

Aphesbero was an intelligence courier for a resistance network operating between northern France and Maule (M. Etchecopar 2005: pers. comm.; Lougarot 2004: 218–27; M. Rodrigo Nicolau 2005: pers. comm.). He had recruited the Hoquigarays to provide a safe house in Maule. The local gendarme intentionally led the Germans to the wrong house that night in order to give Aphesbero time to escape. Unknown to anyone but a few at the time, the officer sympathized with the Resistance. When the German police finally entered the Hoquigarays' house, they found one slightly warm, unmade bed and an open window. Furious, they arrested the couple, who consistently maintained that they knew nothing about Aphesbero's resistance activities. Owing to the influence of a young northern Basque nationalist among high-ranking Nazis, the Germans freed the couple seven months later.[33]

The Gestapo searched unsuccessfully for Aphesbero. For many years later, he wrestled with a suspicion that someone local had betrayed him. Aphesbero tried to understand the circumstances and reasons that might lead a person to betray his fellow citizen but insisted that he had no right to accuse anyone in the absence of formal proof of guilt. One suspect staunchly supported Pétain and opposed the Resistance; another potential source of betrayal had tried to recruit Aphesbero to his resistance group and became annoyed when Aphesbero declined. The courier could not explain that he had already committed himself to an intelligence network that was in fact linked to the disgruntled recruiter's own group, as it was too dangerous to disclose such information. At the Liberation, Aphesbero did not report his suspicions, because he never found adequate proof upon which to base an accusation (Lougarot 2004: 218–27).

For the remainder of 1943 and until the liberation in 1944, the Germans aggressively pursued resisters and their helpers across Xiberoa, assisted by anonymous denunciations, paid informers, and a few pro-German citizens. By infiltrating escape and resistance networks and engaging in military aggression against Xiberoan people, the Milice also greatly aided the Germans and often worked alongside the French Waffen ss unit based in Moumour and responsible for numerous murders, tortures, deportations, and terrifying raids in Xiberoa and Béarn.

By October 1943 the de Gaulle–Giraud quarrel had become the focus of public debate in town and pitched a political battle between "left-wing partisans and the former enemies of the Popular Front." The Maule middle classes feared a communist takeover. The trans-Pyrenean crossings of young sto evaders had all but stopped, but the Resistance—the subprefect advised the prefect—was gaining strength day by day. The maquis were "well-armed and well-received" by the local population in Maule and the surrounding countryside.[34] Although resistance activities had indeed begun in Xiberoa, the two main rival groups were not yet fully organized: Sector IV of the Secret Army (Armée Secrète) and a company of the CFP (Corps Franc Pommiès), which represented the ORA (Organisation de Résistance de l'Armée) in southwestern France. The Secret Army supported de Gaulle, whereas the CFP initially backed his political rival, General Giraud.

The Secret Army was set up nationally as a united military resistance movement, and its forces were often unarmed and untrained (Sweets 1976: 37). Its military role was to prepare for the Allies' landing and de Gaulle's day of national insurrection, intended to liberate France for the French. In Xiberoa the Secret Army was local in origin (Davant 2001: 169). It mainly consisted of insiders to the Xiberoan moral community: civilian volunteers and some reserve officers strongly opposed to Vichy and firmly behind de Gaulle. Its three maquis operated from Maule, the rural hamlets of Larceveau and Larrebieu, and the mountainous zones of Arbailles and Upper Xiberoa. By the end of 1942, dispersed groups of Secret Army resisters had formed in the mountains.

Organization and communication improved locally with the merging of resistance movements across France in January 1943. This led to the formation of both a civil, administrative sector in the department of the Basses-Pyrénées (including Xiberoa) and a military one, which was the Secret Army (Poullenot 1995: 176). The head of the civil sector contacted a Maule Basque of Navarrese origins, Jean-Pierre Hegoburu, to set up an escape network across the Pyrenees. A socialist factory worker, he soon became the widely respected head of the Secret Army maquis in Maule, to which he recruited some three hundred local people.

In May 1944 the departmental chief of the Secret Army asked another Xiberoan Basque, Clement de Jaureguiberry, to take charge of Sector IV, which covered all of Xiberoa and included disparate Béarnais maquis groups formed by exiled Spanish Republicans (Poullenot 1995: 188). Educated, passionate about the Basque language, and of sober disposition, Captain Jaureguiberry was highly disciplined. A decorated veteran of the Great War, he had served in the artillery in 1939–40. When the "phony war" ended, he became the director of a sandal factory in Maule. As head of Sector IV, Jaureguiberry worked closely with a socialist schoolteacher, Jean-Pierre Champo, who served as Maule's cantonal head of civil resistance for the Secret Army. Jaureguiberry's general staff (*état-major*) also included his brother, Jean de Jaureguiberry, an influential and widely respected physician and an officer in the demobilized French Army.

As a committed Gaullist and proud Xiberoan, Clement de Jaureguiberry was zealous in his efforts to uphold the "purely military role of the Secret Army in maintaining order without political action" (Jaureguiberry 1950). Its goal was to defeat the German occupiers while at the same time ensuring the safety of civilians, refraining from armed conflict in or near any Basque community or farmhouses and thus avoiding circumstances that might lead to reprisals against them. For Jaureguiberry, the protection of Xiberoan lives and property was as important as driving the enemy outsiders off Xiberoan territory (M. Joanny 2003: pers. comm.). Following the example of their leader, Secret Army resisters and sympathizers regarded members of their resistance movement as defenders of the Xiberoan community and house. The two rural Secret Army maquis consisted of farmers and shepherds who, by the spring of 1943, had become deeply opposed to the Vichy regime. The maquis based in Maule included many radical and moderate socialists of Spanish and Navarrese descent who worked in the Maule factories or were artisans, tradesmen, or shopkeepers. Its highly respected cantonal chief, Jean-Pierre Champo, was a militant socialist teacher who had long supported workers' attempts to improve their conditions at home and at the factories. Owing to the number of socialists and communists among its ranks and supporters, the Xiberoan Secret Army is now often described by its critics as "very political" and as "the Red Maquis" (J.-L. Davant 2003: pers. comm.). By July 1944 the movement had 477 officers and troops operating in Xiberoa and was poorly armed but well organized (Poullenot 1995: 189).

The founder of the second largest resistance group operating in Xiberoa and Béarn, the CFP, was an outsider to Xiberoa. Born in Bordeaux and a career army officer, André Pommiès was keen to redeem the honor of the French Army, rid France of the German occupiers, and prevent a communist takeover. A captain in the Eighteenth Infantry Regiment in Pau, Pommiès was closely involved in the clandestine mobilization of combat units in the southwest before the Armistice Army was disbanded in 1940 and the clandestine resistance movement of the French Army, the ORA, was created in December 1942 (Lormier 1991: 178). In February 1943 Pommiès became military commander of Region 4 (based in Toulouse) under the auspices of the Giraudist resistance movement of the Armistice Army, the ORA (Céroni 1980: 56), but from September 1943 he liaised directly with the BCRA (Bureau Central de Renseignement et d'Action), the Free French intelligence service in London (Lormier 1991: 180). Although the BCRA was in fact Gaullist, Xiberoan CFP resisters insisted that their operation received support from the British (M. Béguerie 2004: pers. comm.). The BCRA sent French agents to organize resistance in France and was closely allied to the British SOE (Special

Operations Executive, RF section), which provided Pommiès's combat units with money and arms from the British War Office (Kedward 1994: 290). By April 1944 the CFP had recruited nearly nine thousand men in southern France. The CFP had three main missions: gaining enemy intelligence, carrying on sabotage, and harassing the Germans. Through BCRA and the SOE, the CFP in Xiberoa received regular parachute drops and was thus better armed and supplied than its rival, the Gaullist Secret Army (Céroni 1980: 37).

In June 1943 an envoy of Pommiès asked two reserve officers in the defunct French Army to recruit a Xiberoan CFP company: the *patron,* Pierre Béguerie, and his friend, Jean Jancène, whose family owned a sandal factory and a grocery shop in Maule. Privileged as a child, wealthy and successful as a businessman, Pierre Béguerie enjoyed fine things as much as he loved to hunt with his friends in the Xiberoan countryside (M. Béguerie 2004: pers. comm.). Like Clement de Jaureguiberry, Pierre was in his forties and married, with children, when he joined the Resistance. The two men knew each other well socially and belonged to an extensive network of Xiberoan families linked by marriage. Although much respected in the community, Béguerie had highly antagonistic relationships with many local socialists and the communists who remained in Maule. One socialist with whom he regularly clashed over local labor issues headed the Maule Secret Army: the sandal maker Jean-Pierre Hegoburu.

Pierre Béguerie began to form his maquis in June 1943. Aided by other *patrons,* he recruited more than a hundred conservative, anticommunist French Basques, most of whom had military experience. These included officers from the former Armistice Army and former colleagues in the Hussars who remained sympathetic and loyal to Pétain but opposed Vichy's policy of Franco-German collaboration (Béguerie n.d.: 5). Contrary to the assumption mistakenly made by some local people, many of the men recruited by Béguerie were in fact Xiberoans, and one came from the middle-class Rodrigo family of Aragonese descent. Like their Secret Army counterparts, Xiberoan CFP resisters had a vested interest in ridding their community of the Germans, avoiding the destruction of local property, and preventing enemy reprisals. Many local CFP recruits were in their late teens and became involved in the movement simply by chance rather than owing to any strong political commitment (G. Recalt 2003: pers. comm.). Owing to its Giraudist, military links with the ORA and Pommiès, the Xiberoan CFP company is now often remembered as "the White Maquis" of Xiberoa.[35] Its *maquisards* were based in the Xiberoan communities of Ospitaleku (near the internment camp at Gurs) and Sohüta, a small town adjacent to Maule. Although the CFP had more than five thousand active resisters in southern France during the summer of 1944, Béguerie's Xiberoan company rarely had more than a hundred men and often operated with no more than thirty (Lormier 1991: 180).

Conflict between the leaders of the CFP and Secret Army resistance groups in Xiberoa centered on fundamental issues relating to the moral community. Was the Resistance a protector of, or an endangerment to, "here people"? From the spring of 1944, Jaureguiberry headed de Gaulle's French Forces of the Interior (FFI) in Xiberoa. The FFI had jurisdiction over the Secret Army and other, smaller resistance movements, which (contrary to the Secret Army's policy) favored immediate direct action against the Germans, wherever they happened to be. As the Xiberoan FFI leader, Jaureguiberry was thus responsible for coordinating the resistance efforts of his rivals, the right-wing CFP, as well as an armed company of the communist FTP (Francs Tireurs Partisans), a small group of International Brigades, and Guérilleros Espagnols, resisters of Spanish origin who had settled in Béarn (Poullenot 1995: 203). Many of the Brigaders and Guérilleros had been interned at Gurs in 1939. The FTP men, who were of Spanish and Navarrese origin, operated across Xiberoa and Béarn and frequently failed to obey the instructions of Jaureguiberry (L. Blasquiz 2005: pers. comm.; M. Joanny 2003: pers. comm.).

At the beginning of June 1944, Hitler's First Army sent two armored divisions with nearly 5,000 soldiers into southwestern France. The Germans received support from a further 3,500 Italian troops based in the Gironde and Darnand's Milice in Béarn (Lormier 1990: 33). The 276th German Infantry Division was based roughly forty miles north of Maule. The threat of German aggression against Xiberoan citizens forced mutually antagonistic individuals and groups to confront their differences and address their need for solidarity. Shortly before the D-Day landings on June 6, 1944, Clement de Jaureguiberry and Pierre Béguerie made a key agreement as far as Xiberoan Basques were concerned. They recognized that the military mission of the local CFP company would be to disrupt German communication and transport links (Céroni 1980: 122) and that Sector IV of the Secret Army would begin its own military action on de Gaulle's day of national insurrection. The Secret Army would maintain civil order in the province and would in due course achieve political control for the Gaullist Liberation Committees across Xiberoa. From the start, Jaureguiberry insisted that resisters should refrain from combat near civilians.

In July 1944 the Spielberg Battalion occupied Maule, its six hundred troops aiming to eradicate the Resistance in Xiberoa. The battalion belonged to the regiment of General Wolf and received support from the SD (Sicherheitsdienst) in Pau, a division of the ss-controlled security service. Its outposts throughout the department of the Basses-Pyrénées were responsible for gathering information about Jews, resistance activity, intelligence and evasion networks and for surveillance (Poullenot 1995: 103). The Germans were particularly anxious to capture a volatile resister in the CFP known as Bercut, who had moved to Maule soon after the armistice in 1940. Bercut had initially joined a Secret Army combat unit in Béarn and quickly gained local notoriety as a reckless resister who was fond of disguises and enjoyed danger. In September 1943 Bercut led a bold raid on Germans based at Gurs, stole a German truck, and drove off with a substantial cache of weapons and ammunition (M. Béguerie 2004: pers. comm.; Davant 2001: 173).[36] When his audacious behavior drew sharp criticism from Secret Army leaders in the summer of 1944, Bercut defected to Béguerie's CFP company. Some of his former CFP comrades now recall Bercut as "crazy" and "arrogant," while others remember him as extremely charismatic. As one elderly CFP veteran explained, "Bercut arrived at my house one night disguised as a priest! He had a revolver. I remember how exciting it all seemed. I was only seventeen" (G. Recalt 2003: pers. comm.). In June 1944 Bercut robbed a Maule bank to obtain funds for the CFP. When Pierre Béguerie found out about it, he paid the bank back with his own money (M. Béguerie 2004: pers. comm.).

By June 1944 Bercut had taunted, robbed, and ambushed numerous German and SS troops in Xiberoa (Céroni 1984: 101). Following one attack, he and his men seized German intelligence papers; shortly thereafter, the CFP regional commander demobilized Pierre Béguerie. Local opinion and official accounts of Xiberoan resistance are divided on the reasons for Béguerie's departure. Some attribute his demobilization to the disappearance of those enemy papers, while others speculate that Béguerie left of his own accord when senior CFP officers failed to back his attempt to control Bercut's aggression. Denunciations also compelled Béguerie and the cofounder of the Xiberoan CFP, Jancène, to resign (M. Béguerie 2004: pers. comm.; G. Recalt 2003: pers. comm.). Warned in advance, the two Resistance officers escaped arrest and hid on an isolated farm until the Liberation. The official history of the CFP merely mentions "a problem" with the Xiberoan CFP and reports that Béguerie "waited in readiness" to be recalled by Pommiès "as soon as circumstances were more favorable" (Céroni 1984: 102). In one account of Xiberoa's liberation, written by Jaureguiberry, the Xiberoan Secret Army recognized "the tremendous efforts of Béguerie to contend with the insane orders of his [CFP] superiors and the dissoluteness of his subordinates" ("Libération de la Soule" 1984: 11).

A young former French Army cadet, René Lavalou, replaced Pierre Béguerie as head of the Xiberoan CFP. As outsiders to the Xiberoan moral community, Lavalou and Bercut did not share local concerns about the safety of civilians and their property. As soon as Lavalou took over from Béguerie, relations between him and the head of the Xiberoan Secret Army, Clement de Jaureguiberry, deteriorated rapidly. During one intensely hostile meeting between them, the two resisters faced each other across a table with their revolvers drawn (M. Joanny 2003: pers. comm.). Bercut repeatedly violated the July 1944 agreement between Jaureguiberry and Béguerie and displayed little interest in protecting Xiberoans, their property, or their territory from harm. His audacious actions against German soldiers divided public opinion about the Resistance and led many citizens to question whether resisters were their protectors or a source of endangerment to the moral community. Secret Army men branded their rivals in resistance as "criminals" and "terrorists" (G. Althapignet 2004: pers. comm.). CFP men, in turn, called Secret Army men "riff-raff" and "Red terrorists" (A. Barbe-Labarthe 2003: pers. comm.).

From the end of July until the Liberation in August 1944, Jaureguiberry and Lavalou argued heatedly about military tactics, honor, duty, and what constituted criminal behavior in times of war. Secret Army leaders accused their CFP counterparts of endangering civilians by attacking Germans inside or near Xiberoan communities. In the Secret Army's version of events in 1945, the CFP leaders were depicted as "insane" and as "strangers" to Xiberoa, as men who "would have subjected Xiberoans to destruction and bloodshed had it not been for the stubborn efforts of the Basque Secret Army based in Maule." When Lavalou and Bercut shot two German prisoners in their care, Jaureguiberry asked: "And from which side do the terrorists come? From that of the regular [French] Army?" ("Libération de la Soule" 1984: 10).

During the summer of 1944, Dr. Henri Herbille served as a Red Cross delegate and was often called upon to assist the Germans with health care. Herbille, another local doctor, and a Chicourt refugee-nurse ensured that wounded German soldiers received appropriate treatment. The German commander appreciated their professional skills and compassion (ibid.: 17). German officers regularly called upon Herbille and Mayor Aguer to mediate their relations with the local population and knew that both notables worried about the power that a Gaullist victory might give to the communists and socialists in Xiberoa. Herbille and Aguer were well aware that the communist-led FTP and some Secret Army resisters looked forward to overturning the authoritarian, hierarchical social order promoted by Pétain and embodied by Maule's notables. Although the Legion had long been discredited elsewhere in France and Pétainism—in all its varied forms—had largely ceased to exist by the summer of 1944, Henri Herbille persisted in his attempts to promote a Pétainist cult in the Maule Legion.[37] In keeping with the form of Pétainism embraced by the Legion, Herbille was deeply patriotic, largely owing to his military service in the Great War, and retained a personal loyalty to Pétain as a figurehead for French patriotism, order, and national pride (M. Béguerie 2004: pers. comm.; Vinen 2006: 81).

In the spring of 1944, Henri Herbille also continued his efforts to end the class conflict in Maule by negotiating with Vichy authorities for the release of three ex-communists of Spanish and Basque origin whose names had appeared on his own list of "dangerous elements" drawn up in 1942 and in whose arrests he himself had participated. Herbille still hoped that clemency might engender better relations between *patrons* and workers. He succeeded in bringing the three former communists back from Vichy internment camps, but the Gestapo immediately arrested and deported the men to Nazi concentration camps.[38]

As happened elsewhere in France, resistance against the Germans intensified after the D-Day landings on June 6, 1944. De Gaulle had already popularized the expectation that a national insurrection would be an essential part of France's liberation. The drive to mobilize the Resistance into a national army was manifested in several parts of France, including Tulle, where the FTP maquis of the Corrèze attacked a German garrison on June 7. The major skirmish and loss of German lives that ensued quickly brought the Second Armored Division of the ss unit, Das Reich, to Tulle, and the FTP withdrew. On June 9 the Germans hung ninety-nine civilians in Tulle in reprisal (Kedward 1994: 162, 171–73). On June 10, a different unit of Das Reich committed the massacre at Oradour-sur-Glane, near Limoges (Farmer 1999). A pattern of German attacks on maquis, followed by reprisals on local villages, had become established in southern France (Kedward 1994: 167). As news of the massacres reached Xiberoa, fear of enemy reprisal deepened among citizens of all political persuasions.[39] On June 6 another unit of the ss Das Reich joined the Spielberg Battalion based in Mont-de-Marsan in the Landes. On June 27 those combined German forces entered a Xiberoan hamlet in pursuit of CFP resisters based there and the Basques who sheltered them. The tragedy that followed severely tested the resilience of fundamental Basque values, institutions, and codes of conduct. The massive German raid on Ospitaleku and its tragic consequences also tested local notions of legitimate judgment and justice.

8: The Tragedy of Ospitaleku

As deputy mayor of Maule and a local notable, Pierre Béguerie was in close contact with the occupiers from the time of their arrival in February 1943 until he became involved in the Resistance. Many years later, Béguerie recalled the unpleasant task of taking young German officers to their lodgings in Maule and their cold, brusque response to his attempts at civility. Their behavior contrasted sharply with that of German veterans of the Great War who commanded the Wehrmacht in 1940, and who typically showed respect for their French counterparts during the early years of the Occupation, especially when French veterans were also notables (Vinen 2006: 23–24). The German lieutenant who lodged in the Béguerie family's country estate, however, displayed little interest in or respect for his host, in spite of Béguerie's class and experience at the front in 1914–18. Pierre Béguerie later described the German lodger as "not likable" and unable to understand a word of French. In spite of the German's presence, Béguerie listened to the BBC every night and closely followed the progress of the Allies in Africa and Italy (P. Béguerie n.d.: 18).

Béguerie was a familiar figure in the countryside surrounding Maule. Before the Occupation began, he loved to hunt there and knew the innkeepers in the hamlet of Ospitaleku particularly well. Their daughter, Marie-Louise Lasserre, was twenty-five years old when the Germans occupied Xiberoa. Politically moderate conservatives, devout Catholics, and deeply attached to Basque traditions, the Ospitaleku people were archetypal lowland, rural Basques. They derived their social and spiritual identity from the houses in which they lived and valued Basque traditions of mutual trust, aid, and cooperation between first neighbors. Ospitaleku citizens felt deeply about the need to protect their community from external harm. With a population of ninety-two, the hamlet had two inns, a medieval church, a school, and a town hall clustered around a main square, as well as outlying rural *quartiers* where the economy revolved around sheep, cattle raising, and small-scale agriculture.[1]

In June 1943 Pierre Béguerie recruited some Ospitaleku farmers to the CFP resistance group. In August 1943 his maquis received their first parachute drop near Oloron and hid forty-eight machine guns and eighty grenades in Ospitaleku and in the park of the Béguerie family's country home (R. Amigo, M. Béguerie 2004: pers. comms.). The Xiberoan CFP, however, remained largely inactive until late May 1944, when both the local population and the Germans began to anticipate an Allied landing in France. In preparation for military action, Béguerie chose the hamlet of Ospitaleku as the clandestine base for his maquis. Thickly forested hills and vales offered many places for resisters to hide, and meadows offered ideal terrain for parachute drops from the Allies. Only local people used the rough tracks that led to isolated farmhouses. Higher up, their small barns accommodated cattle, farm implements, and men in hiding (Aguerre, Elissondo, and Lasserre Davancens 2004: 9). The cofounder of the Xiberoan CFP, Jean Jancène, and two other CFP resisters owned property in Ospitaleku, but they did not offer their farmhouses to resisters "for fear their property would be burned down" by the Germans (Elissondo 1989: 2).

The local population did not generally know who "the resisters" were or what they would actually do on Xiberoan territory. Some citizens of Ospitaleku and neighboring rural communities feared the resisters as much as— if not more than—the occupiers. People were thus reluctant to accommodate a maquis in their midst until one CFP *maquisard* from the inn at Ospitaleku, François Lasserre, went from house to house, explaining what the Resistance aimed to achieve on local territory, as well as more broadly in France. Lasserre persuaded many households in Ospitaleku and the surrounding countryside to help CFP resisters (Barreix 2004: 1). In June 1944 six households opened their doors to *maquisards* (Aguerre, Elissondo, and Lasserre Davancens 2004: 12; Malharin n.d.).[2] Four were located in Ospitaleku: the Mahourat farm served as the headquarters of Pierre Béguerie and his nine men; the Larlus family in the house Mianda accepted ten of Bercut's commando members; the Auberge Lasserre became the rallying point for CFP *maquisards*. The son of the house, François, and daughter, Marie-Louise, were both resisters but managed to conceal their clandestine activities from their elderly parents. In the house Ostolats, the Puyade family agreed to shelter fifteen former guards at Gurs who had defected to the CFP. In nearby Sohüta, the Espel family in the house Espel took in twenty resisters. Another Sohüta family agreed to receive parachute drops for the CFP on their property (R. Elissondo 2007: pers. comm.). In the adjacent community of Barkoxe, the Baudéant family in the house Heguilla accepted another twenty men. The number of resisters who sheltered in those houses fluctuated from as few as thirty to more than a hundred (M. Béguerie 2003: pers. comm.; Malharin n.d.).

One Ospitaleku woman, Marie Rosier, wrote about the presence of the maquis, in carefully coded terms, to her husband in Germany, a POW who worked on a dairy farm. As the inheritor of her natal house, Mme Rosier felt particularly obliged to protect her property and household, which included her elderly father and young children, from external harm. Also a "here person," her husband urged her not to worry about the resisters; he was related to two families who sheltered CFP resisters, Espel and Puyade, and he favored active participation in the Resistance. On three occasions, Mme Rosier delivered weapons and provisions received from parachute drops to resisters hidden in the house Heguilla in Barkoxe. In an attempt to avoid detection by German patrols, she transported the goods at three o'clock in the morning and greased the hubs of her oxen-drawn cart with pig fat. She withdrew her assistance to the Resistance when her elderly father observed two men behaving oddly in woods near their farm. One of the men, who was a "here person," was using his herding staff to point out various farms and local landmarks to the stranger. Mme Rosier and her father suspected their fellow citizen of "selling" them and the maquis to an outsider who worked for the German police (M. Barreix 2004: 2).

In Xiberoa CFP *maquisards* came from diverse backgrounds and professions; they included young laborers, farmers, shopkeepers, and middle-class professionals, as well as privileged young men such as Micki Béguerie, son of Pierre. The resistance group also included outsiders to the Xiberoan moral community: three young French men who had evaded forced labor in Germany (through the STO), the hot-tempered Bercut (who came from the Loire), and Aurelien Mosso, a former officer in the Hussars whom Pierre Béguerie greatly admired (P. Beguerie n.d.: 11).[3] Led by Bercut, only one Xiberoan CFP commando carried out military operations against the Germans, including the sabotage of electricity lines and the theft of German arms, ammunition, trucks, and motorcycles (Malharin n.d.). Bercut always carried a gun, an infraction of German regulations that usually entailed deportation or some other severe penalty (Gildea 2002: 146).

The CFP maquis hid in Ospitaleku and adjacent rural farms for only fifteen days in June 1944. The requisition of provisions, without remuneration, and the occasional theft of goods by *maquisards* strained their relations with local people, who "feared for their lives, the safety of their livestock and crops" (Elissondo 1989: 3). Many of the resisters were in their early twenties and regarded their stay in Ospitaleku as an adventure. They were at times impolite to their hosts and thus lacked the respect that traditionalist Xiberoans expected of their fellow citizens. On a few occasions, young *maquisards* recklessly fired their guns into the air to amuse themselves, and they often helped themselves to their hosts' food and wine (ibid.: 3). More mature CFP resisters, however, treated their hosts with respect and helped them with chores on the farm (R. Elissondo 2007: pers. comm.).

When the Allied forces landed in Normandy on June 6, 1944, local resistance activity intensified alongside the Germans' determination to stop it. The *maquisards* received an increasing number of nighttime parachute drops from the Allies (Béguerie n.d.: 12). Although highly risky, such anti-German activity concerned local inhabitants far less than the imprudent behavior of some young resisters, caught up in the euphoria generated by the Normandy landings. Citizens worried most of all about the dangerous actions of Bercut, who particularly enjoyed tricking German soldiers by disguising himself as a priest or a gendarme. On June 7 Bercut donned a police uniform in Maule and stole a motorcycle from a startled German officer. On another occasion he borrowed a cassock from a priest at the private Catholic college in Maule and, fully armed, rode it through a German control point (Aguerre, Elissondo, and Lasserre Davancens 2004: 19). His behavior led one local CFP lieutenant to resign in protest.

On June 8 a German aircraft crashed into a field not far from the Béarnais town of Sauveterre. CFP resisters took the pilot to an isolated farmhouse in Ospitaleku, where the pilot gave *maquisards* information about Germans plans for an airfield at Pont Long, near Pau, which the occupiers used regularly. The resisters and the host family treated the pilot well and even took him cherry picking. Both parties expected the war to end soon, and the German pilot made no attempt to escape (ibid.: 15). Relations between Basques and locally based Germans altered substantially, however, when a wave of Nazi reprisals began in southwestern France. On June 10 an ss division massacred 642 women, children, and men in the village of Oradour-sur-Glane, near Limoges. When news of the tragedy reached Maule by June 15, Inspector Carbou noted deep anxiety among all citizens, who feared their town would be a "second Oradour." A bread shortage, further job reductions, and pay cuts in the factories increased discontent among workers. Resisters sabotaged telephone lines between Maule and a principal Basque market town.[4] On June 22 the head of the Xiberoan Secret Army (Sector IV), Jaureguiberry, complained to his CFP counterpart, Lavalou, that armed CFP *maquisards* had openly gone into Maule, whose citizens did not welcome their presence ("Libération" 1984: 10).

As a precaution against German reprisals, after only two weeks in Ospitaleku, Pierre Béguerie ordered his *maquisards* to stop harassing the enemy and leave the hamlet. His commanding officer in Tarbes likewise ordered all but one of the other CFP companies in southwestern France to follow suit. Only Bercut's commando of twenty men remained active and continued to hide in Ospitaleku until June 26, when the commando moved north into Béarn and sabotaged communication lines between Salies-de-Béarn and Orthez. Bercut and his men then ambushed two German officers and took them to the house Heguilla in Barkoxe, whose family had received provisions and armaments for the Resistance from Mme Rosier of Ospitaleku. The ambush infuriated the commander of the Spielberg Battalion, which operated in the Landes, Xiberoa, and Béarn, though he did not yet know the fate of his two officers (Céroni 1984: 289). Unable to control Bercut and lacking support from his own commanding officer in Tarbes, Pierre Béguerie resigned his local leadership of the CFP in protest (M. Béguerie 2004: pers. comm.). He disagreed with the CFP's strategy of aggression against the occupiers and feared for the safety of local civilians.

On the evening of June 26, a column of German trucks pulled into a vacant field near the chocolate factory in Xarritxa-pe, two miles from Ospitaleku. Some six hundred Germans from the Spielberg Battalion had moved into Maule from its base in Mont-de-Marsan on June 6, and a unit from the SS division Das Reich joined them. The German commander knew that the Resistance had received weapons from two parachute drops (in August 1943 near Oloron and in May 1944 in Sohüta) and from the theft of armaments at Gurs by Bercut and his commando. The Germans wanted to capture Bercut as a matter of urgency and, with the help of an informer, knew the names of families who had sheltered and fed the CFP maquis in Ospitaleku, Sohüta, and Barkoxe (Malharin n.d.).

On June 27, 1944, a clear, bright sky promised a beautiful summer day in the green, undulating countryside around Ospitaleku. Families prepared themselves for a day of hay making in the fields. Their children set off for school on a network of rural paths leading into the heart of the hamlet. Life seemed tranquil and ordinary. As one schoolgirl rounded a bend in the path, she saw a column of German soldiers moving methodically toward Ospitaleku from the west (Dihigo 2004). In the house of Mme Rosier, her mother had risen early to prepare some pepper seedlings for planting. She saw a German convoy on the other side of the valley and shortly thereafter heard guttural German voices coming from the hamlet. Fearful that she was about to be arrested for having aided the Resistance, Mme Rosier guided her elderly mother and young children deep into the forest above their farm. Her father refused to join them. "He said he had nothing to fear and wanted to warn the neighbors [about the Germans' presence] before they went into Ospitaleku to buy their weekly supply of wine from a grocery van" (M. Barreix 2004: 2).

In highly organized fashion, three columns of soldiers approached the hamlet's center from different directions and gradually encircled it. At the same time several squads of twenty to thirty soldiers surrounded selected farmhouses in the nearby countryside. Eyewitnesses estimate that between five and six hundred Germans participated in the raid (P.-P. Dalgalarrondo 2004: pers. comm.). The first victim of German violence was Albert Lasserre from the nearby village of Gurs. Through their network of local informers, the Germans knew that there was a Lasserre in the CFP maquis based in Ospitaleku, only a mile away. The German column approached the hamlet through Gurs and asked a local man where the Lasserre farm was located. The man pointed to his neighbor's farm, where Albert Lasserre stood in front of his house, unaware of the nearby Germans. When his dog began to growl, Albert sensed danger and turned to go back inside. When he reached the farmhouse door, gunshots rang out. Badly wounded, Albert Lasserre staggered into the kitchen. Several Germans followed him and began to ransack the house, looking for evidence of resistance activity. Albert's aunt boldly confronted them, saying that Albert was not the Lasserre for whom they were looking and that, moreover, they were not in Ospitaleku but in the hamlet of Gurs. Convinced that she told the truth, a German officer apologized for their grave error and sent for a doctor. In the kitchen, Albert's aunt gave the Germans hot chocolate. While they all waited for medical aid to arrive, the soldiers showed her photographs of their families in Germany. Albert Lasserre died in the ambulance on the way to the hospital.[5] The man for whom the Germans were looking was François Lasserre, son of the innkeepers who lived a mile away in Ospitaleku (Aguerre, Elissondo, and Lasserre Davancens 2004: 25).

In the house known as Mianda, the Larlus family heard gunfire and correctly anticipated what was happening. They had already been warned about the likelihood of a German raid by the CFP *maquisard,* François Lasserre (R. Elissondo 2007: pers. comm.). Family members heard the angry voice of an Alsatian interpreter, who threatened to destroy the farmhouse and shoot its inhabitants if they failed to tell him where "the sons of the house" were. German police pushed M. and Mme Larlus and their daughter, Aimée, against a wall. In desperation Aimée showed them a postcard from her brother, a POW in Germany. Somewhat appeased, the Germans extinguished the fire they had started but continued to search the house and farm buildings. They found nothing and failed to see some parachute cloth hidden in a hay wagon. Still convinced that another "son of the house" remained at large, the soldiers took Aimée hostage and headed for the hamlet's square (Aguerre, Elissondo, and Lasserre Davancens 2004: 26–27).

In another rural *quartier,* a farmer went outside to see what was happening at his neighbor's farm. Known for his generosity, his willingness to help others, and his courage, Jean Puyade knew that he took great risks by aiding the CFP maquis. On numerous occasions, he had transported cartloads of weapons and provisions for resisters in full daylight. When the Germans arrested him at his farm that day, Puyade denied having had any contact with the maquis. His interrogators then produced a photograph in which the barefooted farmer stood beside his wagon, loaded with provisions (Aguerre, Elissondo, and Lassarre Davancens 2004: 27). It is not known whether his denouncer was an insider or an outsider to the moral community.

Further downhill, Jean Mahourat made his way toward a hay field to begin the day's work. Hearing a commotion, Mahourat turned around and saw soldiers banging on his door. When he went to see what the Germans wanted, one soldier hit him in the face and accused him of helping the Resistance, another German beat Mahourat with the butt of his gun, then an Alsatian interpreter struck the farmer repeatedly with a post. Earlier that month, Pierre Béguerie and his *maquisards* had stayed in the house of Jean Mahourat. When the Germans searched the house, they found some cartridges and a few brassards used by CFP resisters. Infuriated, the soldiers fired their guns wildly at livestock in the field and killed some chickens. They pillaged the house before setting fire to it and to the hayloft. Badly injured, Jean Mahourat sat in the road, crying, as he watched his property burn. The Germans took his cattle and the food he had stored, as well as his clothes. They forced Mahourat to carry a heavy sack of corn, despite his injuries (Aguerre, Elissondo, and Lassarre Davancens 2004: 27–28; Elissondo 1989: 4). It is not known whether the Germans were aware that Mahourat had evaded obligatory work service (the STO) in Germany.

Two of Mahourat's neighbors witnessed his beatings and were themselves arrested. Arnaud Elissondo and his fifteen-year-old son, Laurent, were fetching water from the spring near Mahourat's house when the Germans arrived. The Germans also arrested Jean Belhartx, who was riding his bicycle along a path and had no idea what was happening. Unknown to the Germans, Belhartx was a CFP resister, but when the soldiers found his papers in order they released him. Before setting off again, Belhartx looked at young Laurent Elissondo with deep concern: "That boy is too young. He will never endure the interrogations and he'll denounce us." At eleven o'clock that morning, a flare alerted the Germans dispersed among the rural farms that their main operation in the village was now complete. With their looted goods and prisoners, the soldiers made their way down to the village square. In front of the twelfth-century church, they divided the prisoners into groups and began their interrogations (Elissondo 1989: 4, 6).

Local survivors of the roundup speculated that the informer was present during that final sorting process. Several recalled having seen a "French man in civilian clothes" assisting the Germans as they decided whom to release or to detain (A. Barbe-Labarthe 2004: pers. comm.). The Germans often took their principal informers to such events. By early afternoon, fourteen prisoners remained in the square. A German patrol brought in four farmers from the nearby community of Sohüta on suspicion of helping the Resistance. A few miles away, another German patrol arrested Arnaud Aguer, the mayor of Maule, who was traveling to Pau on business. The patrol took Aguer to Ospitaleku and detained him briefly. In his memoirs Aguer described the scene on his arrival: "In the village square, the troops moved people around and confiscated property with efficiency, as their officers shouted orders. Some pigs had escaped, which annoyed [the Germans]. They took all the cattle and calves. In the distance, black smoke rose into the sky from burning houses and barns" (Aguer 1960: 20–21).

It was by then midafternoon. The gunfire and shouting had stopped. On the hillside opposite the house Mahourat, Mme Rosier, her mother, and her children emerged from their hiding place in the woods. They ran to their first neighbor's house to find out what had happened. As one of the children ran down the road, she saw the house Mahourat in flames, an image that remains foremost in her memory of the Germans and the Occupation (Barreix 2004: 2).

That evening the mayor of Maule, Arnaud Aguer, passed through Ospitaleku on his return from Pau. He saw no one on the road or in the village. The shutters of all the houses were tightly closed. He stopped at one house to learn what had happened after his departure for Pau earlier in the day. The Germans had ordered a six o'clock curfew, three hours earlier than usual, and had warned the villagers that anyone caught outside after that time would be shot. Accounts of the hostages taken by the Germans vary. Mayor Aguer and Laurent Elissondo recalled fourteen hostages (Aguer 1960: 24; Elissondo 1989: 4). Local farmer Jean François Aguerre correctly remembered that the Germans arrested nineteen people, who ranged in age from fifteen (Laurent Elissondo) to seventy-three (Bernard Cazenave, the mayor) and included three women (Aimée Larlus Sahouret, Marie Lasserre, and her daughter, Marie-Louise Lasserre). The Germans put the group in a truck at the head of a convoy destined for the Gestapo headquarters in Baiona on the Basque coast. As the vehicles moved along a country lane, the Germans suddenly found themselves face to face with CFP *maquisards*, who quickly escaped into the woods. In reprisal the Germans arrested four farmers working in a field nearby and loaded them into the truck. During their journey to Baiona, Arnaud Elissondo discovered that he had no tobacco. The German who guarded the Basques handed Elissondo a cigarette, an act of generosity that the farmer pondered for the rest of his life (R. Elissondo 2005: pers. comm.).

At the Nazi prison in Baiona, the Germans separated male and female prisoners. When a German officer began to interrogate Arnaud Elissondo, the sixty-nine-year-old Basque angrily retorted: "Me! A terrorist! An old man who served in the Great War, a terrorist?" Arnaud then turned to his young son, Laurent, and said firmly in Basque: "Don't be afraid, and don't say anything." The interrogator approached the boy and asked if he, too, belonged to the maquis. Laurent replied that he did not know what the maquis was. Neither Laurent nor his father received any physical abuse, whereas the other Ospitaleku men were badly beaten (Elissondo 1989: 7). Father and son remained in prison for eighteen days. Laurent vividly remembered their hunger, his father's cravings for tobacco, and the compassion their middle-aged German guards showed when they slipped a cigarette to each of the Basque prisoners every day. On the nineteenth day, the Germans released the Elissondos and eight other Xiberoan men, who returned to their homes. Six of the men taken hostage in Ospitaleku were deported to the Nazi concentration camp at Mauthausen. The Germans sent the three women to Ravensbrück. Only two of the nine deportees survived the camps: the Ospitaleku innkeepers, Marie-Louise Lasserre and her mother. They were not related to Albert Lasserre in Gurs, the first victim of Nazi brutality on that warm summer morning of June 27.

On June 28, 1944, the day after the German raid on Ospitaleku, the deputy mayor of the hamlet wrote to the prefect in Pau:

> I write to inform you that on Tuesday, June 27th 1944, our commune was taken over by troops of the Occupation from early morning until evening. The troops slaughtered cattle and pigs, took food provisions from many houses and burned one farmhouse. The troops also took away many of our people, including the mayor. The troops returned on Thursday, June 29th, between twelve and one o'clock, looking for livestock they had left behind at the Lasserre farm. As they approached the hamlet they fired their guns and watched families flee into the woods near the neighborhood of Larreja in Barkoxe. One of those families arrived only twenty days ago. They stayed in the house Errecondo. In the town hall, we knew nothing at all about their identity and were not even aware of their presence, because of all the numerous passages made by fugitives through our community. That family never declared their residency in the town hall, as is required, and they never collected any ration tickets. The German troops have said that they will return again to Ospitaleku because of that family, because, it is said, they are Jews. But that family has not been seen by us since Thursday lunchtime. Their maid was taken by the Germans, but the family escaped in their truck and managed to take most of their belongings with them,

as well as their identity papers. (Wrong! Their papers have been re-trieved.) In our community, we only wish to live in peace and tranquil-ity. Could you do whatever is necessary to locate this family? For our own part, we verbally advised the gendarme in Maule yesterday at 9:00 am. We, a very frightened people, are counting upon your assistance, M. Prefect, your intervention and your protection. The name of the family is CASTROT, a father, a mother, one son and one daughter.[6]

The Jewish family in question was that of Kaleb Salomon Castro, origi-nally from the Sephardic Jewish community of Baiona–St. Esprit. In Febru-ary 1943 Inspector Carbou and the prefect of the Basses-Pyrénées had granted the Castro family permission to remain in Xiberoa, largely as a measure of respect to a "son of the *patrie*" who had twice served France in wartime.[7] In the wake of German violence against Ospitaleku citizens in June 1944, fear of further German reprisals outweighed local esteem for bravery at the front by an outsider deemed to be the enemy of both Vichy and Hitler.

Two days after the Ospitaleku raid, on June 29, 1944, the Germans did return to the community and once again terrified the local population. Ger-man officers and their interpreters conducted further interrogations. Once again, soldiers pillaged farmhouses and requisitioned livestock and crates of wine. As the Germans prepared to depart, they found that two of their men were missing. The commanding officer reminded a group of frightened Ospi-taleku people that he would shoot ten hostages for every German wounded or killed. Villagers frantically searched their farms and soon found the two missing Germans in a shed near the church as they roused themselves from a bout of heavy drinking (Aguerre, Elissondo, and Lasserre Davancens 2004: 31).

In the wake of the raids, the Ospitaleku people well knew that they had very little control over their territory, their property, or their fate in the face of German aggression. One of their principal moral authorities, the mayor, was in German custody. The priest (their other main moral authority) felt he could do nothing to protect his parishioners from German violence. Thus, the people of Ospitaleku turned to the two external authorities who, they hoped, might be able to protect them from further harm and destruction: the prefect and subprefect, to whom the deputy mayor wrote on June 28 in des-peration over further threats of German reprisal if the Castro family returned to the hamlet and received shelter there.

When local liberation committees formed across Xiberoa in August 1944, people wanted to know who had collaborated with the Germans. One Ospi-taleku man, nicknamed "The American," had aroused a measure of jealousy before the Occupation when he returned from Argentina with substantial funds. In the autumn of 1944, some Ospitaleku people suspected "The American" of having helped the Germans identify supporters of the Resistance on June 27. Unsubstantiated rumors maintained that he had denounced his fellow citizens to gain revenge for the unpleasant things some people had said about his character and good fortune. The former emigrant vigorously denied the accusations made against him. One morning, however, the man wakened to find a swastika painted on his front door, an act of popular justice through which one or more citizens judged a fellow insider (Elissondo 1989: 8). Jealousy and petty grievances may also have been involved. Villagers did know the identity of two men who had betrayed the CFP maquis: a gendarme who came from elsewhere in France and a local man, both of whom had been seen by Mme Rosier's father in the woods shortly before the German raid on Ospitaleku. The Lasserre family lodged a complaint against the gendarme, an outsider to the moral community, but not against the local man.

In preparation for the sixtieth anniversary of the liberation, a high-school history teacher, Robert Elissondo, and his first neighbor, Jean François Aguerre, recorded and transcribed the testimonies of people who remembered the German raid on Ospitaleku. Although Mme Lasserre Davancens rarely spoke about her experiences during the war, she agreed to talk to M. Elissondo about the tragic events that occurred on June 27, 1944, and their terrible consequences. Robert's own father and grandfather, Arnaud and Laurent Elissondo, had been among the Ospitaleku men arrested. Mme Davancens also agreed to talk to students at the Collège de Saint-François in Maule. The panel of speakers aimed to educate students, parents, and other members of the public about "the need to remember" Nazi barbarism so that it might never recur. Mme Lasserre Davancens broke down in tears as soon as she began to read the testimony she had prepared in advance. M. Elissondo prepared and locally printed a full account of her experiences in 2004 as a contribution to local commemorations of the Liberation.

When the war with Germany broke out I was working as a maid in Paris, for a wealthy family in a grand house. My brother Pierre was a prisoner of war. My other brother, François, got called up to work in a Vichy youth group. My parents had little money and struggled to run our little country inn by themselves. So they asked me to come home to help out. I ran the inn from 1939 until my arrest on June 27th, 1944.

By 1940, our inn started to do well. All sorts of customers came, from the town nearby but there were many outsiders, as well. Some were young men trying to avoid being sent to Germany to work. The internment camp at Gurs was only a mile away. There were thousands of Spanish Republicans and Jews there. In the early days, they needed permission to leave the camp [in 1939–1940]. Sometimes as many as fifteen internees would come to the inn. The Jews were easy to please. They liked our spicy sauces! We also fed the camp's guards.

My brother François was one of the first in our hamlet to join the Resistance. He was such a willing type. I did all I could to help him, out of love, but also because I too wanted to take part in liberating our small part of the world. I followed news of the war closely on the radio. Radio London, it was. I knew that the Liberation was approaching. I was prepared to take risks, but I didn't really think much about possible consequences.

Then the terrible day came. On June 27th, at 4 o'clock in the morning, when everyone was sleeping peacefully, I heard someone beating down the door and shouting. I knew straightaway who it was, and rushed to wake my brother. He had just enough time to escape through a back door. He went to warn the others. I opened the door and faced two men: one German and one civilian. Then more soldiers pushed their way inside. They searched the four beds we, as family, slept in. There were only three of us, because my brother had escaped. "Where is the fourth person?" they demanded, knowing my brother was missing. We said we didn't know where he was. Every time the Germans repeated the question, "Where is he?" they hit us with a truncheon. Then they took us into the square by the church. They searched all the houses, wrecking things as they went. There were hundreds of Germans there. They were furious because they could not find any of the resisters whom we had been hiding. They wrecked our belongings, our furniture, after taking whatever they wanted for themselves. They drank our wine and took the rest away.

We were taken away at 2 o'clock in the afternoon. Us three women in one truck, mother, me and a neighbor. The men were in another vehicle. We women were taken to Biarritz to be interrogated, twice. One especially vicious German kept telling us that my brother had been executed. He kept trying to make us say where the resisters were, and who was involved. We would not tell him, so he kept hitting us. Eighteen days later we were shipped to another German prison, in Bordeaux. Then we boarded a train, not knowing where we were going. Germany! Seven hundred people were deported in cattle cars, sixty-two of us were women. My mother was convinced that father was dead. The train kept stopping. The heat was unbearable. We had neither food nor water. The thirst was worst. Twenty-four days later, we reached Dachau. After a few days, we were sent to Ravensbrück to work. A spoonful of soup and a crust of old bread, that was all we were given each day. At night we froze, because we were forced to undress. When my mother tried to put back on her clothes, in the dark, a woman ss officer saw her and beat her badly. She made me watch. She knew I was the daughter. That was one of the hardest things for me to bear. Having to watch the ss women beat up my mother, who was ill. That was more painful than anything else I experienced physically or in my mind. I was forced to watch and could not do anything to help Mother. Oh, the memory of it is too much to bear.

We were paralyzed with fear, and we did all we could not to be noticed. We were not permitted to be sick. We concealed our fevers, our aches and pains. Washing and dressing in the morning were nightmares. For our entire barrack, we had four or five faucets outside. It was always a battle to get there first. No one had soap or a towel. The morning call-up was the worst. At three o'clock, when it was still night and freezing cold, we were forced outside and lined up along one wall. We had to stand there, without moving, without saying a word for hours on end, in our bare feet, in the rain, in the snow. We were guarded by both the ss women and the ss men. The women were far more cruel to us than the men.

During one of these endless nighttime sessions, Aimée Larlus was standing beside me.[8] All of a sudden she collapsed. She suffered from epilepsy and needed to take her pills. But when we entered the camp, they took all her pills away. The ss women took them and made a note of Aimée's identification number. The next day, at the call-up, they took her out of the line, and I never saw her again. Our hut was next to the crematory ovens. Day after day, we smelled the unbearable smell of burned flesh.

After two or three months at Ravensbrück, they divided us into groups. Able-bodied ones went to work. The others were killed. We had to file, naked, past a doctor seated behind a table in a courtyard. He made us show him the palms of our hands, and oddly enough that is how he judged our fitness to work. I filed past him, and then it was Mother's turn. He studied her hands and motioned for her to keep going. I quickly took her arm and led her away. Luckily, the doctor never once looked up. If he had done so, he would have seen a white-haired, weak old woman.

We worked in an aviation factory alongside elderly Germans, who treated us kindly but were strictly forbidden to share their food with us. The ss were never far away. Often, we had to stand outside in the snow to wait for our spoonful of soup and morsel of bread, the only meal of the day. My mother was the eldest worker in that factory and, on many occasions, people told me that she would not last long. I worried about her constantly. I feared for her. It is a miracle that the Germans did not kill her.

In addition to the punishment and ill treatment, we were bombed. We often heard bombs explode in the distance. The noise made by the sirens was incredible. My mother was traumatized by that sound for the rest of her life. In the hut one day, the bombing woke us up. It was around midday. We had worked for twelve hours straight the night before. We woke up with a start. A bomb had fallen on our hut. It killed around fifty deported women. By chance, we happened to be on the other end of the hut. But what terror, what panic ensued! Another bomb had opened up a gap in the wall. We scrambled to escape, but outside the hut it was hell. The entire neighborhood was on fire. The trees were burning, even the boats on the river. The phosphorus bombs and incendiaries gave off black smoke and made the air impossible to breathe. Once outside, I realized that I had lost my mother. I went back into the hut, through the flames, to find her. A Basque friend from Biarritz finally convinced me to get back outside. My clothes were on fire. Outside, I found my mother. What a relief! She had been looking for me and was worried to death.

During our last month in the camp, we women dug trenches with pickaxes in a forest outside Berlin, as the Germans tried to delay the Russian invasion. We walked ten miles a day, to and from the trenches. Our feet were bloody. Allied bombers passed overhead, but we were forbidden to stop digging. Our guards made us suffer a little more by eating in front of us. All day long, we had only a spoonful of soup. The tiny bread rations had been stopped, which was another torture." Soon thereafter, the Germans transferred all deportees to Oranienburg and then evacuated them, on foot, to a site three hundred miles away. Those who could walk no further were beaten.

The road was littered with bodies, mainly men. I concentrated on helping my mother, who had bloodied feet and terrible rheumatism. Luckily, other deportees took turns helping me carry her. Night fell, and we slept in a forest. The next morning when we wakened, we were stunned to see all the helmets, guns and gas masks lying on the ground all around us. Our guards were gone. Then we saw the first of the Russian tanks. [Mother and daughter were taken in by American troops.] They were incredibly kind to us! They put us in their own barracks, which had a dining room and proper bedrooms. The food was wonderful and made especially for our delicate stomachs. Because Mother and I were both very ill, they repatriated us within a day. They sent us by truck to Holland, then on to Lille, where we bathed and received new clothes. Until then we had been dressed like gypsies, in huge robes that fell to our feet like immense blankets.

In Lille we took the train to Bordeaux, where a police commissioner looked at our papers and cried out: "You're called Lasserre?" It was then we found out that my father was still alive, that he hadn't been deported, that he returned to our village when Bordeaux was liberated. What relief, what joy for me and most of all for my mother! The commissioner told us how my father had escaped deportation. He was ill on the day when all the men were put on the train in Bordeaux to go to Mauthausen. The police commissioner was locked up in the same cell as my father, and he convinced the Germans to leave my father there. He said it was useless to take my father to the camp because he would only die along the way. By chance, the commissioner spoke German. He saved my father. When we set off for Maule on the train, the commissioner telephoned the station master there to let him know we were on our way home.

When we got off the train in Maule, what a big surprise awaited us! A crowd had gathered there to welcome us. The square was packed with people. My brother François was there. He had tears in his eyes. Dr. Herbille was there with his car, and he took us back to Ospitaleku. When we got to the inn, we found my father sitting on the bench beside the fireplace. He always ate his meals there on that bench. What emotions! What deep emotions filled us in finding ourselves together again. I weighed sixty pounds. My mother weighed sixty-two pounds. Only our feet were badly hurt. A few days later, my brother Pierre came back from Germany, too. And so we survived the ordeals of war. In order to give thanks to the Virgin Mary, my brother Pierre and I went on pilgrimage to Lourdes.[9]

Sixty years later, when asked how she felt about the CFP maquis whose brief presence in Ospitaleku had caused such suffering and loss of life, Mme Davancens firmly declared that she "would never blame M. Pierre [Béguerie] for what happened. I have never regretted helping him or the Resistance."

Erect and dignified, she added, "But I cannot ever forgive the Germans" (M.-L. Lasserre Davancens 2005: pers. comm.).[10]

Mme Davancens and Pierre Béguerie belonged to a small, face-to-face moral world in which insiders shared a habitus, a set of perceptions regarding what was legitimate and rightful. The German occupation of Xiberoan soil, local armed resistance against the occupiers, and German reprisals against the *maquisards* and their helpers severely tested traditional beliefs about what was morally right or wrong. Mme Davancens and many other Xiberoans citizens resolutely insisted that Pierre Béguerie was not responsible for the terrible events of June 27, 1944. Béguerie was an insider to the Xiberoan moral community. Immediately prior to the German raid, his conduct was not guided by an ethic of conviction, without regard to consequences. Béguerie ordered his *maquisards* to leave Ospitaleku precisely because he feared that the consequences of their presence would trigger German reprisals against local civilians. In making that decision, an ethic of responsibility rather than an ethic of ultimate ends guided the CFP leader (M. Weber 1958: 120).[11] His subsequent decision to step down as leader of the CFP had a foreseeable consequence with which the Basque patron wrestled for the duration of his life (M. Béguerie 2004: pers. comm.). The resignation of Pierre Béguerie left CFP *maquisards* under the command of two outsiders to the Xiberoan moral community who were both guided by an ethic of conviction: namely, that aggression against the Germans was a justifiable means to an end, the liberation of French territory. Most local people did not question the legitimacy of the cause defended by the maquis, yet—as many citizens observed—the community paid dearly for having aided the Resistance.

After the Liberation and for several subsequent decades, the brief presence of the CFP maquis in Ospitaleku and its betrayal by a "here person" and an outsider-gendarme traumatized and divided a rural Basque community that had long valued solidarity and harmony. Two of the households directly affected by the German raid in June 1944 lost their people as a result of German violence in Ospitaleku and Nazi concentration camps; their houses remain empty. A third house was also closed when its members, survivors of Nazi brutality, moved elsewhere soon after the Liberation, a decision that appears to have been driven in part by events on June 27, 1944 (R. Elissondo 2007: pers. comm.). For many years after the raid, the people of Ospitaleku and neighboring rural neighborhoods rarely mentioned events of that terrible summer. It was not until 1989 that the schoolteacher Robert Elissondo first heard about the tragedy from his father, Laurent Elissondo, an eyewitness of Nazi violence against Ospitaleku Basques. In 1989 Robert's father had only harsh words for the Resistance. As the end of his life neared, however, his anger subsided and his views about the maquis softened (ibid.).

Veterans of the CFP maquis gather annually on June 27 at the Lasserre family's inn to commemorate those who suffered and perished as a result of Nazi violence in June 1944. It was not until the sixtieth anniversary of the Nazi raid on Ospitaleku, however, that its victims spoke in public about their horrifying experiences, for the first time, in commemorative ceremonies at the Collège de Saint-François in Maule and in Ospitaleku itself. On June 27, 2004, CFP veterans, survivors of the tragic raid, their families, and other local people gathered for a Mass in the twelfth-century church of Ospitaleku and for commemorative speeches in front of the plaque that lists the names of those who died as a result of the raid. Many citizens perceived the gathering as an act of reconciliation between former *maquisards* and local inhabitants. Most survivors of the raid and deportation insisted that, with the exception of the controversial resister Bercut, the *maquisards* did not deliberately threaten the security of villagers and their property. No one questioned the just cause for which the resisters fought: the removal of German occupiers from Xiberoan territory and the liberation of their *pays*.

A Basque family from Uztarroze, the Erronkari Valley, Nafarroa, c. 1910.
Courtesy of Román Pérez, Maule

"Swallows" from the Erronkari Valley, Maule, c. 1927. Courtesy of Román Pérez, Maule

German officers dining at the Hotel Bidegain, Maule, 1943. Courtesy of Mme
Maitena Etcheverry d'Abbadie, Maule

The town hall in Maule. *Foregound:* war memorial; *background:* medieval fort.
Courtesy Dr. Xabier Irujo, Center for Basque Studies, University of Nevada, Reno

Canon Ithurbide (*first row center,* white hair) with colleagues and pupils at the Collège de Saint-François, Maule, 1943. Courtesy of Jean de Jaureguiberry

Above: A Xiberoan shepherd-*passeur* and a child, 1980. Author's photo, reproduced with the permission of the Bidegaray family.

FACING PAGE:

Top: Clement de Jaureguiberry, leader of the Xiberoan Secret Army (Sector IV) and local FFI leader at the Liberation. Courtesy of M. Joanny, Toulouse
Bottom: Mme Lasserre Davancens, CFP resister and survivor of Ravensbrück, 2005

The Liberation in Maule, with Xiberoan Resistance
leaders and Alsatian refugees from Chicourt, August
1944. Courtesy of M. Joanny, Toulouse

9: Resisting Divisiveness Through Ritual in Urdos

As happened elsewhere in France, denunciations deepened existing tensions and created new divisions in Basque society during the German Occupation. In the purges of the post-Liberation period, accusations of collaboration often pitted relatives, neighbors, and former friends against each other. Denunciations challenged the primary values upon which Basque society was based and tested the resilience of relationships and practices at the core of Basque social organization. In the Pyrenean borderlands of Urdos, people prided themselves on their social and spiritual solidarity and the harmonious relations enjoyed by neighbors. When denunciations led to the arrests of several local shepherds and the deaths of three men, the community struggled to come to terms with such treachery in their midst and to combat the discord it caused.

In their comparative study of accusatory practices in modern European history, Sheila Fitzpatrick and Robert Gellately (1997: 1) consider denunciations "as spontaneous communications from individual citizens to the state (or to another authority such as the church) containing accusations of wrongdoing by other citizens or officials and implicitly or explicitly calling for punishment." Fitzpatrick and Gellately draw attention to the importance of examining the sociocultural, as well as the political functions of denunciation at a grassroots level, where accusatory practices are "an unstudied but important point of contact between individual citizens and the state, one that embodies a whole set of unarticulated decisions about loyalties to the state, on the one hand, and to family and fellow citizens on the other" (1997: 2).

Linguistically, the English term *denunciation* cannot contain the contradictions conveyed by the French terms *délation,* closely associated with betrayal, and *dénonciation,* in which the revelation of wrongdoing may be treated as an act of civic virtue. *Délation* is treacherous, self interested, and motivated by malice; it involves behavior judged to be contemptible and cowardly. By contrast, *dénonciation* can be exalted when it protects public morals and the state (ibid.: 17–18). The authorities and ordinary French-speaking citizens employed both discourses of denunciation during the occupation of the Basque Country, as well as during post-Liberation trials of alleged collaborators.

The Xiberoan dialect of Basque makes nuanced distinctions between accusatory acts that are, in themselves, socially unacceptable but might lead to something "good" in society and accusatory acts that are driven by contemptible motives and bring only harm. The former, less negative act of denouncing is expressed by the verb *salatu* and a range of substantives based on the same root (*salakeria, salatze, salazale*). It also covers the acts of accusing, betraying, and informing on someone (Casenave-Harigile 1989). The term *salakeria* (denunciation, betrayal, treason, informing on someone) can be used to denote both *délation* and *dénonciation* in French. The word also means disloyalty. Among Xiberoan Basques who experienced the Occupation, the most despicable kind of denunciation was an act of betrayal conveyed by *saldu*, literally "to sell" someone, usually someone well known to the betrayer. For that generation, saying that an individual "sold" a fellow citizen to the Vichy or German police has a far more negative connotation than saying he or she denounced (*salatu*) a person. In those troubled times, "selling" a fellow citizen violated key Basque expectations: mutual trust among the members of a community and a neighborhood and their solidarity in the face of opposition to outsiders.

When France's war with Germany ended in June 1940, Urdos Basques regarded themselves as fortunate, for their province lay just inside the Unoccupied Zone and came under Vichy rule. Those who had survived the Great War shared a deep dislike of the Germans and initially most people respected Pétain as a war hero, though very few felt any loyalty toward Vichy (K. Irigaray 1979: pers. comm.). Most citizens were moderate conservatives anxious to protect the interests of the community, their properties, and traditional rights and privileges, but owing to a core of socialists (supporters of the sfio, Section Française de l'Internationale Ouvrière), the community was widely regarded in the largely conservative lowlands as "Red."[1]

The socialists were closely linked with a militant schoolteacher, Claude D., whose wife came from Urdos. The couple visited her friends and family there on a regular basis. An ardent supporter of the Popular Front in 1936, Claude D. organized and distributed socialist propaganda throughout the Basses-Pyrénées and established headquarters for the sfio in Sustary, where he rallied the support of both socialists and communists.[2] According to the Maule police, Claude D. had "fervent partisans" in Urdos and Sustary, where he regularly met his followers at the Café au Trinquet. In August 1940 Vichy officials banned Claude D. from his profession as a "veritable danger" to society, and the prefect finally ordered the militant socialist out of Xiberoa in April 1941. According to Vichy police inspectors, the "Reds" in Urdos and Sustary still required surveillance, for they remained in contact with Claude D., who used various aliases and disguises when he returned illegally to the area.[3] By the end of 1942, Vichy police were likewise concerned about the popularity of Urdos as a point of clandestine passage to Spain for Jews and

House A → House B → House C → House A

The cycle of giving and receiving blessed bread in Urdos

other fugitives fleeing German and French oppression (Eychenne 1987: 158–62; Lougarot 2004: 244–47). As a dispersed, mountainous community, Urdos was not easily patrolled by the small detachment of French customs officers who tried to control the flow of trans-Pyrenean contraband and the tide of mainly Polish, Belgian, and French Jews heading south (J.-B. Hondagneu 1977: pers. comm.).[4]

On the eve of the Occupation, the Urdos people enjoyed a high degree of social and spiritual solidarity. The commune had a population of eight hundred people, whose livelihood revolved around shepherding, cheese making, small-scale agriculture, and trans-Pyrenean smuggling. Its citizens were devout Catholics, suspicious of strangers, and highly protective of their own interests and property. Individuals derived their social and spiritual identity from the house, which had a name, a tomb in the cemetery, and certain rights and obligations. Every house had three first neighbors, an institutionalized relationship that obliged houses to cooperate, trust, and mutually assist each other in a range of secular and spiritual activities. First neighbors also participated in a community-wide ritual exchange of blessed bread, *le pain bénit*. The obligation to give blessed bread passed from house to house around the commune. The ritual took place every Sunday and was a cherished local institution. The female head of the bread-giving household distributed *le pain bénit* among parishioners after Mass and then gave a special gift of bread to the female head of her first-neighbor household, whose own turn to give bread fell on the following Sunday. The bread given and received by first neighbors was regarded as a gift of life and was systematically exchanged in a cycle of giving and receiving that took one year to complete. During the Occupation, the ritual served an especially crucial function, for it promoted social and spiritual solidarity in otherwise uncertain, uneasy times.

When Germany occupied all of France in November 1942, the news surprised few Urdos Basques but gave rise to anxiety and speculation about the likely impact of the Occupation on the region and their own lives.[5] Urdos fell within "a forbidden frontier zone" (*une zone frontière interdite*) accessible, in principle, only to those with an appropriate pass (Poullenot 1995: 27). Relations between the local people and the occupiers were fraught with tension. German patrols regularly searched and ransacked local property in their attempts to find Jews, Allied pilots, STO evaders, and members of the Resistance. The patrols responded brutally to local acts of resistance. By the spring of 1943, German security services had killed one young man suspected of possessing firearms, as well as several fugitives who were trying to cross the Pyrenees into Spain.[6] Most Urdos people deeply resented and feared the Germans. Although one nearby community applied the tradition of *la jonchée* (strewing greenery) to sexual liaisons between local women and their German lovers, the Urdos Basques decided not to use that form of popular justice when two of their own female citizens became involved in affairs with the occupiers.[7] The risk of reprisal was, in their view, too great in a "forbidden" borderland zone where opposition to the enemy so easily triggered German violence.

The Gaullist Secret Army had many supporters in Urdos, including a maquis of fifteen shepherds who were largely inactive until the eve of the Liberation (K. Irigaray 2000: pers. comm.). The occupiers knew about the long-standing trans-Pyrenean relations between Basques on both sides of the Franco-Spanish frontier, but they lacked sufficient manpower to repress the activities of borderland clandestine guides. Thirty-six guides operated regularly in the canton to which Urdos belonged (Eychenne 1987: 148). In Urdos most neighborhoods had several shepherds willing to guide fugitives into Nafarroa (Aytaberro 1983: 129–37; G. Iladoy 1977: pers. comm.). Some operated alone; others worked alongside a neighbor, a brother, or a son and relied upon one or two trusted contacts in adjacent villages to take fugitives to certain safe houses used as points of collection by Urdos shepherds. As happened elsewhere in the Pyrenees, many clandestine guides expected payment for their services, which entailed considerable risk as well as expenses to be met. Escape networks organized by British intelligence services paid the guides a fixed price of five thousand francs per Allied pilot, plus expenses (Poullenot 1995: 125). In 1943 the total average cost per civilian ranged from three thousand to four thousand francs. One notorious Navarrese guide charged ten thousand francs per person when working with an organized escape network (Eychenne 1987: 158–60). Many *passeurs,* however, asked clients for a discretionary payment, according to their financial circumstances (R. Jaureguy 2003: pers. comm.; J.-P. Jonnet 1977: pers. comm.). Some shepherds refused any payment at all, particularly in the case of fugitives trying to escape obligatory work service in Germany (STO). Shepherds often felt sympathetic to the evaders, in keeping with long-standing Basque opposition to conscription of any kind by a foreign power.

The rugged terrain and settlement pattern in Urdos helped people to conceal their clandestine activities from German patrols and overly curious citizens. Fugitives sheltered in barns and haystacks and beneath piles of fern on certain farms. The Urdos innkeepers regularly hid Jews, Allied pilots, and STO evaders delivered to them by a baker, who covered the fugitives with loaves of bread destined for the occupiers. Largely Bavarian customs officers patrolled the neighborhoods, regularly searching houses and barns and intimidating the Urdos people with their fierce dogs. Local citizens found the Germans cold, correct, disciplined, and quick to respond brutally to acts of resistance. The curfew, routine searches, the prohibition on firearms, and limited access to communities outside the reserved zone inconvenienced and annoyed people. Restrictions on the use of mountain pasturage in summer caused deep resentment and greatly reduced cheese-making capability. The presence of Germans on their territory greatly angered Urdos Basques, whose lands were inextricably linked to their personhood and to two primordial Pyrenean institutions—the house and the community. The rules and regulations imposed by the Germans on local citizens interfered with the commune's long-standing tradition of autonomy in the management of its own affairs.

Although the penalties for disobeying German rules were severe, not all citizens obeyed the occupiers. Gabrielle Harispe was an eccentric, mischievous individual who took pleasure in ignoring both the Germans' rules and those of her own society. Contrary to local codes of conduct that required a household to conceal any internal strife from the wider community, Gabrielle quarreled bitterly and publicly with her husband, and when he mysteriously fell to his death in the mountains during the spring of 1937, public opinion widely held his wife responsible. In a society deeply attached to its local form of Catholicism, Gabrielle's open distrust of priests offended devout parishioners, some of whom regarded the slight but physically tough woman as a sorcerer. Gabrielle occasionally used spells and charms to get rid of agricultural pests on her property, and she knew about occult means of dealing with human enemies. When the Germans arrived in Urdos, she threatened to give a "desiccation mass" that would make the occupiers "shrivel and die" (G. Harispe 1978: pers. comm.).

By all accounts Gabrielle unnerved the Germans, who usually avoided contact with her even though she flagrantly disobeyed their orders (A. Carricart, G. Harispe 1978: pers. comms.; J. and M.-L. Lascombes 1979: pers. comm.). She refused to relinquish her late husband's shotgun, an infraction of German regulations that often entailed a severe penalty (Gildea 2002: 146). When the Germans restricted access to the high mountain pastures upon which Urdos shepherds depended, Gabrielle defiantly took her flock to their usual territory. A German patrol threatened her with their fierce dogs, but the diminutive woman held her ground. According to both Gabrielle and the postmistress in whose house the German commander had lived, the patrols kept the shepherdess under close surveillance but never bothered her again (J. Larbonne 1979: pers. comm.).

During the Occupation, Urdos people also resented German demands for a weekly supply of meat, a rare luxury in the community. Initially, the Germans obtained meat and other foodstuffs in an ad hoc manner from local farmers, who were forced to deliver provisions to three German collection points dispersed along the valley and to the mountain herding hut used by patrols on the frontier. When, as often happened, a household had no meat to give, its members turned to a first neighbor for assistance. Some households complained to the priest that the Germans demanded meat from them regularly, while other houses managed to avoid German requisitioning altogether. Such accusations of unfair, unequal treatment typically involved households from different parts of the commune, for people who lived near the Navarrese frontier and those at the northern end of the valley were longstanding rivals in matters of marriage, hunting, and cheese making. The German Occupation exacerbated existing tensions between the two groups. In his dual role as secular and spiritual leader, the Urdos priest was well accustomed to mediating relations between neighbors and relatives divided by quarrels about property. As a native Xiberoan, he understood the desire of Urdos Basques to manage conflict without intervention from external authorities whenever possible.

Thus, in the spring of 1943, the Urdos priest proposed that local households should take turns providing the occupiers with food by following the rotational order of the blessed-bread ritual, which had long served as a means of uniting Urdos people both socially and spiritually. By adapting the structure and principles of the blessed-bread ritual—with its fixed order and clockwise rotation—to the circumstances of German Occupation, the priest argued, Urdos households would share the burden of feeding the occupiers in a systematic and egalitarian fashion. He consulted the mayor and his parishioners, who applauded his proposed solution to an issue that had divided the community.

The priest wanted to keep his parishioners' sacred ritual giving of blessed bread on Sunday separate in time and space from their much despised secular obligation to the Germans. Thus he arranged for the latter obligation to be fulfilled on Saturday and started the cycle by choosing a farm at the other end of the valley from the household whose turn it was to give blessed bread that Sunday. As in the blessed-bread ritual, the obligation to provide food passed from first neighbor to first neighbor in a clockwise direction around the community. When people recalled those anxious, difficult times in the 1970s, they often commented on the sense of unity and order such systematic secular and ritual arrangements gave them during the Occupation (A. and B. Carricart 1979: pers. comm.).

When local denunciations and German violence against Urdos people began to occur in the spring of 1943, the community had an even greater need for the combinative, positive effects of the blessed-bread ritual. The priest urged his parishioners to remain loyal to one another and cautioned them about the potentially tragic consequences of idle talk (A. Carricart 1977: pers. comm.). The German military police and Gestapo based in Sustary needed local informers and encouraged denunciations, a practice most Urdos citizens regarded as socially and morally reprehensible (M. Idiart 1977: pers. comm.). One Urdos man recalled an encounter with the German police, who showed the shepherd a wad of francs and said: "We know your son is a clandestine guide. If you denounce him and let us know when and where his next group is meeting him, we will give you this money, and more." The shepherd declined, declaring that his son was only interested in girls, not in passing fugitives (Aytaberro 1983: 137; A. Bidegaray 1977: pers. comm.). Both oral and written denunciations did, however, occur.

Soon after the arrival of the Germans in Urdos, three Eiherabarra brothers agreed to help a trusted cousin guide a group of Allied officers to Spain.[8] Soon thereafter, the Basques formed an escape network for fugitives fleeing Vichy and German repression. In March 1943 the eldest brother, Eloi, agreed to collect twenty-four clients from a fellow *passeur* at nightfall some ten miles north of the frontier. When they reached the Urdos road, which was regularly patrolled, the shepherd and fugitives hid in thickets until a boy appeared and spoke to Eloi in Basque. The child's father worked the night shift in the hydroelectric factory; every night the boy took his father a snack, a nocturnal task approved by the Germans and vital to the safety of *passeurs* and their clients. The child told the shepherds where German patrols were positioned and signaled to them when the road was safe to cross.

On that March night, the group quickly made their way up into the mountains. Before sunrise, they reached a herding hut near the summit that a second *passeur* had just left with his group of fugitives. Eloi Eiherabarra and his clients crossed a wide bank of snow to join them. Together they numbered more than forty men. Snow fell heavily, and the exhausted group made slow progress. Suddenly, both *passeurs* motioned for their clients to follow them as they ran for some rocks. Eloi had spotted a German patrol at the summit, lying in wait with a heavy machine gun. The patrol killed at least one of the fugitives, a young Basque trying to escape compulsory labor service in Germany.[9] The other fugitives followed their guides through the snow into Nafarroa.

In early May 1943, someone denounced all three Eiherabarra brothers to the Germans in Sustary in an anonymous letter, which a Sustary woman happened to see on a German officer's desk when she applied for a pass to leave the reserved zone (P. Jaureguy 1944: written testimony). The Sustary woman, Mme Urruty, successfully warned the brothers of the betrayal in time for them to avoid capture. (She soon became a liaison agent for the Xiberoan Secret Army and plays a pivotal role in the next chapter.) The Eiherabarra brothers were denounced a third time in July. The Sustary Gestapo showed them three anonymous letters of denunciation, which the brothers were not permitted to read (Lougarot 2003: 246–47). The interrogators repeatedly threatened Eloi, who received particularly harsh treatment from Hammer, a German lieutenant based in Sustary, but they ultimately released the shepherds for lack of evidence (G. Harriguileheguy, J. Jonnet 1977: pers. comms.). The brothers continued to pass fugitives to Spain until the Liberation in August 1944. The identity of their denunciator(s) was never revealed in the post-Liberation purge of collaborators, to the journalists who tried to interview them, or to me (Lougarot 2004: 246).

On another July night in 1943, a German patrol raided the farm of Dominique B., an Urdos shepherd-*passeur*. The patrol showed Dominique a photograph of his alleged denunciator, whom the shepherd instantly recognized as a recent client, but he feigned ignorance. The Germans discussed his response and unwittingly revealed the identity of the denunciator to Dominique's brother, who listened intently to their conversation. As a former POW, the brother understood enough German to grasp that the traitor was a male French spy who infiltrated groups of young men evading the STO. The Germans deported Dominique B. to Buchenwald, which he survived (A. Bidegaray 1978: pers. comm.).

In July 1943 a series of denunciations led to the arrests and deportations of six Urdos men. On the night of July 16, the Germans arrested a father and son, Pierre and Tomas Garat; Pierre Garat's brother; the fiancé of Garat's niece; and two of Garat's first neighbors, Mathieu and Gregoire Doyart. Tomas Garat and Mathieu Doyart were both twenty years old and were close friends. Their respective houses were linked as first neighbors. Tomas Garat regularly passed Jews, Allied pilots, and STO evaders across the mountains into Nafarroa. Matheiu Doyart occasionally helped him. Tomas's father, Pierre, often collected money from the fugitives before handing them over to his son. The fiancé of Garat's niece recruited candidates for clandestine passage in the lowlands and was occasionally assisted by Pierre Garat's brother.[10]

The Germans arrested Mathieu Doyart and his brother Gregoire, ransacked their farmhouse, and treated the young men roughly. Someone had denounced Mathieu as a *passeur* and Gregoire as an STO evader (G. Iladoy 1978: pers. comm.). Soon thereafter, the occupiers arrested Pierre Garat for helping his son Tomas, who had been denounced as a *passeur* and arrested as he led four Jews across the Pyrenees. A slip of paper found on one Jewish fugitive gave the names of a Parisian man and an Urdos farmhouse. A few hours later a German patrol ransacked that farm, owned by Joseph Garat. When the Germans discovered some old hunting guns and ammunition, they arrested Joseph Garat, the Parisian, as well as his fiancée (daughter of Joseph, niece of Pierre Garat).

According to the Vichy inspector's report, the Parisian had met the fugitives in a lowland café and asked Pierre Garat to take them to Urdos. The fugitives paid Garat 8,500 francs before his son, Tomas, collected the group. The Vichy inspector noted that Pierre Garat had been a prisoner of war in 1914–18 and claimed that "although he [Garat] did not appear to have taken an active role in the clandestine passage of the four foreigners, he was well aware of his son's [anti-Vichy] actions." Aided by his father and the Parisian, Tomas Garat regularly worked as a clandestine guide. According to the inspector, Pierre and Tomas Garat, as well as the Parisian, "were all well-regarded in the community."[11]

When the Gestapo in Sustary interrogated the six Basques from Urdos, they reportedly beat and tortured Tomas Garat "because he was the *passeur*." On the following day, the Germans transferred the group to Fort du Hâ in Bordeaux, where further questioning and intimidation took place. From there, the prisoners went to the German transit camp at Compiègne and on to Buchenwald (G. Iladoy 1978: pers. comm.; J. Lascombes 1977: pers. comm.). For the duration of the Occupation and during the process of liberation, the Doyart and Garat households struggled to deal with rumors about the identity of the traitor(s) responsible for the arrests and deportations. Certain "bad tongues" maintained that Pierre Garat had himself denounced his first neighbors (the Doyart brothers), as well as his own son, Tomas. Three possible motives circulated about the betrayals.[12] It was said that the Gestapo had promised Garat a lifetime pension in return for information about *passeurs;* that Garat had made the denunciations "to save his own skin," for the Germans knew of his involvement in clandestine passages (G. Harriguileheguy 1977: pers. comm.); and that Pierre Garat sought revenge against his son for having challenged his authority as head of household during a series of violent arguments.

How did public opinion regard the denunciation and deportation of Pierre

Garat himself? Some people suspected a Navarrese Basque muleteer, as well as his niece's fiancé, the Parisian, had betrayed Garat. The muleteer, a seasoned smuggler who became a clandestine guide during the Occupation, knew many Urdos shepherds, including Pierre Garat. The muleteer competed with the Parisian for clients seeking passage across the Pyrenees. Most people, however, felt certain that Pierre Garat's denouncer was a "here person," an insider motivated by jealousy over the substantial sums of money the Garats made by helping fugitives reach Spain.

Spread by "bad tongues," accusatory rumors about Garat's role in the arrests and deportations of the Doyart brothers and Tomas Garat severely tested the first-neighbor relationship between the Doyart and Garat households. Although the Doyarts did not wish to believe the "bad tongues," they felt deeply anguished and confused by such destructive talk about Pierre Garat (M. Idiart 1978: pers. comm.). The elderly mother and wife of Pierre Garat, together with his teenaged children, likewise wrestled with "the words no one wanted to hear" (G. Harriguileheguy 1977: pers. comm.). The terrible rumors about Pierre Garat infuriated and traumatized his family. Mathieu Doyart and Tomas Garat were age-mates who regularly herded sheep together, and no one was surprised to learn that both young men had become *passeurs*. Their parents and grandparents had long been diligent first neighbors, always willing to help each other. The Doyarts were aware of domestic strife in the Garat household but tried to respect their neighbors' right to privacy (G. Harriguileheguy 1977: pers. comm.; G. Iladoy 1978: pers. comm.).

In an effort to help the two families deal with their painful, difficult situation, other neighbors represented the Garats and Doyarts whenever the seasonal cycle required first-neighbor mutual aid. Such first-neighbor assistance by proxy enabled the two households to uphold local traditions about secular, vicinal cooperation. First-neighbor aid by proxy was not an invention of the Occupation: Urdos households also used the strategy to cope with labor shortages arising from military conscription, its evasion, and trans-Atlantic emigration to the Americas (A. Carricart 1979: pers. comm.).

The strategy was not, however, used in the blessed-bread ritual. Long-standing tradition obliged the house Doyart to give *le pain bénit* to the house Garat once a year when its turn came round in the community-wide cycle of ritual giving. When it was her turn to give blessed bread in 1943, Mme Doyart, mother of the deported brothers, Mathieu and Gregoire, walked to the Garat farm and gave her "gift of life" to Mme Garat, wife of Pierre Garat and mother of the *passeur* Tomas. When the obligation to give blessed bread once again reached the Doyart household in 1944, Mme Doyart gave *le pain bénit* to her first neighbor, Mme Garat, in keeping with the long-standing Urdos tradition that promoted community-wide solidarity and good will among neighbors (M. Idiart 1978: pers. comm.). The two Basque women performed the ritual giving and receiving of blessed bread again in 1945 and in subsequent years thereafter on an annual basis. The deaths of their sons did not end the women's resistance to the divisiveness of denunciation.

Mathieu Doyart and Tomas Garat both died in Buchenwald in 1943. When their families learned the terrible news, the priest gave a special Mass for the two young shepherds. Parishioners filled the eleventh-century church and much of the adjacent cemetery, where people gathered to pay their respects. When a classmate of Mathieu and Tomas stood before the congregation and sang one of their favorite Basque songs, people wept openly (M. Elgoyhen 1979: pers. comm.). Pierre and Joseph Garat, Gregoire Doyart, and the Parisian survived Buchenwald and returned to Urdos in May 1945. The Parisian quickly married Pierre Garat's niece and moved away from the area. Pierre Garat faced the informal courts of neighborhood opinion in his moral community, which wrestled with two conflicting desires: to manage conflict and justice on their own or turn to the external authorities for the administration of legal justice. Well aware of the accusatory rumors about Pierre Garat, the priest exhorted his parishioners to resist the divisiveness of denunciation caused by "bad tongues" and deplored the damage caused by their malicious gossip. Pierre Garat angrily rejected the accusations of collaboration and betrayal that nevertheless continued to circulate in Urdos (G. Harriguileheguy 1979: pers. comm.).

During the process of liberation, the Urdos people were largely uneasy about and unwilling to participate in the process of "denouncing the denouncers" (*l'anti délation*) to the newly established French authorities. No one reported the local shepherd widely suspected of having denounced Pierre Garat and his niece's fiancé to the Germans in 1943. However, in June 1945 the post-Liberation authorities arrested Pierre Garat for "unworthy conduct" in relation to the denunciations of his son, Tomas, and his two first neighbors, Mathieu and Gregoire Doyart. According to a resister who served on the Chambre Civique, the court did not have conclusive evidence that Garat had denounced anyone (A. Barbe-Labarthe 2005: pers. comm.). Prominent members of the Xiberoan FFI testified that Garat had helped their cause on numerous occasions in 1943. Several former resisters pointed out that Garat had himself been denounced for helping fugitives (G. Harriguileheguy 1977: pers. comm.; A. Barbe-Labarthe 2004: pers. comm.). The court acquitted Garat, who returned to his farm and eventually received the Croix de Guerre for his services as a clandestine guide during the Occupation (Poullenot 1995: 131).

Some people still claimed that Garat was a double-crosser who posed as a resister and a *passeur* to conceal his courtship of German favors and whose greed matched his cowardice. His critics argued that Garat rarely put himself at risk during the Occupation and "always sent Tomas" when a *passeur* was required (G. Harriguileheguy, J.-B. Hondagneu 1978: pers. comms.). Pierre Garat had conspired with the Germans, they asserted, to make his arrest seem like a nocturnal raid. His detractors remained convinced that Garat had "sold" his own son and his first neighbors to satisfy his deep-seated greed and self-interest. Those who believed in Garat's innocence regarded him as a victim of Nazi oppression and barbarity who well deserved the Croix de Guerre bestowed upon him by the French government (J. Harrmora 1978: pers. comm.).

Critics and supporters of Pierre Garat were united on one front. Both sides deplored the fact that Garat had himself been denounced twice by fellow citizens from Urdos: once to the German police and, on his return from Buchenwald, to the local liberation committee. As insiders, the denouncers had betrayed not just Garat, but the entire moral community by denying the solidarity of Urdos Basques as a dominant value in the face of German aggression against local lives and property in 1943, and, in 1945, in the face of legal judgment by outsiders to the moral community who represented the French state. Local acts of denunciation breached the community's long-standing tradition of managing internal conflict on its own. Legitimate judgment belonged to those who had been born in Urdos and embraced its traditions and values. The boundaries of legitimate judgment about wrongdoing coincided with those of the moral community.

No one in Urdos ever resorted to post-Liberation vigilantism or violence against Garat after his acquittal. The Garat household never became the focus of popular justice for three main reasons. First, the informal court of neighborhood opinion never reached consensus about Pierre Garat's guilt or innocence. Second, the Garat house was a sociophysical space to which victims of Nazi barbarity belonged. Violating the house with a Nazi swastika or miniature wooden coffin would have violated the memory of Tomas Garat and degraded Pierre Garat's survival of deportation to a Nazi concentration camp.[13] Third, with the encouragement and guidance of their local priest, the Urdos people concentrated upon the restoration of community solidarity in the post-Liberation period. The weekly ritual giving of blessed bread provided them with a vehicle for doing so.

In her study of local purges in three French market towns, Megan Koreman (1999: 178) argues that while the French government sought to establish law and order by means of due process (the sphere of *légalité*), local communities understood the Purge according to a paradigm that focused on right relationships in the community and on redemption rather than punishment. In this conceptualization, the purge served as a means of atonement that would redeem not only the transgressor, but also the entire community. In Urdos the local purge consisted solely in the 1945 arrest of Pierre Garat. Although many Urdos families had prospered from the black market and two local women had had affairs with German soldiers, the community chose not to engage in whistle-blowing when liberation authorities sought information about local acts of collaboration. It was widely known that one shepherd-*passeur* had more than once betrayed Jewish fugitives to the Germans. On one occasion in 1942, the shepherd took his Jewish clients' money, jewelry, and other valuables before guiding them across the Pyrenees. When the group reached the summit of one mountain, the shepherd told the Jews that they were in Spain and watched them descend a trail that led them directly back into Urdos, where a German patrol awaited them. The Jews were transported to Gurs, the nearby internment camp from which nearly four thousand Jews were sent to Drancy and on to Auschwitz (Laharie 1993: 219). During the process of liberation, no one denounced the shepherd to the Purges Commission. People acknowledged among themselves that wrongdoing had indeed taken place in their moral community, but they preferred to handle matters themselves rather than allow the external authorities to manage justice and to preserve silence about matters they had failed to prevent or control and of which they remained deeply ashamed. Their silence about the shepherd's betrayal of Jews reveals the dark side of solidarity in a small, closely knit community whose murky moral universe stood in sharp contrast to the imagined community of France and its heroic profile at the Liberation (Gildea 2002: 358).

In her study of local collaboration in nearby Gascony, Vera Mark locates the pardon in a cycle of forgiving and forgetting that enables a society to reconstitute itself (Mark 2005: 51). Social models of the pardon situate it within cycles of magic and exchange (Abel 1996: 220, 232).[14] The act of pardon replaces an evil act (such as denunciation that leads to deportation, suffering, and death) with a good one and, like the gift, requires something in return: forgiveness. In Urdos the one man upon whom the local purge belatedly focused—Pierre Garat—could not be pardoned by his community, because he steadfastly denied any treachery against his fellow citizens. The cycle of forgiveness was located in the ritual giving of blessed bread.

In Urdos the blessed-bread ritual was a vehicle by means of which the community countered the divisiveness of denunciations and local betrayals; it also facilitated the process of forgiveness. After the deportations of the

Garat and Doyart men, the weekly ritual giving of *le pain bénit* focused people's attention on putting relationships right. The female heads of the Garat and Doyart households both suffered the tragic loss of male kin to Nazi barbarism as a result of local betrayals. Their participation in the ritual exchange of blessed bread served the same function as the pardon. The act repaired damage caused by denunciations and, with the passage of time, enabled reconciliation between the Garat and Doyart households. By 1976 their first-neighbor relationship operated fully in all spheres of activity. A good act (giving blessed bread) had replaced an evil act (denunciation/local betrayal). The Urdos people did not allow the sin of denunciation to destroy primordial vicinal relationships in their community. The ritual exchange of *le pain bénit* by the Garat and Doyart households served as an affirmation of goodness, of life and all that was just and morally right; it helped an entire community recover from its own local experience of occupation and war. The people of nearby Sustary were not so fortunate.[15]

10: Denunciation, Rumor, and Revenge in Sustary

As happened in so many communities across France, betrayals deeply divided the small market town of Sustary during the German Occupation.[1] Located twelve miles north of the Franco-Spanish border, the community was occupied continuously by the Germans from early December 1942 until the town's liberation on August 25, 1944. Such prolonged, daily contact between Sustary citizens and the occupiers gave rise to a network of complex relationships between certain Basques and Germans, as people developed their own strategies for making the best of their circumstances.

During the Occupation, French people sent three to five million letters of denunciation, signed or anonymous, to the Vichy and German authorities (Halimi 1983: 7). In France, as in Germany during the Third Reich, such letters often revealed the instrumental, private motives of their authors (Amouroux 1981: 265–97; Burrin 1996: 208–9; Cobb 1983: 105–6; Gellately 1997: 199–200; Halimi 1983). People used denunciations to get rid of rivals, enemies, and spouses; to settle scores; to gain emotional revenge or material advantage. As several studies of occupied France have shown, rumors served as useful indicators and manipulators of public opinion, especially about developments in the war, the vicissitudes of French political life, and the daily concerns and problems faced by ordinary citizens (Guillon 1997: 247–48, 2005; Laborie 1990). The Xiberoan town of Sustary provides an unusual opportunity to explore accusatory rumors about wrongdoing and the sanctions imposed upon their sources and targets by fellow citizens. In Sustary people accused of wrongdoing ironically referred to the moral community that judged them as "the good tongues" (*les bonnes langues*).[2] When accusatory rumor entailed the malicious denigration of an individual, it constituted slander and thus, in principle, obliged the community to question such information as the work of "bad tongues" (*les mauvaises langues* or *les langues de vipère*; *mihigaixtoak* in Basque). In the compromised moral universe of the Occupation and post-Liberation period, the words and actions of "good" and "bad tongues" deepened tensions in an already divided society.

In Sustary two women figured prominently in a web of denunciations and rumors that interlinked them, their adversaries, their supporters, and certain German officers during 1943–45. A shopkeeper and native of the town, Mme Etxart (née Harbustan) came under the close scrutiny of "good tongues" as a young woman. Her arch rival, Mme Urruty, came from another Xiberoan community and ran the local garage with her husband, an insider to Sustary. According to the Harbustan family and other supporters of Mme Etxart, "good tongues" wrongly accused the shopkeeper of sexual promiscuity as a *femme légère*, of multiple denunciations to the German authorities, and of economic collaboration with them.[3] With the help of Mme Etxart herself, the "good" and "bad tongues" constructed and manipulated a partly imagined, partly factually correct public rumor (*aipu* or *ots* in Basque; *la rumeur publique* in French) with which Mme Etxart playfully and dangerously amused herself before and during the German Occupation.

Accusatory rumors played a key role in the formation of public rumor as information widely accepted to be true, whether or not it was official. Unlike denunciations, accusatory rumors were made to fellow members of the moral community, who had a right to judge each other, rather than to the authorities responsible for the administration of legal justice. Public rumor was created not by a homogeneous public at large, but by individuals who felt concerned about particular events and behaviors and their potential impact upon the community as a moral, socioeconomic entity (Kapferer 1995: 108). Accusatory rumors constituted moral judgments, based upon Xiberoan values and codes of correct social and sexual conduct. Citizens had a right to contest the veracity of such rumors, but once an accusatory rumor became accepted by a majority of citizens as the truth, it entered the domain of public rumor. Interactions among Mme Etxart, her fellow citizens, and certain German officers provide an unusual opportunity to trace the development of public rumor through a series of civic judgments about the shopkeeper. In Sustary public rumor became the focus of local debate about legitimate judgment, popular justice, and legal justice during Vichy, the Occupation, and the process of liberation.

In 1940 Mme Etxart and Mme Urruty were both in their early thirties, strong minded and competitive, and both women enjoyed intrigue and risk taking. They disliked each other intensely. During 1943–44 Mme Urruty served as an undercover liaison agent for the Gaullist Secret Army. She also gained the trust and cooperation of a Gestapo officer, Sasse, based in Sustary during 1943. Her adversary, Mme Etxart, cultivated mutually beneficial relations with a German lieutenant, Hammer, who played a central role in the collection and dissemination of information about anti-Nazi activities in the town.

In 1940 Sustary had around a thousand inhabitants, including farmers and shepherds living in rural neighborhoods outside the tightly nucleated town.[4] Its weekly livestock and vegetable markets regularly attracted rural Xiberoans to the community, which had several hotels, numerous cafés, fabric and hardware shops, a dental practice, a savings bank, a post office, pharmacies, several butchers, and one of the few garages in Xiberoa at that time. In the 1930s and 1940s the Sustary people spoke Basque and French fluently, and many citizens communicated in Spanish and Italian as well, for an Italian entrepreneur owned the sawmill on the edge of town and employed mainly Italian and Spanish workers. In 1943 twenty-three Italians, twenty-four Spanish Republican refugees, and sixty-two Jewish refugees lived in Sustary.[5]

In Sustary every house traditionally had a name, upon which native citizens based their social and spiritual identity, and two first neighbors. Vicinal reciprocity was institutionalized in the ritual provision of mortuary services by a house to its first first neighbor, defined as the first house to the right of one's own. A Sustary house was also traditionally obliged to give blessed bread to that neighbor and to the congregation after Mass when its turn as bread giver came in a community-wide cycle of exchange. As happened in rural Xiberoan communities, the obligation to give blessed bread in Sustary rotated from house to house in a fixed order of giving (M. Eyheramendy 1979: pers. comm.; J. Hastoy 2005: pers. comm.; Lagarde 2003: 196n.). When internal social and political conflict deeply divided Sustary citizens in the 1930s, however, first-neighbor relations began to deteriorate. When neighbors found themselves siding with different, mutually hostile political factions in the town, they began to change the town's network of vicinal relationships. Rather than cooperate with each other, such neighbors often ended their long-standing vicinal relationship, a decision that contravened one of the most important traditions in rural Basque society. By 1935 the Sustary priest was forced to address the situation, because so many houses had refused to give blessed bread to their first neighbor (or to receive it), owing to mutually hostile feelings between them. Initially, the priest obliged all houses to give bread to him for blessing and distribution after Mass, but the practice fell into disuse soon after the German occupation of Sustary began in December 1942.

Local notables included the Harbustan family, the notary, two rival pharmacists, and two rival physicians (Dr. Carricart and Dr. Idiart). Among Sustary's most prominent conservative families, the Harbustans shared political sympathies with their two first neighbors: the notary and Dr. Carricart. A staunch conservative and traditionalist, Dr. Carricart knew Jean Ybarnegaray well. The two men had been classmates at the Petit Séminaire in Uztaritze and later moved in the same political circles (Jacob 1994: 66). Carricart served as general councilor for Sustary for almost two decades. Owing to his political conservatism, Carricart was locally known as "the White doctor." His professional and political rival, Dr. Idiart, was equally devoted to his community, highly competent, and charismatic. Idiart first became mayor of Sustary in 1939, a position he retained throughout Vichy and the Occupation and to which he was reelected in 1945.[6] Although the vast majority of Basque general councilors and mayors belonged to the Right, Dr. Idiart was a radical socialist, a center-Left party member, and thus was known as "the Red doctor" (Larronde 1994: 50). Dr. Idiart was an arch enemy of the powerful Harbustan family.

Mme Etxart and Mme Urruty belonged to the two opposing political factions that divided Sustary before the Germans arrived in 1942: "the Whites" (les Blancs) and "the Reds" (les Rouges). As the Vichy police inspector Carbou noted after one of his routine visits to Sustary, commercial and professional rivalries, as well as personal animosities, often intensified political differences between the two groups.[7] Attached to traditional Catholic conservatism, the Whites were mainly notables who opposed the Popular Front in 1936, railed against communism, and supported Pétain with varying degrees of commitment. In Sustary the Reds backed republicanism and were mainly moderate radical socialists who supported de Gaulle and his resistance movement, the Secret Army, during 1943–44.

The Whites and the Reds were not, however, homogeneous groups either socially or politically. In the 1930s many conservative Xiberoans from Sustary and nearby villages were actively involved in the northern Basque nationalist movement, Eskualerriste, which promoted use of the Basque language in education, the church, and Basque popular culture. Founded by a Basque priest, Abbé Pierre Lafitte, the movement decreed that "for a true Basque, the center of everything is the house [etxea]." Eskualerristes regarded the traditional three-generational family as a cornerstone of Basque society and staunchly defended the preservation of Basque customary law as a means of protecting the integrity and continuity of the household (Larronde 1994: 86, 90). The teenaged son of a Sustary notable, Johanne Harbustan, joined the movement while studying philosophy at the Petit Séminaire in Uztaritze. To the consternation of conservative politicians such as Ybarnegaray, the young Harbustan campaigned for the Eskualerriste movement throughout Xiberoa in 1936–37. An ardent French nationalist, Ybarnegaray vociferously opposed all regionalist movements in France and had an uneasy, sometimes hostile relationship with Abbé Lafitte, whom Ybarnegaray once described as "a red fish swimming in a baptismal font" (Jacob 1994: 63).

The elder sister of Johanne Harbustan, Maienna, first became the focus of accusatory rumors in 1929, when she was eighteen.[8] As the pretty daughter of a prosperous, conservative family in a largely socialist town, the young woman easily attracted public attention. Her flirtatious, socially provocative behavior intensified such scrutiny. Although no conclusive evidence underpinned it, "bad tongues" claimed that Mlle Harbustan ended an unwanted pregnancy in 1932 (G. Harriguileheguy 1977: pers. comm.). In 1933 Maienna Harbustan married a politically conservative shopkeeper, Dominique Etxart, who had been chosen to inherit his natal house. In keeping with Basque custom, she moved into his parents' home and became its younger female head of household. Owing to political and personal animosities and contrary to Basque traditions, the Etxarts were not on speaking terms with their two first neighbors. The Etxart household thus lacked the vicinal solidarity that figured prominently in traditional Basque societal arrangements. Maienna Etxart soon found herself without the domestic support of her parents-in-law and husband, for the elder couple died in 1937 and Dominqiue Etxart was mobilized in September 1939. She resolved to make the business prosper "to please her husband upon his return" and competed aggressively with her commercial rivals (G. Harriguileheguy, J.-B. Hondagneu 1977: pers. comms.). Dominique Etxart became a prisoner of war in 1940, shortly before France surrendered to Germany.

Owing in part to Basque customary law, Xiberoan housewives were accustomed to exercising power and authority. In three-generational households, the wife/mother was advantaged by the support of the elder, retired female head of household in handling the additional burdens and responsibilities brought by the Occupation. Maienna Etxart lacked such additional domestic support and defied Vichy's ideal image of the POW wife (Fishman 1991: 129). The shopkeeper did not behave as one of the regime's "suffering but triumphant mothers," vulnerable and dependent upon men (Diamond 1999: 75). She relished her independence as head of household and as her absent husband's equal partner in business. Xiberoan notions of gender equality did not conform to those espoused by Vichy in its vision of a New France, in which women were subordinate and inferior to men (Ferro 1987: 255–56; Fishman 1991: 125–34; Paxton 2001: 166; Pollard 1998: 6–9, 91). Even as Mme Etxart represented wayward female sexuality in Vichy's definition of womanhood, she also overstepped Xiberoan boundaries of acceptable behavior for a married woman. She flirted openly with men and enjoyed the scandal it caused.

The captivity of M. Etxart in Germany "did not disarm the good tongues" in town, as the notary ironically described those who gossiped about the young POW wife.[9] Rumors spread that she had several lovers. Unlike the Vichy perspective on adultery, which blamed uncontrolled female desire, Xiberoans held male and female adulterers equally responsible for their actions and subject to the same public form of popular justice: the nocturnal strewing of greenery (*la jonchée*) between their houses (see Pollard 1998: 42, 64). Mme Etxart's house was not targeted, because—in spite of considerable speculation—confusion surrounded the rumors about her alleged affairs.

Although they were deeply disturbed by their daughter's behavior and the rumors, the Harbustans lacked the moral authority to confront her, since Mme Etxart belonged to another house over which they had no jurisdiction. Drawing upon traditions of mutual assistance by first neighbors, M. Harbustan asked their neighbor, the notary, to speak frankly to his daughter about the dangers of playing with public rumor. The notary's cautionary words to her, however, had no effect on a person whom the notary described as "greatly amused by tittle-tattle" and who "took a malign pleasure in starting rumors about herself."[10] Mme Harbustan then wrote a stern letter to her daughter, warning that if she "did not change her behavior, the door to the paternal home would be forever closed."[11] Although access was not denied, relations between parents and daughter became further strained when the Germans arrived in Sustary in mid-November 1942.

Sustary fell within the forbidden frontier zone (*une zone frontière interdite*) that extended ten miles north of the Franco-Spanish border.[12] German customs and the security service (SD, Sicherheitsdienst) established a garrison in the town to quell the Resistance and coordinate the interception of anti-Hitler fugitives trying to reach Spain (Poullenot 1995: 103). The occupiers quickly became regular customers in Mme Etxart's shop, and she made no attempt to conceal her social and commercial relations with the Germans from members of the moral community. The shopkeeper also let local people know that she often had detailed knowledge of anti-German sentiment and activity in the town and was prepared to share it with the German authorities.

According to police reports, most Sustary citizens strongly supported de Gaulle. Only a minority remained "completely confident in Marshal Pétain and his government, without being terribly willing collaborationists—except for a very few."[13] Although the socialist mayor, Dr. Idiart, and his deputy were committed Gaullists, both men remained in post for the duration of the Occupation.[14]

The head of German customs, Superintendent Ressel, lodged with Gaullist supporters, the Urrutys, who owned the town's garage. German convoys regularly stopped there and thus increased the Basque couple's contact with the enemy. Mme Urruty also worked in the post office, another public space conducive to gathering information. As an outspoken socialist, Mme Urruty had become a political adversary of the Harbustans soon after she moved to Sustary on her marriage in 1934. A mutually jealous and particularly hostile relationship developed between her and Mme Etxart. When the Germans arrived in 1942, their rivalry escalated.

In February 1943 the introduction of laws on obligatory work service in Germany (STO) greatly increased local opposition to Vichy and aided recruitment to the Gaullist resistance movement, the Secret Army. The socialist mayor, Dr. Idiart, formed a local Secret Army unit that included a socialist butcher and Mme Urruty. She regularly passed intelligence to the regional head of the Secret Army from the spring of 1943 until the Liberation (Poullenot 1995: 189). Other Secret Army helpers included two female hoteliers and several "Red" households who fed and sheltered Allied pilots, Jews, and young STO evaders. Fugitives often met in a café owned by the widowed sister-in-law of Maienna Harbustan Etxart's father, Kattlin Harbustan. Basque farmers regularly liaised with Kattlin before collecting fugitives who sought passage across the border into Spain.

From the spring of 1943 until the Liberation, townspeople regularly saw Mme Etxart in the company of a German soldier, Lieutenant Hammer. Although French citizens had a propensity to report wrongdoing to the Vichy and German authorities in signed or, more often, anonymous letters, Mme Etxart preferred to pass information orally to Hammer in public places such as the square outside her shop. The German officer then decided whether to follow up with an arrest, warn the suspect that action might be taken, or pass the intelligence to the local head of the Gestapo. Rumors circulated that Mme Etxart and Lieutenant Hammer were lovers. In May 1943 Mme Etxart denounced the Urrutys to Hammer for sheltering Allied pilots, but the German merely reproached the couple for their illegal activities, apparently in order to frustrate Mme Etxart, for Hammer enjoyed manipulating the shopkeeper. The Urrutys suspected Mme Etxart, because M. Urruty had "foolishly bought several tins of sardines" in her shop for the fugitives and had attracted her unwelcome attention.[15]

One day in July 1943, Mme Etxart quarreled bitterly with another adversary, Mme Sabalot, whose socialist husband was the mayor's deputy. Later that day, a Vichy economic controller, Duclos, searched Mme Etxart's shop for illegal food stocks, which he found. Duclos asked the mayor to provide "a declaration about the morality of the accused, including not only what public rumor held to be true," but also how her parents viewed her behavior. Through the mayor, the Vichy authorities knew about Mme Harbustan's ultimatum to her daughter to change her ways. When the authorities arrested Mme Etxart, her family negotiated a "house arrest in the paternal home," terms that reflected Vichy's emphasis on male authoritarianism.

Charges against her were soon dropped. Mme Etxart blamed M. Sabalot for denouncing her to Duclos. Mme Etxart's brother, Johanne Harbustan, openly threatened to take revenge against Duclos for having acted upon the denunciation.[16]

By August 1943 the Urrutys had become involved in a web of accusations and secret confidences involving Mme Etxart, local gendarmes, Lieutenant Hammer, and the Gestapo agent, Sasse. Sympathetic to the Resistance, Sergeant-Major Labat (responsible for the Sustary gendarmerie) warned the Urrutys that Mme Etxart had denounced them to Sasse for having a gun. Sasse viewed Mme Etxart with a measure of contempt, for he knew about her fondness for rumormongering and making denunciations. Aware of his disdain for her rival, Mme Urruty encouraged conversations with Sasse during his routine visits to the garage and, at immense risk, gained his confidence. Sasse then warned her that Mme Etxart had denounced the Urrutys to Hammer for helping fugitives cross the Pyrenees. On the same day, ostensibly to prove that he "was not hard on people," Lieutenant Hammer himself warned the Urrutys that Mme Etxart had denounced them. As a favor to Mme Urruty, Sasse released five Xiberoans who had sheltered fugitives.[17]

Police reports and testimonies later considered in French courts of justice show that Sustary civilians and Sergeant-Major Labat had surprisingly candid conversations with Lieutenant Hammer, and to a lesser extent with Sasse, in their day-to-day dealings with each other. In a manner that mirrored Mme Urruty's manipulation of the Gestapo agent Sasse for intelligence about arrested resisters, Sergeant-Major Labat often used Hammer to gain information about Xiberoans held by the Germans and the reasons for their arrest. On one occasion, a local woman asked Labat if he could find out whether her father and brother were still being held by the Gestapo and whether Labat could take them some fresh clothes. When Labat casually mentioned the two men to Hammer, the German soldier explained that he had arrested the two Basques for having hidden twelve American pilots waiting for a passage across the Pyrenees. Hammer then asked Labat, "Why didn't you know that already?" Labat replied, "I don't always hear everything."[18]

The socialist Sustary mayor, Dr. Idiart, and the secretary of the town hall, M. Sabalot, belonged to the Gaullist Secret Army. Owing to their close surveillance by the Gestapo, however, neither man was active in the maquis that operated in the vicinity of Sustary. Dr. Idiart, in particular, used his Vichy connection to resist the Germans in other ways. On one occasion in May 1943, the head of German security in Sustary asked Idiart to allocate two gendarmes to guard the houses in which German soldiers lived, because the Germans had become anxious about the threat of an attack by resisters. Dr. Idiart informed the subprefect, arguing that the Sustary brigade could not afford to give up two men. The subprefect backed Idiart and refused the German officer's request. The matter seems to have been dropped by the German head of security and Superintendant Ressel, who often exchanged political views about international developments with Maule's Inspector Carbou during the weekly market in Sustary.[19]

The occupation of Sustary was, in many respects, a curious one. Intra-community relations between some local people and certain Germans were often characterized by casual exchanges of information and news in spaces of public sociability such as the post office, the marketplace, and local taverns. Many Sustary citizens became acquainted with Lieutenant Hammer in particular. Although Hammer sometimes presented himself as a defender of local citizens, he was not a benign occupier. Located on a hill above the town, the villa to which Hammer escorted resisters, clandestine guides, and other wrongdoers was widely known as a place of Nazi violence.[20]

During the Occupation, Sustary served as a temporary base for numerous strangers involved in resistance groups operating across France. The Sabalots had a lodger, Brigadier General Bertschi, who moved to Sustary after the French Army's defeat in 1940. In October 1943, Mme Etxart warned Bertschi that the Germans had the Sabalot house under close surveillance. She knew that Bertschi had engaged in talks with Xiberoan Resistance leaders.[21] Some people speculated that Mme Etxart's sense of mischief motivated her "favor" to the brigadier; others regarded her warning to Bertschi as an attempt to make him, and the Sabalots, fear her. The brigadier abruptly left town when his name appeared on the Gestapo's list of undesirable citizens (J.-B. Hondagneu 1977: pers. comm.).

Following another denunciation in November 1943, Vichy police arrested Mme Etxart for possessing illegal firearms. She suspected that the denunciation had come from Mme Urruty, because she "knew about the gun and had a long-standing grudge" against Mme Etxart, who went to prison for a month.[22] In a letter to Mme Etxart's lawyer, the notary observed how difficult it was "to control the inane rumors and rancor" that were tearing Sustary apart. He admitted that Mme Etxart "had been spoiled as a child and was capable of saying ridiculous, stupid things about herself." She made enemies easily, "owing to her own imprudence and to the spitefulness and jealousies of her fellow citizens."[23] On her return from prison, Mme Etxart allegedly said "to whomever wanted to hear" that "those who would like to see me arrested again will be shot."[24]

Tensions deepened within the large network of Harbustan kin when Mme Etxart allegedly denounced a cousin to Lieutenant Hammer as they passed

her aunt's café. According to Lieutenant Hammer, Mme Etxart casually remarked, "My cousin is in the maquis." When they parted, Hammer warned
the café owner to tell her son that he had been denounced and should leave
his resistance group, which he did. In the postwar trial of Mme Etxart, Lieutenant Hammer later explained his actions as an attempt to show the community he "meant no harm."[25]

Mme Etxart then denounced M. Sabalot to Lieutenant Hammer for listening to the BBC and was annoyed when the German merely warned her
enemy. When Hammer did arrest a Basque shepherd well known for helping
fugitives, Mme Etxart smugly told a cousin who was in her crowded shop
that "Edward Sabalot will be next." Soon thereafter, Hammer did arrest Sabalot for listening to Radio London and led him past Mme Etxart's house,
which was not the normal route to the Gestapo's interrogation center. According to public rumor, the sight of Sabalot being paraded by Lieutenant
Hammer past her house greatly pleased Mme Etxart.[26]

In the spring of 1944, the Gestapo agent, Sasse, moved to Agen, several
hundred miles north of the Basque Country, but he remained in close contact with Mme Urruty.[27] Rumors circulated about their collaboration in
releasing resisters. Certain "bad tongues" hinted at a sexual relation between
the female agent and a senior Resistance leader, but such idle talk did not enter
the domain of public rumor. Jealous that her arch rival had established such
close ties with a Gestapo agent, Mme Etxart courted the attention of his young
successor in town, known simply as Franz, who quickly arrested two of her
enemies: Mme Sabalot and Mme Etxeberry, who worked in the post office
with Mme Urruty. The Gestapo claimed that the women had been seen in a
car with Brigadier General Bertschi and a local Resistance leader. Mme Sabalot and Mme Etxeberry insisted that they had spent the day in Baiona with
their daughters, but the Gestapo beat them unconscious on two consecutive
days. On the third day the Germans let the women go without explanation.
Through the chauffeur of a Vichy policeman who supported the Resistance,
the women learned that Mme Urruty had gone to Agen as soon as she heard
of their arrests, and that Sasse had authorized their release.[28] Following denunciations allegedly made by Mme Etxart, the Gestapo then arrested two of
her aunts (her father's brothers' wives), who often sheltered fugitives in their
hotels. The Germans eventually released the women, unharmed.[29]

Between the summer of 1943 and August 1944, agent Sasse and Mme
Urruty facilitated the release or prevented the arrest of some seventy Basque
resisters (Jaureguy 1944). During one of Mme Urruty's visits to see him in
Agen, Sasse expressed his surprise that Mme Etxart "hadn't been killed by
someone in the Resistance" and warned the agent that she had been de-

nounced five times by her rival.[30] Mme Urruty was not treated as an "honorary man" by her male colleagues, nor did she regard herself as one. In keeping with the Xiberoan emphasis on gender equality, men in the Secret Army respected Mme Urruty for her courage and commitment to the Resistance (M. Barbe-Labarthe 2003: pers. comm.).

In January 1944, someone placed a small wooden coffin containing a German cartridge on the doorstep of Mme Etxart as a warning from one or more citizens to stop betraying "here people" to the enemy.[31] Another local woman, also suspected of denunciations, received a similar coffin. A few days later, unknown individuals strewed branches (la jonchée) between the woman's house and the lodgings of her German lover. Within a week, three other married women known to be sexually involved with Germans became targets of la jonchée.[32] In keeping with Basque custom, the incidents took place quietly at night and at considerable risk. Townspeople disliked being judged by outsiders who did not belong to their moral community, which had its own internal, traditional means of publicly sanctioning "moral treachery" (les trahisons morales, notably adultery) (Desplats 1982: 181). Adapting a Gascon tradition to the unusual circumstances of the Occupation, those who placed small coffins on the thresholds of certain houses exercised the same right as those who anonymously practiced la jonchée: the right of the moral community to judge not simply the behavior of individuals, but also the houses to which they belonged.

Mme Etxart did not become the target of la jonchée, which her family used as proof of her marital fidelity. Accusatory rumors had, however, circulated about her adulterous relations with both German and Basque lovers.[33] "Bad tongues" insisted that Mme Etxart had prepared two envelopes for her POW husband's return from Germany. According to the rumor, allegedly started by the shopkeeper herself, one envelope contained a million francs, the profits of her black-market dealings with the Germans. The other envelope allegedly contained a list of her lovers. "Bad tongues" claimed that Mme Etxart planned to make her husband choose one of the envelopes "to amuse herself," an accusation that Mme. Etxart steadfastly denied.[34]

This ethnography of accusatory practices, however incomplete, goes beyond the stereotypical image of female denunciators who compulsively wrote letters to the German and Vichy authorities and who, during the liberation, had their heads shaved in front of a jubilant crowd eager for revenge (Brossat 1992; Cobb 1983: 105; Diamond 1999; Lefébure 1993; Virgili 2002). Mme Etxart's choices and experiences need to be placed within the context of values and expectations that shaped her habitus at the time. Contrary to a popular theory about women, gender relations, and denunciation in occupied

France, the shopkeeper was not a disadvantaged member of society (Burrin 1995: 215). She belonged to a powerful family and lived in a culture that promoted equality between the sexes. Both before and during the Occupation, Mme Etxart created problems for herself by continually testing the resilience of Xiberoan values and codes of conduct, as well as the tolerance of her family and friends. Like so many other men and women in occupied France, she used denunciation as an instrumental means of gaining revenge against her adversaries and enjoyed the power it entailed (Gildea 2002: 28–33). The shopkeeper also derived pleasure from rumormongering and causing a stir in her small community.

The prolonged presence of Germans in Sustary enabled her not only to create close social relationships with them, but also to involve some of them in her dangerous games. Why did Mme Etxart engage in oral accusatory practices? By verbally reporting or hinting at wrongdoing to Lieutenant Hammer in places of public or semipublic sociability, the shopkeeper achieved goals that simply could not be reached through anonymous letters of denunciation. She needed other people to hear her words, or at least to see her talking to Lieutenant Hammer and the young Gestapo agent, in order to play with public rumor. Mme Etxart used the dangerous but exhilarating power that accusatory practices and proximity to German authorities could give to men and women (Gildea 2002: 28).

That power enabled Mme Etxart and Mme Urruty to compete with each other. They denounced each other to different authorities, with whom each woman had reached an understanding. The shopkeeper and Lieutenant Hammer were like minded in several respects: they both played with information about wrongdoing to achieve personal and instrumental goals, and, like Mme Urruty, they both tried to manipulate public opinion about themselves. As a power player, Mme Urruty was advantaged by her direct access to both Vichy and German authorities who, with the exception of Superintendent Ressel, were all playing a double game: Duclos was both a Vichy economic controller and a Resistance officer; the mayor was an underground Gaullist serving Vichy in the town hall; and Sasse used his influence in the Gestapo to help Basque resisters and to protect the Urrutys from denunciations.

As a moral community, Sustary citizens were accustomed to judging one another through public rumor, a product of human communication and imagination that was contested and constantly reshaped as people evaluated and responded to accusations of wrongdoing (Paine 1967: 279).[35] As his sister's staunch defender, Johanne Harbustan denied that public rumor held Mme Etxart responsible for any of the denunciations that had torn Sustary apart. Her enemies, he argued, created and manipulated accusatory rumors about the shopkeeper in order to destroy her reputation and her thriving business. Judicial judgment and punishment of collaboration-related crimes, such as denunciation, rested with the French Provisional Government through its courts of justice and the Chambres Civiques (Novick 1968).

As early as January 1944, Inspector Carbou identified Sustary as a "foyer of trouble," where a majority of citizens were Gaullists who eagerly awaited the Liberation.[36] He understood, however, that the increasingly intense mutual hostility between supporters of the Harbustan family and supporters of the Gaullists derived not so much from ideological differences as from personal animosities. The continuous presence of the Germans from early December 1942 until August 1944 deepened divisions between two factions that existed before the Germans arrived. As the Liberation approached, accusatory rumors about acts of collaboration with the enemy increasingly entered the domain of public rumor. In both factions, citizens began to reflect deeply on the prospect of judicial judgment by authorities external to the moral community and to prepare for the possible consequences. The brother of Mme Etxart, Johanne Harbustan, railed against the "bad tongues" in town who accused his sister of sexual collaboration and of betraying so many fellow citizens to the enemy. In Sustary the process of liberation promised to be divisive and uneasy.

11: The Divisiveness of Liberation

According to the departmental correspondent for the Comité d'Histoire de la Deuxième Guerre Mondiale, the department of the Basses-Pyrénées was liberated between August 20 and August 26 "practically without military combat" (Poullenot 1995: 260).[1] On November 30, 1944, a prefectural decree fixed the dates of liberation in a shorter timescale (August 22 to August 26), based upon the liberation of Pau, Baiona, and Oloron. For Xiberoans, the local process of liberation began with a highly controversial skirmish on the outskirts of Maule, on August 10. There are at least two versions of the events that culminated in the liberation of Maule. As might be expected, the Secret Army's account differs from that of the CFP.

On July 25, 1944, the Spielberg Battalion vacated the Collège de Saint-François in Maule to return to its base in Mont-de-Marsan, but a garrison of forty-five soldiers and three subofficers was left in the school. The CFP company leader in Xiberoa, Lavalou, decided to attack the remaining Germans but needed reinforcements, given the close proximity of the Sustary garrison. He met with the Secret Army FFI leader, Clement de Jaureguiberry, in a Maule café to discuss a joint military intervention. Jaureguiberry refused to engage in combat, given de Gaulle's orders to wait for the day of national insurrection, but agreed to harass the enemy provided that such action took place far from Xiberoan communities. At this stage of the narrative, the CFP version agreed with that of the Secret Army.[2]

On August 9, a Maule physician (Dr. Sehabiague) and a pharmacist went to the hamlet of Roquiague to advise Lavalou that the Germans planned to leave Maule the following day. (Dr. Sehabiague often helped Dr. Herbille attend to wounded German soldiers.) Lavalou discussed his plan of attack with them: Bercut's combat unit would ambush the German convoy on the outskirts of Maule, while the other CFP units spread out across the countryside to block escape routes. Lavalou traveled to Pau to request military reinforcement from CFP headquarters and left Bercut in command. When the Germans left their trucks in a Maule garage (owned by a collaborationist) to be serviced for their forthcoming journey, Bercut attached magnetic mines to their chassis, which later failed to explode. On August 10 at the Collège de Saint-François, Canon Ithurbide briefed Bercut about German plans to evacuate the school and town.

The CFP violated the July 1944 agreement reached between Xiberoan Secret Army and CFP leaders (Jaureguiberry and Béguerie) when Bercut's combat unit ambushed the German convoy on the western edge of Maule on August 10. The CFP took two prisoners, and the forty-six other Germans took cover in a nearby manor house, which CFP men quickly surrounded. Resisters and Germans exchanged gunfire all afternoon. In the clinic, Dr. Sehabiague, Dr. Herbille, and the pharmacist treated wounded German soldiers. Sehabiague unsuccessfully tried to persuade a German officer to facilitate a German surrender. The officer refused, then he slipped out of the clinic to telephone the German garrison in Sustary. Two FTP resisters (both Maule communists of Navarrese descent) and one Secret Army man, who came upon the scene by chance, arrested the German officer and three other soldiers in the middle of town. The German officer refused to give his weapons to the FTP communists but agreed to "submit them to the mayor."[3]

According to Secret Army reports, a CFP machine gunner positioned himself in the square at the railway station and opened fire. A crowd of curious onlookers assembled. When citizens noticed a young woman sitting inside a CFP truck, rumors circulated that Bercut had arrested her and had threatened to shave her head as punishment for "horizontal collaboration." A group of First World War veterans unsuccessfully called for the machine gunner to stop firing across the embankment, which was far from the house held by the Germans. They did manage to release the frightened young woman. In the confusion, CFP resisters accidentally killed the French chauffeur of a German vehicle and wounded three of their own men ("Libération" 1984: 8).

In another part of town, two Secret Army men (including the socialist St. Jean Lanouguère) and a former CFP resister (who had left the Resistance after the Ospitaleku raid) armed themselves with weapons abandoned by the Germans and made their way to a hillock overlooking the railway station. Their gunfire narrowly missed the two FTP communists, who had positioned themselves between the hillock and the manor house. Both Secret Army and CFP reports identified this group as the "Secret Army section mobilized by Lanouguère to prevent enemy infiltration" back into the town. According to the CFP, Lavalou took charge of the situation on his return from Pau and on the following morning, deciding to "end matters," sent one of his German prisoners to the manor house with an ultimatum to the Germans there: if they refused to surrender, the CFP would launch a second assault. CFP documents give two different versions of the Germans' response. In the official CFP account, the Germans never replied to Lavalou's ultimatum, whereas in the testimony given by Lavalou and Bercut in 1964, the Germans "would only surrender to soldiers of a regular Army," so Lavalou dispatched a senior officer in the Maule gendarmerie and five other gendarmes to meet the German in charge. None of the CFP documents describe any meeting or negotiations between the CFP and Germans. One account reports merely that "the Germans gave up and filed out of the manor house with their hands in the air, unarmed, with a white sheet serving as a white flag. . . . There was an explosion of joy among the local population, who congratulated Lavalou and Bercut on their success. Thanks to them and their valiant men, citizens could once again walk the streets of Maule wearing their tri-colored armbands without fear. In accordance with the permanent instructions of Pommiès, Lavalou and Bercut handed the German POWs over to the Secret Army, except for two sub-officers." Some CFP resisters involved in these events insist that they never saw a Secret Army resister take part in the assault on the manor house. In their 1964 account of events, Lavalou and Bercut noted that "the facts reported by the CFP cannot be found in the pamphlet written by the Secret Army soon after the Liberation."[4]

According to the Secret Army version of events, the Germans surrendered to both Secret Army and CFP leaders on August 11 ("Libération" 1984: 8). Secret Army resisters took the German POWs to their mountain hideout, and Bercut claimed responsibility for the two German officers in charge of the convoy ("Libération" 1984: 12).[5] Dr. Herbille immediately went to examine four wounded Germans.[6] The mayor of Maule, Arnaud Aguer, called Jaureguiberry and the president of the local liberation committee, Jean-Pierre Champo, to an urgent meeting at his house. Aguer mistakenly believed that his town had been "forcibly occupied by the Resistance" and thus tried to pass civic responsibility for the town over to Champo, on the grounds that the head of the local liberation committee would have to deal with any German retaliations and reprisals. Jaureguiberry and Champo assured the mayor that the town had not been endangered by the Resistance, but "only a part of the Resistance known as ORA [the CFP]," and that CFP leaders would bear full responsibility for any harm done to Maule or its citizens. Jaureguiberry was furious about "the flagrant violation" of the CFP's agreement not to attack Germans near or in Xiberoan communities (ibid.: 13). Later that morning, Jaureguiberry met with senior CFP officers, who proposed to attack the Germans in Sustary, the only Xiberoan canton still occupied, and to leave the Secret Army in charge of liberated communities. Jaureguiberry angrily rejected their "grotesque plan" and later wrote that the CFP men selected to lead the attack had "become overly excited by alcohol" and "fought over a machine gun" before falling asleep (ibid.).

In retaliation for the CFP ambush, a German airplane bombed Maule on August 12, killing seven local people.[7] During the air strike, Maule citizens rushed into the hills nearby and remained there for several days (M. Joanny

2004: pers. comm.). The ambush and capture of forty-six German soldiers also brought eight hundred Germans from the Spielberg Battalion back to Maule under the command of Captain Racke.[8] On August 14, following a denunciation, a German patrol found and shot three wounded CFP resisters on a farm near Maule, one of whom died. In retaliation the CFP resisters, Lavalou and Bercut, shot the two German prisoners of war in their care.[9]

On August 15 the German battalion leader, Captain Racke, wrote to the Maule notable Dr. Henri Herbille, as president-elect of the Red Cross, asking him to negotiate the immediate release of the German prisoners held by the FFI ("Libération" 1984: 17–18). On their release, the German officer promised to hand over the six resisters he held and to ensure that no reprisals against Xiberoans took place. Racke gave Dr. Herbille and the Resistance twenty-four hours, after which hostages and other retaliatory measures would be taken. With little choice, Herbille fulfilled his duty, as a holder of civic and moral authority, to mediate relations between Xiberoans and the external authorities who endangered them.

Mayor Aguer and Dr. Herbille at once made their way to the resisters' mountain hideout, where they found most members of the Liberation Committee (including the FFI leader, Jaureguiberry; the cantonal head of the Secret Army, Champo; the socialist head of the Maule Secret Army, Hegoburu; and the trade unionist, Lanouguère). The negotiators and resisters then discovered that Lavalou and Bercut had killed the two German officers in their custody—information that had not yet reached Captain Racke. Resistance leaders spent several tense hours with Herbille and the mayor. Both sides understood that the German commander would require the return of his two missing (and now dead) officers. The threat of reprisals weighed heavily upon the consciences of all men involved (M. Joanny 2003: pers. comm.). The Xiberoan FFI leader, Jaureguiberry, rejected Racke's proposal, because he felt obliged to uphold "military law." Dr. Herbille and Mayor Aguer returned to Maule to convey the news to the German commander ("Libération" 1984: 18).

On August 15 the Allies landed in Provence, marking de Gaulle's day of national insurrection. Without any provocation from Xiberoan resisters, the Germans abruptly left Maule. Jubilant and relieved, some citizens declared that the Maule people had liberated themselves. The FFI leader, Jaureguiberry, described the sudden departure of the Spielberg Battalion as "the miracle of Maule" and ascribed it to the evident "dangers" posed by Secret Army resisters. "Thus, by obeying the orders received, by being disciplined and combative in spirit, the Maule company of the Secret Army with its three hundred-strong volunteers, overcame eight hundred far better armed Germans" (Jaureguiberry 1950: 12). One Basque CFP veteran wryly noted, however, that the "miracle" of Maule might have been more accurately described as "the miracle of Saint-Tropez," owing to the Allied landings in Provence (Davant 2001: 178).

The Xiberoan FFI leader ordered his victorious men not to seek revenge against local citizens suspected of collaborating with the Germans. Jaureguiberry appealed to communist resisters, in particular, for calm and discipline. Many of them came from the Navarrese community in Maule; others belonged to a maquis of the communist resistance group FTP and to a group of Guérilleros Espagnols that had been operating in the region since November 1942 (Poullenot 1995: 199).[10] The communists had scores to settle and talked excitedly about the need for purges to root out "undesirables." The FFI had not yet completed its mission, however, for a German garrison still occupied Sustary, the only canton from which the Germans did not depart "spontaneously" (ibid.: 262).

Protected by more than one mile of barricades and barbed wire, 163 well-armed Germans still held Sustary and a nearby hamlet.[11] On August 17 Jaureguiberry met with the CFP battalion leader, as well as Lavalou and Bercut, in the hamlet of Ospitaleku. Jaureguiberry quarreled violently with the CFP men over weapons and ammunition obtained from guards at Gurs who had defected to the Secret Army and forbade the CFP to take part in the liberation of Sustary. On August 18, Secret Army resisters and Guérilleros Espagnols began to surround the town and intercepted parachutes intended for the German garrison. Mme Urruty had already advised Jaureguiberry that the German commander in Sustary, Ressel, "planned to fight to the end" ("Libération" 1984: 20). Rumors circulated in Sustary that the Resistance planned to attack the town, a decision deplored by the Sustary priest, Canon Arricar. In his memoirs, Canon Arricar recalled that "without any authority in the matter, without any mandate, but eager to protect my parish from harm that, with a little patience, could be avoided, I asked the mayor [Dr. Idiart] if I could intervene with the French forces to persuade them that their proposed attack threatened both their own safety as well as that of the local population" (Arricar 1962: c). By August 19 some 300 Secret Army, FTP, and Spanish resisters surrounded Sustary. The mayor and Jaureguiberry both feared that the mayor's close involvement in the Resistance, as well as in the political and personal animosities that divided Sustary, would jeopardize negotiations with the Germans. FFI leader Jaureguiberry thus turned to another traditional source of mediation between community and external authorities: one of the town's priests, Canon Arricar.

Through an intermediary, Jaureguiberry asked Canon Arricar to deliver a letter to Superintendent Ressel. When the priest discovered that no one on duty in the German headquarters spoke French, Canon Arricar sought the assistance of Lieutenant Hammer, who located Ressel and translated the letter for him. In the letter Jaureguiberry advised Ressel that Germans who remained in southern France had been effectively cut off from German troops in the north. He asserted that his FFI forces constituted "an Army, not a maquis or a band of terrorists" ("Libération" 1984: 21). Both Superintendent Ressel and Lieutenant Hammer questioned the legitimacy of the letter, because it had not been signed. Canon Arricar assured them that the author "was a decorated French Army officer widely admired for his high moral standards." Sensing their suspicion, the priest tried to persuade the Germans "that they had been forgotten by their commanding officers." The priest argued that German customs officers, not "true soldiers," held the Sustary garrison. Superintendent Ressel retorted that they were very well armed and would "defend themselves until death." The priest judged Ressel to be "loyal and correct . . . not a 'hard' type," but Ressel remained suspicious about the "honorability" of the letter's author. Canon Arricar debated whether he should reveal Jaureguiberry's identity, given the dangerous circumstances, but did so on condition that Ressel swore on his honor not to tell anyone else and to treat Jaureguiberry "correctly, as an officer" if the Germans ever captured him. Ressel promised, and the two men shook hands. As he was about to depart, Canon Arricar discovered that he had lost a button from his cuff. The Basque priest and the German officer searched for it unsuccessfully (Arricar 1962: C). The interlude befitted the oddity of German-Basque relations during the occupation of Sustary. On the next day, Ressel rejected Jaureguiberry's terms of surrender.

On August 21, German customs officers abandoned their headquarters in Oloron and headed for Spain through Urdos and other borderland communes. Citizens and FFI members arrested thirty known collaborators and Milice sympathizers in that town.[12] On the same day, Secret Army resisters and Guérilleros Espagnols ambushed a German convoy with fifty troops in the Xiberoan commune of Montory. Five Germans were wounded and one Guérillero Espagnol, Julio Lopez, died accidentally when a grenade exploded in his hand. Superintendent Ressel's doubts about the feasibility of an honorable surrender deepened in the face of such "terrorists" ("Libération" 1984: 22). On the following day, Ressel delivered the missing button to Canon Arricar at the presbytery, and the two men spoke briefly about Jaureguiberry's "deep regret" over Ressel's decision not to surrender. The German commander declared in halting French that he would "protect Sustary from the communists," who had recently stolen weapons from the Secret Army in Pau. The boundaries of the moral community had, once again, become blurred. An outsider and potential source of harm (Ressel) offered to defend insiders from another potential source of harm that was both external and internal to Xiberoa: the communists. The Sustary priest replied that "the French [would] handle the threat of communism themselves" (Arricar 1962: C).

Meanwhile, the Secret Army liaison agent, Mme Urruty, pursued her own diplomatic mission with Ressel, who had lived in her house since early 1943. According to Jaureguiberry, Ressel finally agreed to negotiate with him "due to the tenacity and intelligence of Mme Urruty." During prolonged and tense negotiations between Jaureguiberry and Ressel on the night of August 22, two of Sustary's three remaining Gestapo agents disappeared ("Libération" 1984: 22). In the terms and conditions of surrender, Jaureguiberry promised Ressel that the Xiberoan FFI would protect the occupiers from harm and safely transport them to the nearby camp at Gurs; that it would ensure the Germans' rights as prisoners of war would be upheld; that German officers would remain in their lodgings, if their Sustary hosts agreed, until Jaureguiberry arranged for their transportation to Gurs; and that Superintendent Ressel could keep his own revolver as a sign of trust, but all other German weapons and ammunition would have to be relinquished. Ressel surrendered to Jaureguiberry on August 23.

While Jaureguiberry dealt with the German surrender, the postmaster of Sustary, widely known as a collaborator, attracted a crowd of citizens in the main square. The postmaster "violently criticized" the manner in which Jaureguiberry had conducted negotiations with the occupiers. A group of "bellicose" communist resisters then added to the unrest by calling for summary executions of German prisoners. That evening, Superintendent Ressel asked Jaureguiberry if he still hoped to be able to maintain order in the town and, once persuaded, ordered the German troops to disarm. On August 24 "all the church bells in Xiberoa rang out" at noon to celebrate the liberation of Xiberoan territory from German occupation. By nightfall, however, many Sustary citizens became anxious when a group of resisters asked Jaureguiberry "if the time had come to execute the Plan, about which everyone had heard but about which no one knew anything for certain." According to public rumor, the plan had been devised by resisters who did not belong to Sustary; it called for the arrest of certain Sustary citizens, the creation of a popular tribunal, and summary executions. Jaureguiberry insisted that neither he nor the other FFI men had any right to administer justice ("Libération" 1984: 24). When some resisters arrested the alleged collaborator, Mme Etxart, Jaureguiberry released her and angrily reminded people that responsibility for such matters rested with the Departmental Liberation Committee. The FFI leader called for calm and discipline in the town as people gathered to celebrate (M. Joanny 2004: pers. comm.).

The FFI took charge of the camp at Gurs and prepared barracks for 250 German prisoners of war captured in the Maule area.[13] The rest of the camp came under civilian control and soon held some 3,000 additional prisoners, half of whom were suspected collaborators whose arrival aroused considerable curiosity in the community (AMCB 1995: 152). The other half was made up, once again, of Spanish Republicans, arrested by the FFI as "preventive internees" in an attempt to stop the guerrilla warfare still being waged by bands of Spanish communist resisters along the frontier (Laharie 1993: 261–62). During the night of August 29, Jaureguiberry accompanied a convoy of nearly 200 German POWs to Gurs. Heavily guarded, the convoy traveled by night and avoided Maule, where communist resisters still called for revenge against the Germans. In Jaureguiberry's absence, a twenty-four-year-old man and two teenaged brothers ignored local and regional FFI orders not to carry out acts of reprisal against suspected collaborators in Sustary.

The young men committed an act of violence performed on some twenty thousand women in France between 1943 and early 1946 (Burrin 1995: 213; Diamond 1999: 135–36; Virgili 2002: 1): they shaved Mme Etxart's head, as well as the heads of two other women who happened to be in town that day and who had had German lovers. Only a small crowd witnessed the head shavings (G. Harriguileheguy 1977: pers. comm.). Jaureguiberry was furious that FFI orders had been breached and that no one had stopped the young men. He jailed the eldest man for one month and sharply admonished the two boys for their disrespectful behavior. Only one other instance of head shaving (*la tonte*) occurred in Xiberoa: the May 1943 hair-cutting incident in Maule involving youths whose own heads were shaved by German soldiers seeking revenge.

Some male resisters applauded the Sustary head shavings as a "just punishment" of women who had slept with Germans (P. Béguerie n.d.: 12). For many men and women, however, *la tonte* violated Xiberoan moral codes relating to men's respect for women (A. Carricart 1977: pers. comm.; A. Jonnet 2003: pers. comm.; M.-L. Lascombes 1977: pers. comm.). In Xiberoa the ritualized practice of *la jonchée* provided an anonymous, nonviolent alternative to the "ugly carnival" of female head shaving (Brossat 1992; Virgili 2002: 231). The spreading of greenery and the appearance of small coffins on doorsteps symbolized the grave disapproval of one or more members of the moral community and served not as a punishment, but as a pointed and usually effective warning to traitors who had collaborated with the Germans.

From late August through October 1944, Inspector Carbou observed joy, anxiety, and confusion among Xiberoans, who hoped that a new government would be formed as quickly as possible. Most people wanted the disparate elements of the Resistance to be mobilized into one national army. Conservative citizens feared the communists in their midst, as well as the military and numerical strength of Spanish Republicans who had gathered along the international boundary and eagerly awaited an opportunity to continue their armed struggle against Franco. Farmers and shepherds feared that they would be abandoned by the new government, while workers in Maule firmly believed that the plight of the "proletarian class would be improved."[14] During September, a group of Guérilleros Espagnols regularly crossed and recrossed the Xiberoan-Navarrese border at Larraiña, and in late October 1944, five hundred Guérilleros passed noisily through Urdos, en route to Maule, along the road taken by so many young "Swallows" from Aragón and Nafarroa during the late nineteenth and early twentieth centuries.[15] In nearby Oloron, exiled Spanish Republicans formed a Committee of National Unity (Comité d'Unité Nationale) that attracted more than a thousand supporters.[16]

By mid-September 1944, young *maquisards* assigned to Gurs began to complain about inactivity and boredom. Most of them realized that "they would not be sent to the front without military training" and that the "combat" in which they had participated in Xiberoa "bore no relation to the combat seen by a regular army." Hoping to capitalize on the youths' new spirit of patriotism, certain communist resisters from the FTP tried to draw the young Xiberoans into their groups by promising them military action.[17] In the first months of liberation, rural Xiberoans and their Béarnais neighbors also feared the CFP resisters posted to their communities by the FFI. In mid-September CFP resisters caused three civilian deaths by shooting weapons randomly in Xiberoan villages. One hundred CFP resisters guarded the borderland Béarnais commune adjacent to Urdos. The local population warmly welcomed the resisters' departure at the end of September, following CFP requisitions of food and wine and the three fatal accidents caused by young, inexperienced CFP recruits who did not know how to handle weapons properly.[18] Published accounts of the CFP's role in the Resistance in southwest France omit such incidents (Céroni 1980; Lormier 1990). At the end of September, when the CFP was assigned to the first armored division of the French Army, its men were given a choice. Those who "wished to end the war in Germany" committed themselves contractually to the army when the CFP was reorganized as an infantry regiment; the others went home (Lormier 1990: 103). Lavalou, Bercut, and some members of their Xiberoan company continued the war in Germany (M. Béguerie 2004: pers. comm.; Lormier 1990: 104–30).

In Maule many workers firmly believed that the Liberation would quickly improve their socioeconomic situation. Militant communists and anarchists briefly occupied a sandal factory until gendarmes removed them (R. Pérez 2004: pers. comm.). The factory owners quietly followed local, regional, and national events with intense interest. By November townspeople finally began to see some improvements in food distribution, promised by the authorities in August. Milk and wine became available, but pigs were scarce and the Maule factories operated only three days a week. In the countryside, Xiberoans felt "unhappy and abandoned" by the new government, which fixed prices on wheat, corn, and haricot beans, which had not been raised since 1942. Rural Xiberoans realized that an era of black-market prosperity had ended. The public, recognizing that most farmers had dealt in the black market on a small scale, sought justice only in relation to large-scale profiteers. Anxieties among rural Basques deepened when police arrested several farmers who had been notorious black marketers. Farmers and their families also fretted about the rural exodus that had begun after the Liberation. Many Xiberoans chose to leave their farms "rather than relive the economic hardships that characterized their way of life before the rural black market economy developed."[19]

In November 1944 the Communist Party convened a meeting in Maule, and its members began to distribute leaflets and an article from *Étincelle* that accused certain gendarmes in Maule of having hindered the Resistance. Founded by the Communist Party, a military and political resistance movement, the National Front, opened an office in the town. Soon thereafter, a few young CFP resisters returned to their homes after having been detained by the FFI for refusing to participate in an attack against Germans during the last week of the Occupation. In self-defense the youths blamed the FFI for having given them insufficient weapons and ammunition "to ensure their success and safety." Many townspeople dismissed the youths' assertions as exaggerations, but the matter nevertheless exacerbated local animosities between rival resisters and their supporters. According to a sub-lieutenant in the Maule gendarmerie, local people seemed to have forgotten that the Liberation of France had not yet been completed. He found them "absorbed by their personal interests, local quarrels and intra-community animosities. Factions have once again formed along old, familiar lines," concerned with differences in socioeconomic class, religion, and ethnicity. Politics, he observed, was only one of several factors that divided Maule citizens during the process of liberation.[20]

During 1944–45, the French government and local communities engaged in continual dialogue over the meaning and construction of justice. At its first meeting (August 28, 1944), the Departmental Liberation Committee of the Basses-Pyrénées gave priority to the identification of those who belonged to the Milice and the collaborationist organization Groupe Collaboration. The committee created a Purges Commission (Commission d'Épuration et de la Justice) to identify people who had voluntarily assisted the German authorities or had opposed or hindered the Resistance. The Purges Commission relied heavily upon local liberation committees for information about suspected collaborators. Between August 22, 1944, and June 30, 1946, the commission compiled 2,700 dossiers (0.65 percent of the total population of 415,000) (Poullenot 1995: 272–73, 277).

In September and October 1944, public opinion was divided over the speed and means by which the authorities identified collaborators and collaborationists, including members of the Milice. Some Xiberoans complained that the purge (*épuration*) progressed far too slowly and had allowed known traitors and members of collaborationist groups to escape into Spain. Other citizens insisted that proper judiciary structures needed to be in place.[21]

In Maule the schoolteacher and Secret Army officer, Jean-Pierre Champo, headed the local liberation committee, which was dominated by socialists and communists and included numerous factory workers. Champo also represented the arrondissement of Maule on the Departmental Liberation Committee. Champo and many workers belonged to the socialist party, the SFIO (Section Française de l'Internationale Ouvrière) and had long regarded the mayor of Maule, Arnaud Aguer, and Dr. Henri Herbille as their adversaries. When the mayor and Herbille appeared on a local list of suspected collaborators, the Xiberoan FFI leader, Jaureguiberry, strongly encouraged clemency, in keeping with directives from the new prefect and de Gaulle's pronouncements about the need to forgive and forget (Novick 1968: 157; Poullenot 1995: 272). Champo was a committed Gaullist who greatly respected Jaureguiberry as a leader. Using a strategy not unlike that of Herbille during local campaigns against communists in 1939–42, Jaureguiberry argued that clemency would prevent a deeply divided community from further tearing itself apart. In spite of their political differences, Champo, Jaureguiberry, and Herbille shared a fundamental desire to protect their province and community from harm. Neither Herbille nor the mayor appeared on the list of suspected collaborators sent to the Purges Commission (Commission d'Épuration et de la Justice), which passed information about collaboration to the Court of Civic Justice in Pau.

On September 9, 1944, the Purges Commission arrested Mme Etxart at her home in Sustary on charges of denunciation and "amicable, commercial and intimate relations" with the enemy. She spent nine months in an internment camp while investigations took place.[22] Her brother, Johanne, wrote to the departmental police commissioner, claiming that his family was "the victim of local political machinations conceived by a member of the Purges Commission." In the absence of his sister's POW husband, Harbustan felt duty bound to defend Mme Etxart from "accusations that emanated not from Public Rumor, but from rumor created and manipulated by a minority" in Sustary.[23] In a letter to the Purges Commission, Harbustan denied that his sister had dealt in the black market, had committed adultery, or had denounced anyone. He outlined her efforts to aid the Resistance.[24] Harbustan also asked seven Sustary citizens to write testimonials on his sister's behalf. He turned to a political enemy, the socialist butcher who had belonged to the Gaullist Secret Army. In February 1945 the butcher testified that Mme Etxart "knew our group existed but did not denounce us. . . . She came to my house four or five times with provisions for the men. She preferred giving the supplies to me, rather than to the leader of the local resistance group, Duclos, because of what he did to her."[25] As Vichy's regional economic controller, Duclos was responsible for the arrest of Mme Etxart in July 1943. Harbustan's mother's sister's husband also wrote to the Purges Commission to complain that the post-Liberation roundup in Sustary had been "a one way street" that allowed certain notorious collaborators "to live in peace and freedom," while his niece found herself under arrest as "a defenseless victim of denunciation whose husband was still a prisoner of war."[26]

During the next few months, the Purges Commission received testimonies from forty people who had been directly involved in the web of denunciations and rumors in which Mme Etxart figured so prominently. The witnesses included the German POWs, Ressel, and Hammer. In separate interviews, Hammer variously accused his former friend of multiple oral denunciations "in public" and then denied that she had ever betrayed anyone. When asked about Mme Etxart's propensity for denunciations, Ressel told the authorities to "ask Hammer."[27] Several townspeople expressed a reluctance or inability to identify Mme Etxart as their denunciator, although they all suspected she was directly responsible or at least closely involved in their betrayals. In two cases individuals feared reprisal from the powerful Harbustan family. In another instance a female relative refrained from denouncing her mother's denouncer because she felt that the town had already done enough damage to itself. Although evidence provided by the Sabalots supported the prosecution's case, Mme Sabalot said she did not know who had denounced her to the Gestapo. The two aunts of Mme Etxart who had been arrested for hiding fugitives "could not be sure" about the identity of their denouncer, although they suspected their niece. The resister/Vichy controller,

Duclos, had little to say: "I knew [Mme Etxart] sold food illegally to the Germans, but I never asked that woman for food for my men. I can't say anything about the alleged denunciations. I knew she was on very good terms with the Germans."[28]

Only the Urrutys, M. Sabalot, the mayor (Dr. Idiart), and an FFI officer produced testimonies that unequivocally held Mme Etxart responsible for providing denunciations and intelligence to the enemy. In her own brief defense, Mme Etxart denied all charges against her but admitted to "hostile feelings" toward the Urrutys, the Sabalots, and the mayor and to selling cigarettes to the Germans. She described ways in which she had helped resisters.[29] During the interrogations leading up to the trial of Mme Etxart, several of her long-standing adversaries felt unable to accuse her of betrayal. When confronted with external judgment by outsiders who represented the French state, some Sustary citizens preferred to remain silent about shameful matters that their moral community had failed to prevent or control. Many other Xiberoan Basques made the same decision when the process of "denouncing the denouncers" (l'anti-délation) took place during 1944–45. Their widespread reluctance to testify against members of their own moral community may explain, in part, the extremely low incidence of collaboration-related crimes by Xiberoans brought before the courts.[30]

In October 1944 the president of the Purges Commission reflected on the cultural milieu in which Mme Etxart lived. He had prosecuted her in 1943 for possessing firearms and, although an outsider, he knew a great deal about Sustary, "a prototypical village in which all quarrels—especially political ones—readily transformed themselves into implacable hatred . . . a village in which the worst possible accusations circulated through rumor and gossip." He described Mme Etxart as a

> young and pretty woman whose extremely independent ways and inconsiderate prattle gave rise to malevolence among more austere citizens. She earned a reputation for frivolity and thoughtlessness that was no doubt undeserved or exaggerated, but which all the same gave rise to controversy. Her parents were very stern and welcomed my attempts to set their daughter straight in the summer of 1943. Mme Etxart continued to behave like a spoiled child. In the lengthy sessions I had with her, I still had the impression that she was very capable of saying stupid things, but not of committing villainous acts, such as denunciation.[31]

Led by Johanne Harbustan, a group of Sustary citizens launched a public campaign against Mme Urruty in late 1944. In response the mayor and Jaureguiberry issued a detailed account of the former agent's resistance activities.

They challenged her critics to "check the facts" and to compare their own contributions to the resistance with those of Mme Urruty. They dared Sustary citizens to accuse her of collaboration (Jaureguy 1944). The document did not mention her trips to see the Gestapo in Agen. Harbustan, among others, openly asked why Mme Urruty's dossier with the departmental Purges Commission had never been opened (Mme Harriguileheguy 1977: pers. comm.). In May 1945 the Court of Justice for the Basses-Pyrénées found Mme Etxart guilty of giving intelligence to the enemy and sentenced her to two years in prison with national degradation.[32] Between November 1944 and June 1948, the Chambre Civique of the Basses-Pyrénées heard 567 cases and found 272 people guilty of "reprehensible actions." The court acquitted a further 126 people (Poullenot 1995: 277).

On the second anniversary of Sustary's liberation, a regional leader of the Secret Army (Colonel Boudoube) and senior FFI officers from the Basses-Pyrénées joined the Xiberoan Secret Army for a Mass and ceremony at the war memorial to commemorate "martyred resisters" and to honor four "authentic resisters": Clement de Jaureguiberry (commander of the Secret Army, Sector IV), Mme Urruty, and two other male Xiberoans, all of whom received the Croix de Guerre. Jaureguiberry and the Maule Secret Army leader, Hegoburu, received Resistance medals. The mayor of Sustary, Dr. Idiart, praised "the forces of the Resistance" for having "judiciously forced one hundred sixty Germans to surrender" with little loss of life. Colonel Boudoube, Jaureguiberry, and Hegoburu called upon all members of the Secret Army "to regroup without delay" and "rise up against certain organizations that, in the name of the Resistance," were distributing resistance cards to "undeserving individuals, to persons sentenced to prison and national indignity for acts of collaboration." They called for an immediate inquiry "into a scandal that brought dishonor to the Resistance" and for the immediate public identification of the "imposters."[33] The ceremony and speeches outraged the Harbustan family and their supporters. One of them insisted that Mme Urruty had "done more harm than good to the citizens" of Sustary.[34] The incident set the stage for other contested judgments about "authentic resistance" during the process of liberating Xiberoa; it also marked the beginning of commemorations that exacerbated and perpetuated long-standing divisions in both Sustary and Maule.

12: Uneasy Commemorations

Two days after the liberation of Xiberoa, Charles de Gaulle proclaimed that Paris had been "liberated by its own efforts, liberated by its people with the help of the armies of France, with the help of the whole of France, of fighting France, of the one and true France, of eternal France!" The Gaullist myth of the Resistance maintained that most French people had behaved well during the Occupation, that the Resistance had been "pure and heroic," and that "the French had liberated themselves by their own efforts" (Gildea 2002: 377). The Gaullist version of the Liberation made only passing reference to the role of the Allies. Although the resistance myth aimed to achieve consensus, rival versions of what happened during the Occupation sprang up across France and divided the French, as well as the Basques of Xiberoa. The towns of Maule and Sustary once again provide a microcosmic view of local efforts to establish a "true version" of history that gave legitimacy to those responsible for organizing and leading the resistance. As happened across France, rival resisters created competing versions of events in the summer of 1944, in pamphlets and in commemorative acts, with different heroes and different villains (ibid.: 378).

Group memories are formed through social practices and social acts. Commemoration is itself a social practice that entails remembering and memorializing past events in public as members of a group (Farmer 1999: 3); it has the power to unite and to divide people. In Xiberoa dissenting memories of resistance and occupation can be traced in part to the political battlefield of Maule in the aftermath of the liberation. As municipal, cantonal, and general elections approached in 1945, the battle lines were drawn between resistance leaders and their communities in many parts of postwar France (ibid.: 38; Koreman 1999: 227–57). Conservative French citizens were often indebted to local notables who had protected their best interests during the Occupation (Gildea 2002: 354–55). In April and May of 1945, municipal elections tested the depth and extent of that gratitude. In Maule socialists drew up an electoral list that campaigned under the banner of the Resistance and republican legitimacy. The list included two prominent figures in the Maule branch of the Secret Army: the schoolteacher and Maule representative on the Departmental Liberation Committee, Jean-Pierre Champo; and the former sandal maker of Navarrese descent, St. Jean Lanouguère. The list also included a Maule factory owner who (unusually) belonged to the socialist party (SFIO) and a communist of Spanish descent. The opposing list consisted primarily of patrons who had studiously avoided anything to do with the Resistance and two former CFP resisters who had been recruited by Pierre Béguerie. The socialists dominated the list in the first and second rounds, and Maule became a stronghold for the SFIO. Champo became mayor; the socialist patron and Lanouguère became his first and second deputies in the town hall.[1] The election results broke the long-standing political hegemony of notables and the traditional Right in Maule and inverted the local power structure.

A similar shift from Right to Left occurred in many villages across Xiberoa. In the mountains of Upper Xiberoa, Urdos citizens "showed little fidelity toward the Right" and elected an entirely left-wing municipal council. Sustary remained a socialist stronghold under the leadership of Dr. Idiart. In the hamlet of Ospitaleku, political diversity characterized the municipal council, but most citizens supported a moderate brand of republicanism. The right-wing URD (Union Républicaine Démocratique) remained a dominant force only in the borderland commune of Larraiña, with six hundred inhabitants, and in a hamlet near Maule.[2]

In November 1948 Maule became the only town in southwestern France to receive a citation from the French Republic for "having liberated itself." According to the citation:

> [Maule was a] particularly resistant town throughout the Occupation. In its struggle against the enemy, Maule carefully and cautiously prepared its own citizens for the national insurrection. Led by their dutiful and competent commanders, the men of the Resistance harassed the enemy and engaged in combat at the very gates of the town where their families lived. After having seized numerous prisoners, weapons and supplies, the Maule people liberated themselves on August 10th and 11th 1944. Due to the intelligence and initiative of their local leaders, Maule citizens intimidated the enemy, yet also prevented reprisals against the civilian population. The resisters of Maule then went on to take part in the siege and liberation of a neighboring community where they took nearly two hundred more prisoners. The small Basque town has served the *patrie* well. The citation permits the conferment of the War Cross for the 1939–1945 war, with a bronze star. Paris, 11 November 1948.[3]

Perfectly in keeping with the Gaullist myth of the Resistance, the citation was signed by the secretary of state for the armed forces, Max Lejeune. The text immediately gave rise to a local myth of the Resistance in which the heroes all belonged to the Secret Army and the villains were either uncontrollable communists or dangerous CFP resisters. The text ignored the fact that the CFP-led attack "at the very gates of the town where [resisters'] families lived" was regarded as "a flagrant violation" of the Secret Army/CFP agreement not to engage the enemy in combat in or near Xiberoan communities. In keeping with de Gaulle's own failure to give the Allies much credit for the Liberation, the text makes no mention of the Allied landings in Provence, which provoked the abrupt departure of Germans from Maule on August 15.

In 1984 the local Liberation Committee of Sustary published a pamphlet, "Libération de la Soule." In the foreword, the committee maintained that Sustary was the only town in southwestern France that resisters "actively liberated." By contrast Pau, Baiona, Oloron, and Maule "were evacuated by the occupying troops, and when the local population realized that the Germans had gone, they celebrated their deliverance" ("Libération" 1984: 3). The pamphlet reproduced the military journal of the Xiberoan Secret Army, a day-by-day account of events in Xiberoa from June 4 until September 1, 1944, written by Jaureguiberry. The foreword stressed that the Xiberoan Secret Army consisted of local people, led by "men born in the province" whose sole mission was to liberate Xiberoa without harming civilians or their property. The pamphlet maintained that the CFP leaders "did not have the same concerns" about protecting Xiberoa and its people; they were "strangers to the *pays*" who would have subjected "beautiful Xiberoa to destruction and bloodshed if certain tenacious Maule citizens had not joined the movement. Providence protected Maule and Sustary from irreparable harm" and prevented "catastrophes of incalculable proportions. . . . It is time for the truth to become known by everyone. There are responsibilities to establish and myths to destroy. . . . Certain judgments will seem less harsh, certain appreciations will appear less severe if one bears in mind that this military journal was written by someone who understood and was constantly troubled by the gravity of the situation" ("Libération" 1984: 4).

The author of the pamphlet, Clement de Jaureguiberry, drew upon the long-standing, deep-seated commitment of native Xiberoans (insiders) to protecting their houses, communities, and territory from external harm. That commitment had its roots in sixteenth-century customary law and moral codes of practice. The FFI leader also emphasized the fundamental distinction between insiders and outsiders. Insiders belonged to an imaginary, unified Xiberoan moral community; they shared a habitus. By contrast, outsiders were "strangers" to that sociophysical space who had no appreciation of what that space meant to the local population. Xiberoa was not merely a geographical place but a lived environment in which people shared certain values and expectations about correct behavior and were subjected to the sanctions of legal and popular justice (Thompson 1991: 102). Jaureguiberry saw himself as a key holder not simply of military authority, but also of civic and moral authority. Only an insider could properly appreciate, intellectually and emotionally, the grave dangers posed by those "strangers to the *pays*" who commanded the rival resistance group, the CFP. As insiders, the "tenacious Maule citizens" who joined the Xiberoan CFP (its cofounders, Pierre Béguerie and fellow notable, Jean Jancène) had the ability to control those "strangers" until denunciations and lack of support from the CFP regional commander led to their resignations. Although Béguerie's resignation, in particular, placed CFP control in the hands of two strangers intent upon harming the Germans without much regard for civilians' safety, Jaureguiberry did not publicly judge his fellow Xiberoan harshly. Jaureguiberry merely acknowledged Béguerie's valiant efforts to "go against the insane orders of his [CFP] leaders" ("Libération" 1984: 7).

The pamphlet reported that the liberation of Xiberoa had occurred with "none of the bacchanalia that so rapidly leads to bloodshed, with no violence or plundering." No mention was made of head shavings, the public tirades against the Resistance launched by the postmaster of Sustary, or the clamor caused by angry communists when Jaureguiberry took their weapons away. In one final criticism of the CFP, the pamphlet noted that "numerous CFP detachments invaded Xiberoa" after its liberation and "pretended to occupy the frontier and main towns." Their actions "gave rise to inquietude about the true intentions of the CFP, whose hostility to the FFI had decreased somewhat. Luckily, no serious incident marked their inopportune presence in Xiberoa. Thanks to the spoils of war seized in Sustary, the Secret Army remained much more powerful [than the CFP]" ("Libération" 1984: 19). An official version of the CFP's role in the liberation of Xiberoa was not written until 1964.

The Secret Army pamphlet began with an entry that identified Béguerie as *chef local* of the CFP and Jaureguiberry as *chef local* of the Secret Army. Those first lines infuriated a fellow Secret Army resister from Sustary, Captain Borgès, who had been approached by the regional head of the Secret Army, Paul Boudoube, in August 1943 to organize disparate groups of resisters in Upper Xiberoa into Secret Army maquis. When that failed to happen quickly enough, Boudoube assigned the task of coordinating and leading the Secret Army of Xiberoa to Clement de Jaureguiberry (Poullenot 1995: 188–89). Borgès was assigned to the Sustary Secret Army unit, along with Mme Urruty. In January 1946, soon after the pamphlet appeared, a resister (code named Johanne) sent an irate letter to the *Républicain du Sud Ouest* in Baiona "to reestablish the truth about the Secret Army" in Xiberoa, which "was organized and led by Captain Borgès from start to finish." The letter identified one of Borgès's deputies as Brigadier General Bertschi, who was briefly involved in the web of denunciations and confidences created by Mme Etxart in Sustary. The other deputy was Jean de Jaureguiberry, brother of Clement. The document also listed the names of Borgès's Sustary unit, including the postmaster who had given Jaureguiberry so much trouble in the immediate aftermath of Sustary's liberation and who was arrested and accused of collaboration in November 1944.[4] The letter claimed that Borgès had gone into hiding following a denunciation on June 6, 1944, but continued to lead the Xiberoan Secret Army through the town crier in Sustary, who visited Borgès once a week until the Liberation. The letter maintained that Jean de Jaureguiberry (not Clement) met with Béguerie on June 4 to discuss Xiberoan resistance but failed to tell his "true leader" (Borgès) about the meeting. The letter accused Clement de Jaureguiberry of "illegitimately claiming to be head of the Xiberoan Secret Army" and of "disloyalty to his true leader [Borgès]." The letter was also sent to the editor of the Maule newspaper, *Le Miroir de la Soule,* which declined to publish it.[5] The battle for the truth was thus not confined to the arena of rival resistance movements.

In the decades that followed, the socialists and communists in Maule continued to press for improved remuneration and working conditions in the sandal factories and to engage in heated disputes with Maule factory owners. Jean-Pierre Champo served as mayor of Maule until 1971, alongside a predominantly socialist municipal council (J. Lougarot 2003: pers. comm.). Dr. Herbille remained out of the limelight and avoided involvement in the town's political squabbles and industrial disputes. The 1950s brought further bitter strikes between militant left-wing workers and factory owners, with one strike lasting forty-five days (Ikherzaleak 1994: 78). Strike leaders once again asserted the legitimacy of their revolt against the *patrons,* who battled with them over issues of pay and benefits (R. Pérez 2004: pers. comm.). In Maule industrial strikes continued to be a form of resistance in themselves, as workers struggled to improve their socioeconomic position in a society that was becoming more and more egalitarian.[6]

In the 1950s people spoke about "the miracle of Xiberoa's liberation"; the boundaries of the imagined miracle had been extended to the entire province. In commemorative speeches and newspaper articles about the Liberation, Secret Army veterans still applauded the restoration of order by the Resistance "without loss of French lives, without destruction of Xiberoan property." Veterans made no mention of the numerous farmhouses burned by German patrols in Ospitaleku and other rural communities, of the Ospitaleku deportees and the Barkoxe people who had lost their lives. In a commemorative speech on November 12, 1950, Clement de Jaureguiberry reiterated that the "purely military mission of the Secret Army was to maintain order, without political action; that the struggle against the Germans always took place far from local communities and isolated farmhouses to avoid reprisals against civilians." He accused "warlike strangers in the region" of having "used the word civilian with wanton contempt," whereas "members of the Secret Army understood the term to mean their families, their friends." In recounting the liberation of Maule, Jaureguiberry made no mention of the CFP or the chaos and random gunfire on August 10 and 11. He recalled that the forces of the Resistance "were absolute masters of the town for three days" and that "everything was in order. There were no quarrels. . . . Through its discipline, its combative spirit, the Maule company of the Secret Army—300 Maule men—imposed their will upon 800 infinitely better armed Germans." Jaureguiberry then paid special tribute to the sandal maker of Navarrese descent, Jean-Pierre Hegoburu, who had "recruited, armed and commanded those men" ("Libération" 1984: 27–28). Nearly all of the Maule Secret Army men were at their mountain hideout when the German battalion abruptly left Xiberoa on August 16, following the Allied landings in Provence. Jaureguiberry made his speech in 1950, at the inauguration of a stele erected in honor of the Guérillero Espagnol from Huesca, Julio Lopez, who had died near the village of Montory on August 21, 1944, during a skirmish and was buried in the Montory cemetery. The stele marked the first use of commemorative space by the Xiberoan Secret Army veterans' group, the Amicale des Anciens de la Résistance du Secteur IV.

In the skirmish near Montory, some forty resisters had immobilized a convoy of fifty Germans and prevented their attempt to reinforce the Sustary garrison. When combat ceased, the Germans removed their wounded men. Contrary to orders from the Secret Army maquis leader, the Guérillero Espagnol tried to throw a grenade into a German vehicle and accidentally killed himself.[7] No Xiberoan Secret Army resister was killed during the Occupation. In spite of the fact that Julio Lopez had disobeyed orders and was a "stranger" to Xiberoa, the Spanish resister nevertheless provided a focus for a commemorative monument in a space associated solely with the Secret Army. Located on a roadside embankment, that space gave the veterans a place of remembrance (*lieu du souvenir*), where they continue to meet every August to pay homage to Lopez by laying a small bouquet of flowers beside the stele. The ceremony is nonreligious; it serves as a group tribute to a fallen comrade and, most importantly, as a physical focus for a group memory that has gradually formed over the decades as veterans exchanged individual memories through social interactions (see Cappelletto 2003: 9). The Secret Army pamphlet written by Jaureguiberry established a narrative convention that has shaped veterans' and supporters' group memory of events in 1944 for the past sixty-three years. The pamphlet's narrative represented the good, heroic, and responsible resisters as insiders to Xiberoa and members of the Secret Army. The Other resisters, the CFP, represented endangerment to the *pays* as irresponsible, arrogant resisters who cared nothing for the well-being of local civilians, their property, or their community.

Earlier that summer, on June 27, 1950, General Pommiès, Pierre Béguerie, and other members of the Xiberoan CFP established their own *lieu du souvenir* in Ospitaleku, the site of the massive German raid on villagers who had briefly sheltered CFP resisters in June 1944. After Mass in the tiny medieval church, Pommiès unveiled a plaque commemorating the citizens who had been deported to Nazi camps and died there. The plaque was placed on the external wall of the church, where Germans had lined up citizens believed to have supported the Resistance. During the ceremony, Pierre Béguerie spoke at length of his lingering, deep-seated guilt and grief for those who had perished on account of his maquis' brief presence in Ospitaleku and asked for the forgiveness of their families, friends, and neighbors (M. Béguerie 2004: pers. comm.). General Pommiès, Xiberoan CFP resisters, the Ospitaleku mayor, and the priest then shared a meal with the Ospitaleku innkeepers, the Lasserres. As the sole survivors of Nazi concentration camps, Mme Lasserre and her daughter, Mme Marie-Louise Lasserre Davancens, were the CFP's guests of honor. (The plaque and CFP plans to hold annual commemorations in Ospitaleku spurred their Secret Army rivals to create their own *lieu du souvenir* in Montory.)

Both CFP and Secret Army commemorations at their respective "places of remembrance" had a unifying effect on each group of veteran resisters and their supporters (M. Béguerie, M. Joanny 2004: pers. comms.). The divisive potential of commemoration came into play in the public sphere of municipal efforts to selectively remember past events that still form a dynamic part of the present. The twentieth anniversary of Xiberoa's liberation became a battleground for competing versions of what happened during the summer of 1944.

Although the French government delivered the Croix de Guerre to Maule in 1948, the town did not celebrate its receipt until August 1964. The socialist mayor (former Secret Army resister) Jean-Pierre Champo rekindled old animosities between Secret Army and CFP veterans when he organized commemorative events to mark Maule's liberation of itself. When issuing invitations to the ceremony, Champo included all surviving men of the Xiberoan Secret Army, as well as a Secret Army company from Béarn; but Champo invited only Pierre Béguerie from the CFP, which incensed its veterans and General Pommiès. Béguerie wrote to Mayor Champo three days before the ceremony to accept his invitation "with pleasure," but he also reminded Champo of a recent conversation in which Béguerie had urged Champo not to forget the sacrifices of all those who had actively taken part in the Resistance in Xiberoa. He reminded Champo that the Xiberoan CFP had taken part in numerous dangerous missions during 1943–44 and had "abandoned their families and their jobs to accomplish their military mission" in Xiberoa. Béguerie deeply regretted that Champo had "forgotten the brave men of the CFP." He lamented that Champo's "well-known desire for equity and justice" had not moved him to reserve a space at the ceremony for CFP resisters "who had done their duty, without any recompense, to help liberate" Xiberoa.[8]

On August 30, 1964, General Sarrazac, military commander of the Basses-Pyrénées, presented the Croix de Guerre to Champo and a municipal councilor whose father was of Navarrese descent and had died in a Nazi concentration camp. During speeches by Champo and Jaureguiberry, the Secret Army version of events dominated the process of public remembering. In the aftermath of celebrations, both CFP veterans and communist veterans of the FTP complained to the mayor and the local press about the "incomplete" and "unjust" representation of liberation given by Secret Army veterans during the commemorative events (J. Jaureguiberry 2005: pers. comm.).

In early August 1964, General Pommiès asked a Xiberoan CFP resister, Maurice Malharin, to write a history of his resistance group in Xiberoa. Pommiès wanted to present the document to the mayor of Maule before the town received the Croix de Guerre, so that Mayor Champo would fully appreciate the contribution made by the CFP to Maule's liberation. Held the day after Maule's receipt of the War Cross, commemorative events in Pau featured the CFP's contribution to that city's liberation. Both Pommiès and Champo participated in the ceremony, after which a lively discussion between them ensued. General Pommiès confronted Champo about his decision to exclude the CFP from Maule's festivities. Champo argued that "receiving the Croix de Guerre was an event solely for Maule people" and that he had thus invited only Maule Resistance leaders. Pommiès questioned the inclusion of the Béarnais Secret Army maquis, to which Champo reportedly responded with a series of expletives. When asked why Champo had excluded Lavalou, "the Maule CFP *chef*," Champo retorted that Lavalou did not reside in Maule in August 1944. Lavalou was not a "here person" (*hebenkua*), not an insider to the moral community. When asked why Bercut had not been invited, for he did live in the town at that time, Champo pointed to Bercut's violent, reckless actions as a resister and said "his presence would not have been welcomed." Pommiès castigated Champo for his complete lack of gratitude to the CFP for its role in liberating Maule and decided "to make public a complete history of the Resistance in Xiberoa." In a letter to Malharin, Pommiès asked whether the local Maule newspaper might agree to publish his text and whether the paper had any particular political tendency.[9]

Rivalry and animosities between the Secret Army and the CFP were once again rekindled during commemorations in 1984. On the fortieth anniversary of Liberation, the Veterans' Association of the Secret Army (Sector IV), the socialist mayor of Maule, and its municipal council inaugurated a street on the edge of town in memory of the Secret Army resister Jean-Pierre Hegoburu, who had formed the Maule maquis in 1943. The Allée Jean-Pierre Hegoburu thus became the second *lieu du souvenir* to be visited annually by Secret Army veterans and supporters when they gathered for their own commemorative ceremonies on August 15. CFP veterans and their sympathizers repeatedly protested to the mayor and the municipal and regional councils that naming a street after Hegoburu displayed unfair bias in favor of the Secret Army and its version of local history. In keeping with a long French tradition of treating street names as a reflection of and means of preserving the public memory of a community, opponents of the inauguration argued that certain other Maule citizens were more deserving than Hegoburu (Milo 1997: 365). Some citizens felt that streets should be named after Pierre Béguerie and Dr. Herbille (M. Béguerie, R. Pérez 2004: pers. comms.). The socialist mayor pointed out that the town already had a street named Béguerie (alongside the row of modest houses built by Louis Béguerie in the 1920s for his employees) and an avenue named after the elder Dr. Herbille. In the decades following liberation, alternative memory communities emerged in Xiberoa, as happened elsewhere in the Basque Country and in France (Kidd 2005: 126, 128), and debates between rival mnemonic groups often dominated sociocultural agendas created by local mayors and municipal councils.

Soon after the inauguration of the Allée Jean-Pierre Hegoburu, Maurice Malharin and General Pommiès wrote a competing version of events in the summer of 1944. Excerpts from the two documents appeared in the local press, and copies of the full text circulated among Xiberoans.[10] Some supporters of the Secret Army refused to touch or read the CFP account of liberation. Some CFP supporters treated their rivals' text in the same way. As one woman explained, "I could not bear to touch the pages of that document [the Secret Army pamphlet], even after all these years. It would make me feel ill to read their lies about the past" (R. Amigo 2004: pers. comm.). The two texts provided rival narratives that spawned divided memories.

To mark the fiftieth anniversary of liberation, the biweekly Xiberoan newspaper, *Le Miroir de la Soule,* published an extensive range of interviews with former Secret Army and CFP resisters, survivors of deportation, and clandestine guides, as well as accounts of the German raid on Ospitaleku and the liberation of Maule and Sustary. The editor of *Le Miroir* also published the lengthy memoirs of the Vichy-appointed mayor of Maule, Arnaud Aguer, who gave his own account of Maule's liberation, carefully avoiding mention of local attempts to try him as a collaborator in the French court of justice. Xiberoans read the articles avidly and often wrote to the editor if they disagreed with a representation of the past authored by a CFP or Secret Army veteran (R. Amigo, M. Etcheverry, M. Udoy 2004: pers. comms.). In Sustary a group of Secret Army veteran-resisters and the socialist mayor decided to honor the late FFI leader, Clement de Jaureguiberry, on the fiftieth anniversary of liberation. During the commemorative ceremony in the town hall, a sister of Jaureguiberry unveiled a marble plaque. The mayor praised the bravery and competence of Jaureguiberry and made special tribute to Dr. Idiart, the former socialist mayor and Secret Army supporter. The commemoration and plaque enraged the Harbustan family and their advocates.

In 2000 the mayor of Sohüta, Michel Béguerie, and his constituents decided to perform a popular play about the Resistance in Xiberoa. As the son of Pierre Béguerie and a former resister himself, the mayor had a personal interest in the play, *The Maquis of Xiberoa,* written by a local Basque scholar. More than six thousand Basques watched the play during its two performances, and both the text and the play gave rise to considerable controversy across Xiberoa. Some elderly veterans refused to watch or read it. Others did so and were furious about the play's misrepresentation of their own experiences. For Michel Béguerie and many others, however, the play celebrated the liberation of their beloved territory. In the play, rival maquis did not quarrel or compete. Two characters were called Jaureguiberry and Béguerie. At one point, the actors sang "On the Road to Moscow," in recognition of the Spanish and Navarrese immigrants and anti-Franco Republicans who had fought in the Resistance. Although not terribly pleased by that particular song, former CFP resisters consented to its inclusion and thus showed their willingness to participate in a process of healing. Both CFP and Secret Army veterans asked the playwright to remove a scene involving Gurs, the internment camp located so close to Xiberoan space and so far from Xiberoan public memory. The playwright did so.

More than sixty thousand men, women, and children had been interned at Gurs between 1939 and 1944. Of these, nearly four thousand German and

Austrian Jews were deported to Drancy and sent on to Auschwitz (Laharie 1993). No resistance group ever tried to stop their deportation. Virtually no trace of the camp remains. Near its former entrance, a large commemorative sign advises passersby that the "former French concentration camp of Gurs" was located there. A short distance away, weeds grow thickly around a sentry box. A barrier straddles the dirt road, which leads into a dense, damp forest, planted to conceal land where rows of wooden barracks once housed the changing enemies of France before, during, and after the German Occupation. Beyond the forest, a cemetery harbors the graves of more than a thousand Jews, as well as those of men who fought against Franco during the Spanish Civil War. Gurs has long been a *lieu de mémoire* for survivors of internment and deportation, their families and friends, and others for whom it is a duty, a *devoir,* to remember what happened on that site during its short, tragic existence. Gurs is a place in which the material, symbolic, and functional aspects of embodied memory coexist; it is a place in which history and memory interact (Nora 1992: 14). Continuing efforts are made to "keep the memory of Gurs intact," both nationally and internationally. The camp has an official association (l'Amicale du camp de Gurs), in which the Maule librarian actively participates as the daughter of a deportee who perished in a Nazi concentration camp. At the same time, Gurs is a place that many people in Xiberoa and Béarn wish to forget.

During commemorations marking the sixtieth anniversary of Xiberoa's liberation in 2004, the legitimacy of moral judgments about the Resistance featured prominently in many conversations with elderly Xiberoans. As war veterans, former resisters, and politicians gathered to honor the memory of those who had fought for democracy in France at various memorials across the province, an undercurrent of discontent and anger became apparent among men who had belonged to Xiberoa's rival resistance groups in 1943–44. In Maule the socialist mayor, socialist general councilors, and two Xiberoan priests, along with the mayor of another town, formed the committee charged with organizing commemorative events in 2004. Owing to bitter debates over commemorations and their relation to Xiberoa's public memory, the committee also included an outside negotiator from Oloron, who sought to ensure that all sides (Secret Army, CFP, FTP, International Brigaders, and Guérilleros Espagnols) had equal representation during the festivities and solemnities. The group decided that the main commemorative ceremony in Maule, on June 6, 2004, should pay special homage to Guérilleros Espagnols and International Brigaders who had fought in the Resistance and the armed forces during the Second World War.

At the back of the original Maule cemetery, a boulder serves as a monument to those who died upon their return from Nazi camps, those who died in combat as soldiers during the war of 1939–45, and those who fought against Franco during the Spanish Civil War. Twelve plaques honor the dead; six of them pay tribute to men who were Spaniards or Navarrese Basques. One of the men, Antonio Aroix, fought against Franco in the International Brigades and was killed in the battle of Jarama. Aroix was born in Maule to Aragonese parents. On June 6, 2004, dignitaries, representatives of associations for evaders of STO and German prisons, survivors of deportation, and members of the Resistance gathered around the boulder to commemorate Aroix. The organizers thus shifted their special tribute away from the Secret Army and CFP and, for the first time, sought public recognition of some of Xiberoa's other, previously unheralded heroes. The mayor's late mother had emigrated to Maule during the 1920s as a "Swallow." A former militant communist in Maule, Román Pérez, congratulated the mayor for his decision to honor a Maule man who had fought against Franco. Pérez also invoked the memory of his father, Eustaquio Pérez, the communist activist watched and pursued by Maule police in the last year of the Third Republic and during Vichy and never targeted for clemency. The Maule mayor's decision to honor a "Red" International Brigader at the Maule ceremony in 2004 highly displeased the elderly CFP veterans in attendance, who expressed outrage that an anti-Francoist communist should receive such public recognition and that, for the first time, the annual commemoration did not focus on the Resistance. To make matters worse, the mayor's speech had given credit to the Gaullists and communists for their part in the liberation of Xiberoa.

A second public event took place at a Secret Army *lieu du souvenir,* the street named after the Secret Army resister Jean-Pierre Hegoburu. The mayor unveiled a large marble monument dedicated to the Secret Army and its Maule maquis leader, Hegoburu, a factory worker of Navarrese descent. The municipal council and departmental authorities provided funds for the monument. CFP veterans and their supporters felt outraged by both the monument and its sources of funding. A third event took place in the Collège de Saint-François, the private Catholic college occupied by the Germans during 1943–44. With the support of the municipal and cantonal councils, the director of the college and the socialist mayor unveiled a plaque in honor of the Secret Army and Clement de Jaureguiberry. The plaque and the speeches annoyed the few CFP veterans who attended the event. (Several veterans insisted upon boycotting the ceremony.) CFP attendees once again complained that the commemorative ceremony did not reflect "what really happened" during the summer of 1944. One CFP veteran wrote to the local newspaper to express his disgust and dismay. Some supporters of the Secret Army, in turn, complained that Jaureguiberry had not received the public acclaim he deserved, both as a military strategist and as a "here person" who had taken his moral responsibility to the civilian population very seriously indeed. Secret Army veterans pointed out that the CFP leaders, Lavalou and Bercut, were outsiders who had no attachment to place or to Xiberoan culture. One elderly veteran argued that the CFP leadership had felt no moral responsibility to protect Xiberoans from German reprisals and thus acted irresponsibly by attacking German troops in and near Xiberoan communities during the summer of 1944. Once again, the public dimension of social remembering rekindled old animosities and showed that memories were still deeply divided in Maule.

The sixtieth anniversary of the Liberation also turned some Sustary citizens against each other. The socialist mayor invited members of the Jaureguiberry family and Xiberoan veterans of the Secret Army to a private ceremony in the town hall, where they had champagne. The event was not advertised, but the Harbustan family easily found out about it and communicated their displeasure to the mayor. When the mayor and his entourage briefly gathered at the war memorial opposite the town hall (and adjacent to the Harbustan family home), a member of the Harbustan family joined the group and unnerved some Secret Army supporters. The mayor made a brief speech, and the group dispersed quickly.

Sixty years after the liberation of Xiberoa, former rival resisters and their supporters were drawn into a web of judgments about the respective military strategies, political convictions, and moral responsibilities of their rival leaders during the summer of 1944. Both sides continued to weigh the consequences of choices made by Resistance leaders and to judge their actions as morally right and responsible or morally wrong and reprehensible. In their evaluations of the past, people often emphasized the moral duty of Resistance leaders to take responsibility for their actions, to embrace an ethic of responsibility that entailed understanding the possible consequences of military aggression against Germans: reprisals against the civilian population. Resistance leaders such as Lavalou and Bercut had rejected the ethic of responsibility in favor of an ethic of ultimate ends, which took no account of consequences. In the summer of 1944, the two "outsiders" in charge of the Xiberoan CFP embraced Max Weber's ethic of conviction: for Lavalou and Bercut, aggression against the Germans was a justifiable means to an end, the liberation of France from German occupation (Weber 1958: 120). For Xiberoans the ethic of responsibility provided the only legitimate means of achieving that end by seeking to protect the Xiberoan house and community from external harm.

For many years after the Liberation, Dr. Henri Herbille also figured in local debates about responsibility, conviction, legitimate judgment, and justice during the 1930s and 1940s. Advocates of Herbille had confidence in him as a holder of moral and civic authority who took seriously his duty to protect his community from danger and harm (M. Rodrigo Nicolau 2004: pers. comm.). Many people still insist that Henri Herbille "did what he believed was right" when he helped the French authorities arrest militant communists who posed an internal and external threat to the conservative moral community of Maule. Some citizens remember Dr. Herbille as "one of the few real heroes" during the Occupation. They point out that the physician exposed himself to danger from both the Resistance and the Germans. His supporters argue that unlike many other citizens, Herbille accepted responsibility as a defender of his moral community rather than remaining indifferent to or uninvolved in events that threatened to harm Xiberoan lives and property.

By contrast, some of Herbille's former enemies remember him with rancor as the embodiment of an authoritarian, hierarchical regime that oppressed and exploited the working class. His critics insist that Henri Herbille was an intolerant, manipulative elitist who used his civic power and authority only to serve the best interests of Maule's landed gentry and notables during the interwar years, Vichy, and German occupation. From their perspective, Herbille had no regard for the well-being of citizens whose political beliefs threatened the hegemony of Maule *patrons*. His critics argue that for Herbille, the arrest and deportation of militant communists were justifiable means to an end—the preservation of a conservative, Catholic, hierarchical society. Few people know about the appeals for clemency made by Dr. Herbille to the prefect and subprefect or his attempts to counter the negative effects of denunciations, arrests, and deportations and to resolve class conflict in the town. In the twenty-first century, Dr. Herbille is rarely mentioned by local and external authorities when citizens gather to commemorate the liberation of Maule and Xiberoa.

In Sustary few people wish to talk about Mme Etxart. She completed her prison sentence and returned to Sustary in 1947. In spite of the humiliation she suffered in 1944, Mme Etxart chose to face the ongoing moral judgments of fellow citizens (Virgili 2002: 196–97). Unlike many French women who had experienced head shaving, she decided not to withdraw from society. Mme Etxart resumed married life with her husband and continued to run her shop until the 1980s. The feelings of injustice she shared with her brother, in particular, increased her determination to rejoin a deeply divided society as a victim (ibid.: 197). She spent her final years in a nursing home, where she shared its public spaces with elderly "patriots" and another woman whose head had been shaved in 1944. A tacitly agreed upon silence reduced the chances of reconciliation between long-standing enemies, even as it prevented the resumption of their quarrels (Christian 1969: 137).

13: Remembering the Resistance in Popular Theater

With its roots in a genre that combines drama, history, and oral tradition, Xiberoan popular theater provides an unusual opportunity to explore the long-standing Basque preoccupation with the need to protect the moral community from external harm and danger. Like the process of remembering itself, the plays (*phastoralak,* in Basque; *pastorales* in French) creatively construct representations of the past. The genre, often said to be "seventy-five percent legend and twenty-five percent history," probably has its origins in the medieval mystery plays (Davant 2001: 18). *Pastorales* use verse, music, costume, and dance to tell a story about the struggle between Good and Evil, between insiders (the moral community) and outsiders (Veyrin 1975: 287). Goodness and the insiders always prevail. The plays are written in the Xiberoan dialect of Basque, in verses of four lines each, with assonant rhyme used in even-numbered lines (Aulestia 1995: 5). Never recited, the dialogue is sung in a highly stylized, monotonous chant. When a Xiberoan community decides collectively to perform a play, the mayor assembles a committee responsible for choosing the subject of the *pastorale* and, if a new play is to be presented, the playwright, who is always a native Xiberoan.

Until the nineteenth century, the genre drew its themes from the Old and New Testaments, hagiography, *chansons de geste,* French history (the French Revolution and earlier), and Basque legend (Hérelle 1922: 4). During the interwar years, Xiberoan communities tended to select themes such as the life of Abraham, Joan of Arc, and Napoleon. In 1929, however, the commune of Barkoxe performed a new play that focused on the Great War and followed its Basque hero from the assassination of Archduke Franz Ferdinand in Sarajevo to the signing of the armistice (Lauburu 1987: 45).[1] The play was unusual in several respects: it used "modern" accoutrements such as bicycles, automobiles, canons, and gas masks; its subject matter related to events directly or indirectly experienced by members of the audience rather than to the distant past; and, most important of all, the hero of the play was an ordinary Xiberoan man, not a king or emperor, cardinal or pope, martyr or saint. The hero was a soldier (*poilu*) in the French infantry who came from Barkoxe, a character whom the audience felt they knew as a neighbor and fellow citizen. On his deathbed, the hero bade farewell to his natal village and *patrie* in a manner that rooted French experience in a world war firmly in Xiberoan territory (ibid.: 47). In many respects the play reflected the impact of that war upon northern Basque society, as some Xiberoans began to feel truly French for the first time.

From the 1950s, new *pastorales* focused entirely upon Basque history, Basque heroes, and the battles Basques had waged to protect their houses and communities from external harm and invasion by enemy strangers. In one *pastorale*, performed in Barkoxe during 1953, the Xiberoan house, its tomb in the cemetery, and the hero's strong sense of attachment to his beloved *pays,* the mountains, and his natal village figured prominently in the play. Another play, written and performed in 1958, featured a well-known fifteenth-century song and oral tradition about rival factions in Maule: the hero, a Xiberoan shepherd, embodied Goodness, while the royal owner of the Maule château (an outsider) represented the forces of evil. In the 1970s Xiberoan *pastorales* began to contest official French versions of Basque history and to rectify matters by presenting a Basque interpretation of events, such as the defeat of Charlemagne in Roncevaux by the Basques rather than by the Franks (ibid.: 49–50).

In 1976 a priest (and much acclaimed author of several *pastorales*) broke convention by making his natal community the hero of a play. *Santa Grazi* traced the origins of the commune to the tenth century, but the play was also highly ethnographic in content. Shepherds extolled the virtues of preserving traditions and pastoral rights rooted in sixteenth-century customary law, bringing a small flock of sheep onto the stage to emphasize their deep attachment to their animals and mountains. The play depicted trans-Pyrenean smuggling, the solidarity of Santa Grazi shepherds as they confronted a marauding bear (an external threat to the community, its men, and their livestock) in the high mountain pastures, and the anguish of an elderly couple whose heir never married (an internal threat to the moral community) and thus jeopardized the preservation and continuity of their house. In the text of the play, house names and local place-names constantly provided locally appreciated sociospatial markers for the actors and audience. At one point the returning hero proudly proclaimed that the *indarra* of his natal community derived from its firm commitment to the preservation of Santa Grazi customs and traditions (Casenave-Harigile 1976: 35). With Santa Grazi, the genre of the *pastorale* took a new direction. The play was not about the life of any particular individual, but about the life of a collective entity, a Xiberoan moral community (Lauburu 1987: 52).

In 2001 the community of Sohüta performed a *pastorale* about Xiberoan Resistance, depicted as a unified collectivity whose *maquisards* and leaders worked harmoniously together to rid Xiberoan territory of the enemy occupier who threatened Xiberoan lives and property. When the play was performed on two occasions, it gave rise to considerable local controversy over the relationship between history and popular theater and rekindled longstanding animosities about events in the summer of 1944.[2]

When a community decides to perform a *pastorale,* the organizing committee appoints a "teacher" who helps them choose a topic in conjunction with a Xiberoan playwright. The process of "making a *pastorale*" normally begins one year before the actual performance. The teacher studies the text closely, recruits the actors, assigns their parts, and directs them in weekly, lengthy rehearsals. All actors and musicians are amateurs, and they are almost always local. The number of roles ranges from twenty to seventy-five or more. Deciding to take part in a *pastorale* is a serious commitment, a source of collective pride for the group and their community. It requires dedication, a good voice, a good memory, and at least some fluency in Basque.

The classic structure of the *pastorale* pits the Good Ones (the protagonists, the Christians) against the Bad Ones (the antagonists, the Turks), with goodness ultimately prevailing over evil. The bipolarization of the stage reflects the opposition of Good and Evil, with the Good always using the door to the right, whereas their enemies go to the left. The Bad Ones are aided by Satan and his devil-servants, who tempt the Good Ones and promote discord and evil. Satan's dancers are beautifully costumed, and their movements are elegant. By contrast the devil-servants are buffoons who amuse the crowd with grotesque commentaries. Basque popular theater is by and for the people who perform and watch it. The day begins with a parade through the host community of all the actors and organizers, as well as the flock of sheep that inevitably appears on stage at some point, with its shepherds. Basque flutes and drums play, bells tinkle. At midday the actors, organizers, and members of the public mingle to eat and drink. The performance starts either in midafternoon or early evening; it is always an impressive, colorful spectacle, lasting three to five hours without intermission. Traditionally unique to Xiberoa, these popular plays are usually watched by some six thousand (mainly Xiberoan) people, who follow the performances both attentively and critically. The audience often applauds the Good Ones, insults and boos the Bad Ones, laughs and jeers at the devils. After a performance, the audience lingers to socialize and discuss the strengths and weaknesses of the play and its representation on stage. For many months thereafter, Xiberoans continue to measure the success or failure of the play. The local press follows public opinion, the final arbiter in such matters. In some Xiberoan communities, actors and their families hold annual celebratory meals, at which they sing excerpts from the play that brought them so closely together during the course of one year. In a successful *pastorale,* audience and actors "feel that they are one big Xiberoan family" (Idiart 1987: 119).

The actors perform in a highly stylized manner, with largely expressionless faces, both actors and dancers holding their bodies rigidly. The genre does not permit much individual interpretation of roles, and the characters are usually fictional or represent famous figures in the Basque Country's medieval or modern history. Tradition dictates that characters should not be based upon the lives of real people who are still alive, who knew members of the audience, or whose actions and experiences are still remembered by Xiberoans. There is always at least one battle, in which movements are highly regulated. The Good Ones and Bad Ones line up on their respective sides of the stage, then advance, one against another, striking their staffs in unison. When Good triumphs over Evil, the Good hero recounts the main events of the story or history that formed the play's subject matter. He or she thanks the audience for having been so numerous and for their attentiveness during the performance and wishes them "a good meal, a good night, and a safe journey home."

In the summer of 2000, the community of Sohüta decided to perform a *pastorale.* Its long-standing mayor, Michel Béguerie (son of the factory owner and Resistance leader, Pierre Béguerie), knew that a Xiberoan writer had been working on a play about Xiberoan resistance. Given his own involvement in the CFP as a young resister and his father's crucial role in the formation of that resistance group, Michel Béguerie had a personal interest in the topic. The organizing committee and Béguerie met with the playwright, Jean-Louis Davant, many times to discuss various drafts of the play. Davant also had personal reasons for wanting to write about the resistance in Xiberoa. He had been nine years old when he saw his first *maquisard,* a nineteen-year-old agricultural worker who emerged from the woods near Davant's home with a small herd of cattle destined for farmhouses where CFP men sheltered. The playwright still has vivid memories of the young *maquisard,* dressed in khaki, a machine gun at his side. "For me, as a child, he was like Robin Hood!"[3] Now an elderly CFP veteran, that *maquisard* jokes that his sudden appearance behind M. Davant's farm in late 1943 must have inspired Davant to write his *pastorale* about "the maquis of Xiberoa" (J. Loustau 2004: pers. comm.).

In the introduction to *The Maquis of Xiberoa* (*Xiberoko Makia* in Basque), Davant (2001: 18) recognizes the delicate nature of his topic, stating that he "has treated the two *maquis* [Secret Army and CFP] with the greatest possible respect"; yet he anticipates a measure of dissatisfaction with his representation of the past. Each side, he predicts, will see itself as having been the better of the two, but he "leaves that debate to the historians." The writer of a *pastorale,* he continues, must not decide on such issues, "even though he has his own opinion and preference." Davant (ibid.: 11) identifies his play as a memory work in which the Sohüta people and other Basques could participate, not merely as an audience but through their own individual remembering. He seeks to commemorate the role that both maquis played in the Liberation and, by writing the play, to show how the Basque province of Xiberoa helped to end German tyranny in France in its own small way.

The *pastorale,* Davant continues, is not "realist theatre, but symbolic. The details are imagined, as so often the dialogues as well" (ibid.: 18–19). In this spirit the play "deliberately ignores the tactical disagreements which divided the Resistance in Xiberoa." Davant argues that the key point of this *pastorale* lies in the "common struggle for freedom" in which both sides engaged. It is not his intention "to reawaken old quarrels, but on the contrary to rise above them and to unite the local population in an amicable fervor in celebrating a difficult and finally glorious page" in the history of the Resistance in Xiberoa (ibid.: 19).

To this end the author limits himself "to the visible, military aspects" of the Resistance by focusing on five battles in which Xiberoans lost their lives or were wounded (ibid.). He asks the reader to "leave the rest to the historians" and to treat his play as a "hymn to universal freedom, as well as a love song to our mother Xiberoa, above all nationalisms" (ibid.). Structurally, his *pastorale* follows the classic format. The Good Ones are represented by the men and women of the Resistance and their supporters (including the Basque clergy); the Bad Ones are represented by the Germans, the Lady Turks, and Devils who stir up trouble. The supporting cast includes a range of townspeople, angels, and shepherds. The principal male hero, Battitta, is a fictional resister who joins the Secret Army and falls in love with a Gaullist supporter, Maddi. With these exceptions, most of the characters are named after real people who supported the Secret Army and the CFP in 1943–44.

The Good Ones include five characters representing Secret Army resisters (including Jaureguiberry and Hegoburu) and five characters representing CFP resisters (including Béguerie, Lavalou, and Jancène). They are aided by (among many others) the head of the Red Cross in Maule (Mme Bidegain); the Vichy-appointed mayor of Maule, Arnaud Aguer; and Canon Arricar. The fictional character and hero, Battitta, passes messages between Jaureguiberry and Béguerie as their *agent de liaison* and helps the two Resistance leaders coordinate their efforts without conflict or rivalry. Contrary to the normal boundaries of the Xiberoan moral community, the Good Ones include the outsider, Lavalou, but his character is briefly depicted as cooperative rather than destructive. The inclusion of controversial insiders upset some elderly citizens who remembered them as "double agents." Elderly communists, the families of Spanish Republicans who settled in Maule in the late 1930s, and others keen to resurrect the memory of Spanish "Reds" who fought in the French Resistance complained that the play failed to recognize properly the "third maquis," consisting of FTP partisans and Guérilleros. The play portrays the Germans as comically correct but menacing. The main German character, Spielberg, threatens to burn Xiberoan houses, rails against resisters as "terrorists," and questions the ability of Mayor Aguer to control them (ibid.: 119). No mention is made of the Gestapo agent, Sasse, or of Lieutenant Hammer, but Superintendent Ressel appears in scenes about the liberation of Sustary.

Davant portrays Secret Army characters as loyal Gaullists, poorly armed, whose mission is to prepare for the day of national insurrection. One Secret Army actor, whose part corresponds to that of a real resister, cautions Battitta: "Don't provoke combat close to any community or house. Follow the laws of the war by respecting the local population" (ibid.: 75). In representing the CFP, Davant (ibid.: 74–79) portrays Béguerie as a leader prepared to complement the resistance work of the Secret Army. Béguerie is last seen in scene 11, where he shares Battitta's excitement about the Allied landings and confidently proclaims that the Secret Army and CFP will stand united, each maquis in its proper place, committed to ridding Xiberoa of the Germans. The timing of Béguerie's disappearance from the play is correctly placed in the chronology of the battles fought.

The controversial CFP leader, Lavalou, appears only once in the play. With their respective maquis, he and Jaureguiberry fight the Germans and liberate Maule. In his four lines, the character Lavalou merely reminds Jaureguiberry that they should share the German arms just seized and that the CFP still has two German POWs under guard (ibid.: 106–7). The playwright does not mention their fatal shooting by Lavalou and Bercut. What of Bercut himself, the audacious CFP officer whose fondness for risky, spectacular military action so annoyed and upset Captain de Jaureguiberry and many other Xiberoan citizens? Although no character in the play is called Bercut, the Turk Ladies appear in scene 13 to joke about finding themselves in such a backward place as Xiberoa. "Is it really part of France?" they ask, and propose some mischief. As one says to another, "You must know what happened between the two maquis. Let's cause a lot of confusion between them!" To which her fellow mischief maker replies, "I'm sure you know who Bercut is, the lunatic! If only we could stir him up, that would be such a splendid trick!" (ibid.: 96–97). Bercut never appears in the play.

In the *pastorale*, negotiations with the commander of the Spielberg Battalion and the liberation of Maule follow the unseen denunciation of the fictional Secret Army agent, Battitta. The skirmish between Secret Army resisters and Germans in Montory ends with the "martyrdom" of the Spanish resister, Julio Lopez. Triumph of Good over Evil is completed as the FFI leader, Jaureguiberry—aided by Canon Arricart—convinces the German commander, Ressel, to surrender his garrison in Sustary. In keeping with the Gaullist myth of the Resistance and with Xiberoan public memory, the people of Xiberoa liberate themselves.

The fictional "unknown resister," Battitta, and his fictional fiancée, Maddi, also celebrate the return of their brothers from prison in Germany just in time to attend their wedding in 1945 (ibid.: 145). The cast members join together to celebrate the victory of love, love of liberty, and love of Xiberoa, symbolized by the marriage of the young resisters. The cast thanks the audience for their kindness in forgiving any offence taken by the portrayal of events in the play. One actor notes that they are all forever indebted to unknown heroes such as Battitta for their part in defeating fascism, promoting and defending freedom, and forgiving the enemy "of yesterday who is today our best friend in Europe" (ibid.: 151). The performance ends with the entire cast on stage singing a song about Sohüta, the community whose people "made the pastorale" during one year in their lives. Romantic and poetic, the song extols the beauty of the countryside, their love of the Basque Country, its liberation, its culture and language, and their hope for the future, invested in the young people of Xiberoa.

In the annex to his play, Davant (ibid.: 174–80) quotes directly from official versions of Secret Army/FFI and CFP history ("Libération" 1984; Céroni 1980). He cites the names of villages, including Ospitaleku, where the maquis operated and where local civilians experienced German brutality. Yet when both the play and its annex are compared to official accounts of events in 1944, there are striking omissions: the author carefully makes no mention of quarrels between the rival Resistance leaders or of CFP actions that contravened accepted military conventions. In the annex Davant cites many local events that are still part of community-centered group memories of the German Occupation. He notes, for example, the burning of Basque farms by the Spielberg Battalion in Ospitaleku after its unsuccessful attempts to find any CFP *maquisards* sheltering there. He recalls the murder of a Gurs man by Germans as he attempted to escape and the arrest of Ospitaleku citizens, nine of whom were deported to Nazi concentration camps. Davant "remembers" the denunciation of CFP resisters who were caught by Germans in the Xiberoan hamlet of Barkoxe. He invokes the memory of elderly Basques in the village of Ezkiule who saw or heard about the punitive German raid in which one farm was destroyed and two youths arrested. He recalls denunciations of the Secret Army maquis in the village of Altzükü, and how the warning provided by a female resister enabled the resisters to flee before the Germans arrived. Although Davant notes that the Spielberg Battalion did take revenge on the people of Altzükü, his annex gives no details. These and other "omissions" in the text were the focus of criticism by some Basques during the summer of 2001, when some seventy local amateur actors performed *The Maquis of Xiberoa.*

In 2001 public reaction to the play varied widely. Conversations with Xiberoans and with the playwright revealed four often intermingling interpretative approaches to the play: as an artistic performance, as a commemoration, as a historical representation of past events, and as a culturally unifying form of social interaction. Many Basques appreciated the play as an artistic performance and did not treat literally either the text or the acting out of roles on stage. Many expressed pleasure in Davant's use of the classic, complex structure of a proper *pastorale,* with the battle between Good and Evil clearly depicted and the triumph of the former over the latter duly observed. For these spectators, the performance successfully rose above lingering animosities and tensions between veterans of the rival Resistance groups. As one man put it, "the play isn't about politics. I'm sick of people dragging up the politics of 1944, and arguing about who the real terrorists were—the Germans or certain CFP leaders. Arguing about the communists, arguing about de Gaulle and Giraud. It's a play, for heaven's sake!" (M. Béguerie 2004: pers. comm.).

For many people the performance provided an enjoyable spectacle, to which the audience members themselves contributed through their sheer numbers, as well as through their participation. When Spielberg and his German troops first goose-stepped through the audience to take the stage, people booed and hissed. Some laughed aloud and whistled at the sight of local shepherds, farmers, factory workers, and professionals dressed up as Nazis. The actors themselves grinned at times, sharing a sense of comedy with the audience. When the Gaullist heroine defiantly stood her ground in opposition to a German patrol, people applauded her pluckiness, recognizing in it the characteristic readiness of a Xiberoan woman to stand her ground among men and to defend her beliefs. When the German troops and resisters engaged in battle, the genre required them to strike a pose that seemed comical to some at first sight. The uniformed soldiers took mincing, skipping steps toward their Basque adversaries, with one hand on a hip, the other wielding the wooden staff that is a hallmark prop of Xiberoan popular theater. The resisters did the same. Among some elderly people, it was the Germans who provoked laughter, edged with bitterness. They enjoyed seeing the former enemy portrayed by people whom they knew and behaving in such a ridiculous fashion, even if the conventions of Basque popular theater dictated that it should be thus. When a resister "died" on stage following combat, a murmur rippled through the crowd. Young and old alike were thoroughly engaged by the spectacle. Some of the children onstage suppressed a giggle, because the "dead" resister was himself somewhat embarrassed by his playacting. His discomfort did not draw a laugh from the older people close enough to the stage to see it. Even as it entertained on one level, the spectacle also brought back memories in which humor played no part.

As a public commemoration of Xiberoan victory over the German occupiers, the play called upon the mnemonic community to engage in an act of remembrance. Although the playwright insists that the genre is not "realist theater" (Davant 2001: 18), the process of remembering was aided by his use of real names, real places, and official accounts of events written by rival Resistance groups. By identifying key people involved in Xiberoan resistance, Davant intended to symbolically commemorate their brave actions. Having seen the play, the daughter of one female resister wrote to Davant to express her sincere gratitude, feeling that her mother's instrumental role in Xiberoan resistance had finally been recognized. The play brought back childhood memories, both good and bad, which, "until then, had been completely buried" by the daughter.[4] Before the final version of the play was published and performed, Davant closely consulted many Secret Army and CFP veterans and their relatives. Most agreed with him that the play absolutely must not be treated literally, as history. Some people did ask Davant not to use the real names of local people, a few of whom were still alive. Nearly all of them still had close kin in the area. As many Xiberoans remarked, "the subject matter of the play [was] too recent, too sensitive." Using real names did not, in their view, square with the playwright's insistence that the genre cannot be treated as a "strict lesson in history" and ought to be seen more as "a historical novel in verse with mimicry" (Davant 2001: 18).

In August 2001 the Secret Army veterans' association met to discuss the play. Some members argued that the *pastorale* was never intended to be an accurate, complete representation of the past; they largely appreciated the performance as a spectacle. Having both read and seen the play, a few veterans insisted that Davant had left out "whole chunks of history" in his theatrical representation of Xiberoa's recent past. Some had read the text but not seen the play. A few had ignored it altogether. For much of the afternoon, the group debated whether the play could both be a subjective, imagined depiction of the Resistance in Xiberoa and at the same time selectively seek to be historically accurate in some respects. They asked themselves whether it was possible, in Basque popular theater, to capture reality without falsifying it (M. Joanny 2003: pers. comm.).

One Secret Army veteran was publicly critical of Davant and his play in a regional newspaper article.[5] He asked why so many figures active in the Resistance, as well as those who died in deportation, had been "forgotten" in the play. He accused Davant of having written "an incomplete text" that failed to recognize the important part played by many local heroes not mentioned in the *pastorale.* He railed against Davant for having given too much credit to certain individuals, having got certain details of history wrong, having failed to tell the whole story of a German raid on the veteran's natal village. According to one account of that raid, a female resister persuaded the Germans to release their hostages. Another version attributes the successful negotiation to the village's mayor, who bravely offered himself to the Germans in an attempt to secure the citizens' release. The irate veteran insisted that the mayor's "selfless courage prevented a second Oradour!" A small group of people from Barkoxe felt similarly forgotten by the playwright, because the play did not include a scene about the tragic arrest and deportation of Barkoxe citizens and the fugitives they had hidden in 1943. Davant mentions the Barkoxe tragedy in the annex to the play, but his exclusion of local experiences from the play itself violated the group memory of the Barkoxe people, who insisted upon a literal interpretation of the *pastorale.* Critics acknowledged that thousands of Basques had enjoyed the two performances as a theatrical spectacle, but they feared that the text would be treated as a definitive history of resistance in the Basque Country.

Among other audience members, appreciation of the play as a theatrical spectacle sat uneasily alongside concerns about historical accuracy. They resisted a literal interpretation of the text but nevertheless felt compelled to point out certain "factual errors" to Davant. In one case a real character in the play was confused with his "real" nephew in a particular scene; it was the nephew who had had the experience, not the uncle, who was a character in the play. At times the play was at odds with autobiographical and family memories. Of particular interest is the manner in which the play, as text and as performance, contested and corrupted both autobiographical and group memory in its theatrical representation of the recent past. One elderly Secret Army veteran whose real name was used in the play had great difficulty treating the play as a performance. On one occasion when he talked about the *pastorale,* he read the text aloud at the point where his character appears. In his four lines, the character tells the fictitious hero, Battitta, that their maquis could never successfully attack the Germans; they were too poorly armed to do so (Davant 2001: 99). Turning to the annex, where Davant briefly outlines what happened on that particular day in 1944, the veteran read aloud the words: "A group of maquis, commanded by [the veteran], attacked the soldiers stationed at Ahusquy. . . . One German was killed. The enemy abandoned the area. The massif of Arbailles was thus under the control of the resisters. But some shepherds and some men from Altzai [a nearby village] were taken hostage by the Germans." They were freed thanks to the diplomacy of a female Secret Army agent (ibid.: 175). "That is what happened!" the veteran exclaimed, "This is right," he asserted, tapping his finger on the passage from the annex before flipping back to the verses of the play and frowning. As a symbolic representation of events in 1944, the play was unacceptable to him. It violated his own life narrative, the stories central to his experience of self and to the social identity of the dwindling group of veterans who gather annually to commemorate the accidental death of the Guérillero Espagnol in Montory, to remember Secret Army resister Hegoburu at the street named after him on the edge of Maule, and to remember together the experiences they shared in the summer of 1944. Even as the play contested the elderly veteran's own autobiographical memory—all the things he personally remembered about the Occupation and Resistance, as well as all the things he had been told over time about them—the play also contested the group memory of fellow veterans.

Far fewer complaints focused on Davant's treatment of the two rival Resistance groups. One man objected that an early draft unfairly favored the Secret Army over the CFP. The mayor of Sohüta (son of Pierre Béguerie) was pleased with the play. He and Davant had discussed various drafts, and the scenes with which the mayor was unhappy had been altered. Davant's playful treatment of Bercut's character did not give rise to any adverse comments from Xiberoans who remember the Occupation. (Bercut has not returned to Xiberoa in many years and only communicates with one of his former CFP comrades.)

For many people who participated in *The Maquis of Xiberoa*, the play was an instructive and culturally unifying form of social interaction. The vast majority of actors and spectators had no direct experience of the German Occupation. Some people in their forties and fifties had secondhand memories of their parents' experiences during the war but admitted that until they had seen the play, they had never thought much about that difficult period of Xiberoan history. For them, the performance of the play was a catalyst to individual memory and thus contributed to the formation of family memory. As one shepherd told me, "Papa was a POW in Germany. Maman never talks much about what happened in our valley. The neighbors don't, either. So when my wife and I saw the play, we wanted to talk to Maman about it all. I heard things I never knew before, about the Resistance, some of the bad things that happened here, in the same household."[6]

For many people, *The Maquis of Xiberoa* helped local Basques "learn the story" of occupation and resistance at a grassroots level (Cappelletto 2003). Watching the play and acting in it often led to conversations about the experiences of individuals and groups during the 1940s. As memory work that brought back remembrances of those times, the play often induced people to share their knowledge of what happened. Such sharing was particularly marked among the actors and their families during the yearlong process of "making the play." For them, as for the thousands who watch and take part in Xiberoan popular theater every summer, "making a *pastorale*" is a culturally unifying form of social interaction. It entails the intense social involvement of many in the host community, who differ widely in age, political views, and, to a lesser extent, socioeconomic background. "Making the play" promotes the Xiberoan Basque dialect and culture, particularly among young people whose fluency and interest in their heritage were previously minimal and whose social identity as Xiberoan Basques was not yet clearly formed.

In March 2003 students at the Collège de Saint-François in Maule put together an exhibition about the Resistance that broadly covered the period 1940–44 at national, regional, and local levels with newspaper articles, old photos, maps, and some handwritten personal histories of local evaders, deportees, and resisters. The director of their school and a history teacher were keen to use the exhibition not only as "history-telling" (Young 2003), but also as a socializing process in which memory practice by local war veterans would enable the students to participate in Xiberoan public memory (Cappelletto 2003). During one of two evening presentations, the students, their teachers, and some fifty members of the public gathered to hear the testimonies of local men from the Secret Army and the CFP. Another man spoke of his experiences of deportation, imprisonment, and escape. Among some adults in the audience and in the body language of certain speakers, there was a measure of tension. The last man to testify was a former CFP resister from Maule, who talked briefly about the accomplishments of his resistance group in Xiberoa and then at length about their victories outside the Basque Country. This drew grumbled complaints from audience members, who did not want to hear about events outside their own space, their own moral community, and their own beloved *pays*. When the organizers commented on the importance of preserving Xiberoan collective memory, they referred to the valuable lessons in history that Davant's play had provided. Some people stirred uneasily in their seats. When the school's director went on to say that Davant had given his apologies for not attending the event lest his presence provoke tension or discord, one of the Secret Army veterans looked greatly relieved.

In his play Jean-Louis Davant reached out to the mnemonic community of Xiberoan Basques, seeking to unite them and to rise above long-standing tensions between rival Resistance groups. The performance of the play did rekindle animosities in some veterans by history telling. The play was an agent of remembrance, and it provoked in some a fear that its incomplete story would become a definitive representation of a Xiberoan past that continues to be contested by a handful of elderly people. Concerns about the historical accuracy of the play echo ongoing disagreements about the actions and motives of rival resisters who argued with each other more than sixty years ago.

In his essay "History as Social Memory," Peter Burke (1997: 47–48) considers five of the many different media employed in the transmission of social memory: oral traditions, written records, images, actions (especially ritual ones, such as acts of commemoration or remembrance), and space. As oral tradition, with a written text performed in a quasi-ritual style, *The Maquis of Xiberoa* constitutes a hybrid media that shapes and transmits Xiberoan public as well as individual memory. Its ability to do so seems to lie at the core of the controversy surrounding its publication and, more importantly, its performance. The play was intended to be a public celebration of both liberation and memory work; it is the latter which aroused the most intense emotion among some veterans, for whom the *pastorale,* as a "social history of remembering" was incomplete and therefore unacceptable (ibid.: 46). For others, the play was both performance and commemoration, kept apart from the ongoing polemic over what really happened in the summer of 1944 in the borderland Basque province of Xiberoa.

Conclusion

The primary aims of this book have been fourfold: to understand the ways in which Xiberoan Basques tried to manage conflict and justice before the Germans arrived in 1942; to show how they did so during the Occupation and its aftermath; to examine the ways in which Xiberoans responded to the Germans, to other strangers in their midst, and to one another during those difficult decades; and to explore their divided memories of that past, which is still a part of the present. Xiberoans have a long-standing and deep-seated desire for order and stability. During the first four decades of the twentieth century, an international economic depression, world wars, and civil wars brought disorder and uncertainty into people's lives. Unlike the citizens featured in Lawrence Wylie's classic local study of a French village in the Vaucluse, where neither Germans nor Americans set foot during the Occupation, Xiberoans lived in a place of refuge, conflict, transit, exile, and foreign occupation.

In the 1930s and 1940s, the enemy had many different faces in the borderlands of southwestern France. Xiberoans felt variously threatened by communists, militant socialists, extreme right-wing activists, certain sectors of the Resistance, locally known collaborators, the Gestapo, the Milice, Jewish fugitives, and other strangers whose presence was perceived to threaten the security of local citizens. In the complicated moral universe of those decades, the boundaries of legitimate judgment and legitimate behavior became increasingly blurred. During such extraordinary times, insiders felt an even greater need to protect themselves, their families, their property, and their community from potential sources of destruction. At times people did not know which category of enemy Other posed the greatest threat to their safety and security. As the daughter of Clement de Jaureguiberry once recalled: "When I was a child during the Occupation, I couldn't decide who was the most dangerous enemy: the Germans, the communists, or the men of the 'other' Resistance" (M. Joanny 2004: pers. comm.). As Xiberoans came to appreciate, both insiders (those who belonged to a house and its community) and outsiders (strangers who lacked such memberships) were potential sources of endangerment.

By the 1940s the various moral communities of Xiberoa shared a habitus, a matrix of perceptions and appreciations about what constituted legitimate behavior in a household, a neighborhood, and a community. Their habitus contained inherited expectations about human relationships and taught people the value of cooperation, trust, and mutual aid; it provided a basis upon which to distinguish right from wrong and to recognize legitimacy in human judgment and actions; it contained rules that society expected insiders to follow. When insiders committed wrongdoing, citizens applied sanctions and sought justice in one or both spheres: *legalité/legetarzün,* the upholding of formal laws decreed by the state through its judicial system; and the popular justice of *légitimité/züzenbide,* based upon a bundle of rights, privileges, and obligations rooted in sixteenth-century Xiberoan customary law and unwritten codes of practice, some of which I have traced to the eighteenth century and many of which still had currency in the 1940s. In historical interpretations of the village community (*la communauté villageoise*), the notion of *légitimité* constituted a "second law" (*second droit*) that gave the community a durable structure and a principle of autonomy (Assier 1987: 356). In Pyrenean borderlands such as Xiberoa, popular justice was more than a set of customary laws and shared perceptions about what was legitimate and rightful; it was inextricably linked to a person's emotional and jural attachment to particular sociophysical spaces (the Basque house, neighborhood, community, and local *pays*). People felt that attachment particularly deeply in the mountain communities of Upper Xiberoa.

Pyrenean traditions of autarky and valley autonomy underpinned Xiberoans' long-standing desire to manage their own justice, as well as intracommunity and intercommunity conflicts. From the twelve century to the present, Xiberoans and neighboring Pyreneans have used pastoral treaties to regulate access to their territories and resources. Over the centuries, neighboring valleys in the *pays basque* and Béarn and adjacent valleys along the Franco-Spanish border have often sought to resolve conflicts between shepherds over the illegitimate use of space and resources by means of intercommunity negotiations and the ritual exchange of gifts. Such negotiations typically involved the holders of moral and civic authority (mayors, notaries, and clergy), who were responsible for the local management of justice.

At its most fundamental level, conflict within a household constituted the greatest internal threat of harm in Xiberoan society. Failure to resolve a dispute among its members jeopardized the unity and continuity of the house as a social, jural, and economic entity in Basque society. The gravest disputes focused on issues of inheritance, when siblings refused to recognize the legitimacy of the inheritor selected by their parents. In their attempts to avoid such conflict, Xiberoans used the *légalité* of the French judicial system in contracts that upheld Napoleonic law and then applied the *légitimité/züzenbide* of Xiberoan customary law to ensure that the house and associated property passed to only one child. When conflict did turn the members of a house against each other, Xiberoans expected that household to conceal its disordered condition, as well as possible, from other members of the moral community, for a household's inability to prevent or control domestic conflict was a shameful matter. Domestic and extradomestic conflict also arose from other forms of illegitimate behavior, such as disobeying Xiberoan codes of correct sexual conduct.

I have argued that an individual's right to judge a fellow citizen derived from both customary law and long-standing, unwritten rules about legitimate conduct in Xiberoan society. Through forms of popular justice, both individuals and entire communities had a right to address wrongdoing that threatened the integrity and safety of two primordial Pyrenean institutions: the private sphere of the house and the public sphere of the community. Rituals of popular justice such as the charivari and *la jonchée* forced the members of those two powerful institutions to confront each other, as citizens exercised their right to judge wrongdoers in their midst. During the Occupation, people applied the tradition of "strewing greenery" to sexual liaisons between local women and German soldiers. *La jonchée* constituted an informal tribunal on which public rumor served as both judge and jury. In an entirely different way, the strikes that crippled Maule sandal factories so frequently during the 1920s and 1930s also constituted a quasi-ritualized form of popular judgment, aimed at factory owners and led by militant socialist and communist workers.

The origin and nature of intracommunity conflict varied considerably in Maule, Sustary, Urdos, and Ospitaleku, and each community handled its internal problems in different ways. The four communities also responded differently to the Germans in their midst. A wide variety of factors gave rise to tensions and conflict in Maule during the interwar years and the 1940s: political, religious, and class-based differences; perceived difference in race and ethnicity; industrial strikes; and personal animosities. The local notables, Dr. Jean-Baptiste Herbille and his son, Dr. Henri Herbille, were principal holders of civic and moral authority. As the newly elected mayor of Maule in 1918, Jean-Baptiste Herbille initially tried to manage the patron-worker conflict without the intervention of departmental authorities, who nevertheless involved themselves in local disputes, championed workers' rights to better pay and conditions, and at one stage castigated the elder Herbille for his repressive, illegitimate treatment of factory employees. Henri Herbille involved the external authorities in his own attempts to manage conflict and justice in Maule, cooperating with the prefect and subprefect as a national campaign against communists in France took root in Xiberoa. Herbille utilized their power and authority in his attempts to eradicate the class conflict in Maule and remove militant communists—whom he perceived as agents of destruction—from his small, face-to-face society. Vichy's regulations and the minister of justice provided Henri Herbille with mechanisms for removing "dangerous elements" from Xiberoa, as well as for bringing ex-communists back to Maule through state-delivered acts of clemency.

The arrival of the Germans in Maule did not unite a community divided against itself until German violence directly affected people's lives. Both the occupiers and the occupied tried at first to establish nonconfrontational relations with one another through the efforts of Vichy-appointed Mayor Aguer and the first German commander in Maule. Both men hoped for "correct relations" between civilians and occupying troops. Nocturnal raids by the Gestapo, its brutal treatment of four local youths, and the arrests of clandestine guides and others who actively resisted against the Occupation triggered a fundamental shift in citizens' perceptions of the Germans, and Maule people began to unite in their opposition to Hitler's troops on their territory. Most citizens feared and largely avoided contact with the occupiers, unless their professional or political duties required communication with the Germans. Households and hoteliers who provided lodgings for German officers rarely spoke to them; neither side sought sociability (M. Béguerie, M. Etcheverry 2004: pers. comms.).

In Maule Basque-German relations became increasingly tense as opposition to Vichy laws about obligatory work service in Germany (STO) and local support for the Resistance grew. Rather than contributing to community solidarity, however, the STO legislation caused further conflict between workers of Spanish origin and indigenous Maule citizens; almost all of the men sent to Germany came from the town's Navarrese community. Notables and workers bitterly disagreed about the legitimacy of that unofficial policy. As happened elsewhere in France, Maule citizens began to treat acts defined by Vichy as illegal as a legitimate response to a regime that increasingly allowed itself to be manipulated by Hitler. Evading the STO and joining the Resistance became legitimate, patriotic acts, and the developing "culture of the outlaw" in Maule "inverted the notion of legality and proclaimed the rightness and legitimacy of revolt" (Kedward 1994: 283). Even as the discourse of the Resistance had particular appeal among militant socialists and communists in town, talk of legitimate revolt greatly enhanced anxieties among conservative Xiberoans, who feared that a Gaullist victory would bring the communists to power in France. From the spring of 1943 until the summer of 1944, the formation of rival, mutually hostile resistance groups in Maule and the surrounding area introduced an additional agent of divisiveness in intracommunity relations and struck at the heart of local debates about what constituted legitimate and illegitimate judgment and behavior. At the time few people realized that Clement de Jaureguiberry commanded the military operations of the Xiberoan Secret Army and had the extremely difficult task of coordinating all local resistance efforts from June 1944 until the process of liberation ended. As an insider to the Xiberoan moral community, Jaureguiberry instinctively understood the need to protect Xiberoans from German reprisals, even though he often managed conflict between himself and rival resisters (both CFP and communists under his own command) in provocative and potentially dangerous ways. Weber's ethic of responsibility guided the FFI leader's decisions; he accepted responsibility for the consequences of his actions and struggled constantly against the ethic of conviction that guided the reckless actions of Bercut and, to a lesser extent, Lavalou.

The citizens of Sustary managed their own conflicts, justice, and the Germans' presence in quite a different way. Political differences, commercial rivalries, and personal animosities created deep divisions in the town at least a decade before the Germans arrived. Although the town had a factory that employed mainly foreign workers, Sustary had none of the industrial or ethnicity-based conflicts that plagued Maule. In the 1930s militant socialist schoolteachers pitted themselves against powerful conservative notables, who strongly opposed the Popular Front. When Vichy rule began, political rivalry and discord increased between the socialist mayor and the general councilor, the "White" physician in town (who was also a first neighbor of the Harbustans). Personal animosities and commercial rivalries also shaped the boundaries of Sustary factions and contributed to the breakdown of vicinal relations in much of the town, as well as to the cessation of certain religious practices that had traditionally promoted social solidarity.

Unlike the Maule people, Sustary citizens experienced continuous occupation from early December until the Liberation in 1944. Although German customs officers often manned the garrison, the Gestapo maintained its sinister presence there throughout the Occupation. Relations between the Germans and local people varied greatly in their degree of intensity and purpose. In contrast to the situation in Maule, Sustary citizens who housed German officers established relationships with them that were at times cordial and sometimes even friendly. Archival records show that many Sustary people, including Canon Arricar, often conversed with the occupiers—especially Lieutenant Hammer, who socialized with local people in Sustary cafés and restaurants, on market days, and in the post office. Even as Hammer manipulated local people (especially Mme Etxart), they often manipulated him in their pursuit of information, in their attempts to settle scores and to achieve personal goals. When Inspector Carbou visited Sustary, he often discussed current events in the war with Superintendent Ressel, who commanded the garrison. Ressel also had an unusually sociable relationship with Canon Arricar and Mme Urruty, who in turn had a close, mutually manipulative relationship with a Gestapo agent. The occupation of Sustary was far from benign. Brutality figured regularly on the agenda of the Gestapo. Xiberoans who lived through the Occupation often claim that Sustary was the most dangerous place to be during those difficult times, not only because of the Gestapo. Many people claim that Sustary had the highest incidence of denunciation in the province.

The rural communities of Urdos and Ospitaleku provide contrasting pictures of Basque-German relations, the experience of occupation, and the administration of justice. The Germans occupied Urdos continuously. Although the number of men based there rarely exceeded ten, people felt the Germans' presence keenly and regarded it as an illegitimate invasion of territory through which Urdos Basques defined their personhood and collective identity as "mountain people." The German authorities imposed rules and regulations that violated long-standing Urdos traditions, rights, and privileges that were rooted in customary law. Patrols from Sustary and Oloron regularly searched local farms for Hitler's enemies and tried to intimidate the local population. With few exceptions, most rural people avoided contact and conversation with Germans and their interpreters. Like their Sustary neighbors, Urdos Basques felt that they, too, lived in a highly dangerous space during the Occupation.

Unlike Maule and Sustary, Urdos was not a deeply divided society before the Germans arrived. Political disagreements and local rivalries did exist, but they never gained enough agency to turn the community against itself. As in other rural Basque communities, in Urdos people retained a range of traditional practices and societal arrangements that provided a highly structured framework within which to achieve and maintain order and stability. The first-neighbor relationship, religious rituals such as the giving of blessed bread, systematically organized shepherding syndicates, and institutionalized forms of reciprocity and cooperation promoted a high level of social and spiritual solidarity in the commune. When German demands for meat on a daily basis threatened to divide the community, the Urdos priest devised an imaginative plan for coping with the problem. Similarly, when local people betrayed certain fellow citizens to the German police, the two women most closely affected by denunciation, deportation, and death responded courageously to their difficult circumstances and gave new meaning to a ritual that resisted the divisiveness of denunciation. Still, one or more "here people" in Urdos chose to denounce their fellow citizens to the Germans in 1943–44 and to the Liberation authorities in 1944–45. In Urdos people revealed deep-seated confusion over the legitimacy of "denouncing the denouncer," a process that took justice out of their hands and thus contravened long-standing traditions of autonomy in such matters. During the process of liberation and its aftermath, Urdos people relied upon other traditions in their attempts to handle the intra-community and intra-neighborhood conflict caused by local denunciations: they adapted their vicinal traditions to address an emotionally fraught situation involving two first neighbors; they called upon traditional values of neighborly cooperation and mutual aid to cope with their local crisis, locating the cycle of forgiveness in the ritual giving of blessed bread.

The people of Ospitaleku faced different challenges during the Occupation. Its people saw CFP resisters far more often than German troops, even after the tragedy of June 27, 1944. The presence of *maquisards* and of a Jewish family caused acute anxiety among members of the local population, who were not divided by any significant differences of political opinion. The Ospitaleku people shared a conservative Xiberoan habitus and a deep-seated yearning to protect themselves, their houses, and their property from harm. As in Urdos, the institution of first neighbors remained strong during the Occupation and in its aftermath. Numerous forms of reciprocal exchange, in both secular and spiritual spheres, fostered community solidarity and harmony. The brief presence of a CFP maquis threatened to turn the hamlet against itself. The massive German raid in June 1944 left citizens stunned and terrified. The arrests and deportations of so many local people—and visceral fear—united the rest of the population against the Germans.

Some citizens continued to resent the Resistance long after the tragedy occurred, but the passage of time and public memory of the Resistance, shaped by local, regional, and national discourses, fostered an ethos of forgiveness. That ethos is annually reinforced by the people of Ospitaleku when they participate in acts of commemoration organized by CFP veterans every June 27. Such forgiveness was not, however, extended to the "here person" responsible, in part, for the denunciation of the CFP maquis in June 1944. Yet no one ever "denounced the denouncer" during the process of liberation. Citizens chose to remain silent about his wrongdoing rather than to enable his judgment and punishment by authorities external to their moral community.

Xiberoans did call upon the formal courts of French legal justice to punish political and civilian collaborators for the harm they had done to Xiberoans and to the *patrie*. Legal judgments made by the courts during the Liberation did not, however, always bring closure to the process of community-based judgment in Xiberoa. More than sixty years later, some survivors of the Occupation and their families continue to contest the legitimacy of both civic and legal judgments that sent their loved ones to prison or punished them by other official means. In the twenty-first century, many Xiberoans have divided memories of the interwar years, German occupation, the Resistance, and the process of liberation. I have traced the roots of ongoing divisiveness to local disagreements about the legitimacy of legal and popular judgments and to the various ways in which Xiberoans tried to manage conflict and justice during those difficult decades. Nowadays, Xiberoans often attribute continuing animosities between rival resisters to insults they exchanged long ago and sometimes continue to repeat. Some supporters of the CFP still dismiss the Secret Army as "riffraff," men with no military training or experience who were "too political" (a euphemism for left-wing militancy) and who rarely engaged in actual combat. In turn, some Secret Army supporters still criticize the CFP as having been "too military" and brand its leaders as "terrorists" and "criminals" who gravely endangered Xiberoan lives and property. Political disagreements and both class-based and religious differences often did divide rival resisters, but neither of the two main Resistance groups was in fact politically or socially homogeneous. Their maquis included many young people who became involved in the Resistance merely by chance or because they happened to trust the person who recruited them. The lingering hostility felt by former rival resisters and their supporters is embedded in their habitus, in those lasting dispositions that integrate past experiences with experience in the present.

Neither popular nor legal justice ever provided rival resisters with a framework for establishing the legitimacy of their decisions and actions. Rival resistance leaders sought to establish "the truth" in their competing accounts of what happened during the summer of 1944 and during commemorative events to celebrate the twentieth anniversary of liberation. Although those leaders were no longer alive on the fortieth and sixtieth anniversaries of liberation, their friends and former comrades sometimes perpetuated feelings of hostility between rival groups through their own commemorative events, which still wrestled with issues of legitimacy, judgment, and a long-standing Xiberoan obligation to protect the community from harm.

In Xiberoa as elsewhere in France, "the need to remember" is today a compelling, selective social process in which young and elderly are alike involved. The voices of war veterans, former resisters, and survivors of Nazi atrocities dominate the public dimension of social remembering in that part of southwestern France. They speak passionately about the "need to remember" those who fought against fascism in France and Spain and against Hitler, exhorting people of all ages to "never forget" those who suffered and died in those struggles. These survivors, their civic supporters in the town halls and schools, and the local press all assume that a "collective memory" exists in the popular imagination. Preserving that collective, public memory is itself treated as a form of resistance to the socially unacceptable act of forgetting (*l'oubli*). They insist that a duty to remember (*un devoir de la mémoire*) underpins that collective process of remembering. Some elderly survivors of war feel a sense of urgency to share their private memories with the public. A few are accustomed to giving their testimonies at educational events designed to instill in today's youth a need to learn from the past and to protect democratic freedoms. Such public remembering seeks to unite Xiberoan people across generations and political differences. It seeks to rise above hostilities and rivalries stemming from events in the 1930s and 1940s by addressing moral and ethical issues of global importance.

In some individuals, a "need to know" accompanies the need to remember. It is most visible and intense in their efforts to learn as much as possible about the experiences of loved ones in wartime, about their circumstances, about the people who helped and harmed them. These Xiberoans were typically children or teenagers in the early 1940s. As adults, for a range of personal reasons, they have a keen interest in recuperating the memories of those loved ones. Some elderly Xiberoan people are profoundly absorbed by the need to remember, as well as by a "need to know." Their attachment to the past structures much of their daily lives and gives rise to a range of intense emotions. Anger and hatred often wrestle with deep-seated sorrow and lingering love. Some were victims of Nazi barbarity. Others endured the war and the Occupation at home and lost loved ones who are still mourned. Some elderly survivors of war avoid public attention and refuse invitations to attend or speak at civic functions. At times individual remembering is simply too painful, and silence serves as a refuge.

Yet, as many Xiberoans are aware, a social process of remembering, rooted in the 1930s and 1940s, continues to divide some members of Xiberoan society, especially in relation to denunciations made long ago; the long-standing, bitter *patron*-worker conflict; and the rival resistance groups that formed in Xiberoa. In 2004 the process of translating private memories into public remembering became intensely divisive when elderly veterans of the Resistance felt compelled to "tell what really happened" in their small province during the German Occupation. They did so in locally published memoirs, newspaper articles, and local radio programs and at civic events. Although some people claimed to be tired of the polemic surrounding the long-standing rivalry between the "Red" and the "White" maquis, they seemed unable to forget aspects of the past that still troubled them deeply. Yet even as they called for an end to the rivalry and animosity, some people were irresistibly drawn back into the web of hostility that surrounded commemorative events on the sixtieth anniversary of the Liberation. Disagreements about the past simply did not go away. Sensibilities continued to be offended. The need to forgive wrestled constantly with a reluctance or stubborn refusal to do so. For these veterans and their families, the need to remember had an emotional, competitive foundation, inextricably linked to their intense desire to ensure that their own "correct" version of events, especially during 1944, be treated as the definitive one.

In all four communities explored in this local study of borderland Basques, citizens used the popular justice of public rumor, ostracism, accusatory practices, and ritualized forms of public ridicule to address wrongdoing in their midst. As I have shown, citizens did not always turn to the official judiciary system created to administer justice during the process of liberation. Rather than testify against a fellow citizen locally known to have betrayed one or more individuals, people often refrained from making incriminating statements and thus refused to engage in the widespread process of "denouncing the denouncers." I have argued that their decision to do so derived from longstanding Xiberoan desires to protect two primordial Pyrenean institutions, the house and the community, and to manage their own conflict and justice. Parallel processes operated in the Basque house and community. Even as household members sought to conceal intradomestic conflict—a source of shame—from other citizens, Xiberoan communities likewise attempted to conceal intracommunity conflict that they could neither prevent nor control. Intense disorder arose from moral treachery by "here people" during the Occupation and the process of liberation. Betrayal of one insider by another gave rise to deep-rooted shame and revealed the dark side of solidarity in small, face-to-face communities whose complex moral universe in the 1940s sometimes stood in sharp contrast to the heroic profile of liberated France.

In 2001 a Xiberoan play about local resistance and liberation celebrated the solidarity of "here people" during the German Occupation. In 2004 numerous civic and educational events commemorated those who had suffered and perished in the war and honored those who had helped Xiberoans liberate themselves. In doing so, the borderland Basques of Xiberoa located the pardon in a cycle of forgiveness and forgetting that will, in due course, break down their divided memories of the past.

NOTES

1. Christian's (1969) community study of Saint Pierre examines the deep divisions between Gaullists and Pétainists on an island off the Newfoundland coast. Jacob (1994, chap. 3) provides an excellent overview of French Basque culture, clericalism, and politics from 1920 until 1945. The best accounts of occupation and resistance in the Basses-Pyrénées in French are provided by Jiménez de Aberasturi (1996) and Poullenot (1995). A useful account of the German Occupation in the Basque town of Kanbo is given in Halty (1985). In Lougarot (2004) the narratives of men and women who helped fugitives escape Vichy and Nazi oppression provide rich ethnographic detail and invaluable historical information about the Basques under German occupation.

2. Collaboration took many forms during the Occupation, including denunciation (intelligence with the enemy), large-scale profiteering in the black market, and sexual liaison with the Germans. Collaborationism refers to membership in pro-Nazi political movements and associations.

3. Dutourd's novel *The Best Butter* (1955) is a moral tale about profiteering on the black market. Grenier's novel *Another November* (1998), set in Pau, explores the ways in which the Occupation permanently changed the lives of friends who variously joined the Resistance or collaborated with the Germans.

4. Todorov (1996) uses the ethic of conviction and the ethic of responsibility conceived by Max Weber (1958) as an analytical tool in understanding the choices resisters made in one French town during the Occupation.

5. Very little has been published about the experiences of northern Basques during the interwar years, under Vichy and German occupation. Basques refer to the three Basque provinces of Lapurdi, Behe Nafarroa, and Xiberoa in the French state as "the northern side." The four Basque provinces of Gipuzkoa, Nafarroa, Bizkaia, and Araba are located in the Spanish state. Basques often refer to the area as Hegoalde, "the southern side."

6. In order to preserve anonymity, protect the interests of individuals and their families, and honor agreements relating to the departmental archives, I have changed the names of two communities and, with some exceptions, the names of persons whose experiences are recounted in the book.

7. Through the Conseil Général of the Pyrénées-Atlantiques, the minister of Culture and the director of Archives in France kindly gave me permission to consult classified documents in the Archives Départementales (noted hereafter as AD, P-A). The Social Behavioral Institutional Review Board at the University of Nevada, Reno, reviewed and approved the English and French versions of the consent documents for protocol SB03/04–64, "War, Occupation and Memory in the Basque Country."

INTRODUCTION

1. On the eve of the Occupation, the department of the Basses-Pyrénées had a Jewish population of 400 and two synagogues (in Baiona and Pau). For unknown reasons, the synagogue in Pau functioned throughout the Occupation for the 100 to 150 Jews who remained there, in spite of the Gestapo (A. Laufer 2004: pers. comm.; Poullenot 1995: 54).

2. Wylie (1974: 27) had a similar experience in the Vaucluse village of Peyrane.

1: INSIDERS, OUTSIDERS, AND TRANS-PYRENEAN RELATIONS

1. The concept of habitus, much like Thompson's own concept of the moral economy, has been widely reworked as an analytical tool in a range of disciplines (Thompson 1991: 257–351).

2. The word *xokho* makes an affective link between a person and a space in which one feels at home. The term is often translated as *le coin* in French (Lauburu 1998: 31).

3. The distinction between *arrotz* ("stranger to the house") and *etxeko* ("of the house") dates at least from the eleventh century. Basque proverbs recorded in the sixteenth and seventeenth centuries often used the word *arrotz* in a pejorative sense (Peillen 1997: 453).

4. Northern Basques used another pejorative term ("black bones," *ezurbeltzak* in Basque; *os noir* in French) for Spaniards who came from communities south of the Ebro River (ibid.: 446).

5. Cases in which the moral community judged Xiberoan men and women are found in the departmental archives of the Pyrénées-Atlantiques, AD, P-A, B5380, folio 38 (1737); B5365 folio 89 (1721).

6. In 1721 the jurats of the Béarnais village of Monein went to the lodgings of a young, impoverished woman who had given birth to an illegitimate child in their community. Reluctant to use community resources on the outsider, the jurats appealed to external magistrates, who ruled that Monein had a moral responsibility for the nourishment of mother and child (Desplats 1982: 61).

7. The charter (1704) of the Basque valley of Baigorri promised recompense to denunciators who reported wrongdoing to the local authorities and treated such denunciations as "positive acts" (Bidart 1977: 55). In many different societies, denunciation has been the subject of two opposing discourses: one exalts denunciation as a civic duty to the state, while the other deplores it as betrayal (Fitzpatrick and Gellately 1997: 17). Lucas (1997: 22–39) explores the contradictions between "good" and "bad" denunciation (the problem of *dénonciation* versus *délation*) during the French Revolution.

8. The seminal article by Cavaillès (1910), "Une fédération pyrénéenne sous l'Ancien Regime: Les traités de lies et de passeries," has been reprinted in collected essays on trans-Pyrenean treaties and pastoral agreements (Société d'Etudes des Septs Vallées, 1986).

2: URDOS, A BORDERLAND MORAL COMMUNITY

1. This figure is taken from the 1911 census, reported in the *Annuaire administratif, judiciaire et industriel du départment des Basses-Pyrénées (1831–1911)*.

2. In attenuated form, the pastoral institution of the *olha* still exists today.

3. The Basque spoken in Urdos still contains expressions and vocabulary that are unique to that commune.

4. In rural Xiberoan communities, the offer or withholding of hospitality by the female head of household still defines the status of a visitor as a welcome or unwelcome guest. In 1977 a woman refused to offer food or drink to a French graduate student who had been doing fieldwork in another valley. When he left the house, she explained that she had no respect for the man because he had made no effort to learn the Basque language and had no interest in the local culture. She described the student as *auher*, which means both "useless" and "lazy" (K. Irigaray 1977: pers. comm.).

5. A French law mandating the equal division of property, passed in 1793, was modified further in the Civil Code of 1803. It was not until February 1938 that the law permitted impartible inheritance, on condition that nonheirs receive compensations from the inheritor (Jacob 1994: 43, 414n.).

6. In the various Pyrenean patois, the terms *vési, vésiau, vézin, bezi* denoted neighbor (Fougères 1938: 92).

7. According to Basque customary law, an individual could not leave his or her birthplace and settle in another community without first having been accorded the status of "neighbor." In Nafarroa, customary law required an individual who moved into a community to keep a fire burning in the hearth for one year and a day and to pay a tax in order to become a neighbor/citizen (ibid.: 93n.).

8. For a detailed explanation of vicinal relationships, see Ott (1993b: 63–81).

9. Of the 114 marriages contracted by Urdos Basques between 1900 and 1979, 97 were endogamous to the community and 81 involved people from the same half of the community.

10. In seventeen cases, a "here person" married an outsider (Ott 1989: 255).

11. I discuss the strategy in greater detail elsewhere (ibid.: 259–60).

12. People expected men to control their sexual force by means of coitus interruptus (J.-P. Jonnet 1978: pers. comm.; D. Prebende 1979: pers. comm.).

13. In July 1920 the French state passed a law aimed at the suppression of birth control, particularly abortion (Pollard 1998: 11). In 1939 the Third Republic changed aspects of that law in its Family Code. Women who habitually had abortions and their professional accomplices became liable to prison sentences and fines (ibid.: 175).

14. As recently as 2001, a Xiberoan shepherd explained to me as we admired the snow-capped mountains against a clear blue sky: "I've never understood your love of words and books. Those mountains, the earth, my animals—they are my university. They have always been my teachers."

15. In the 1970s elderly Xiberoans often talked about "the old religion" (*errelijion zaharra* or *la vieille religion*) and felt deep nostalgia over its gradual disappearance during the 1950s and 1960s.

214 Notes to Pages 29–40

16. The priest used the relic for these purposes (and also to banish mice) until the 1950s.

17. Desplats (1982: 163) reports a similar incident in the Béarnais town of Higuères. During the winter of 1916–17, a group of local women enacted a charivari and composed "very lewd verses" to ridicule and punish the wrongdoers.

3: BASQUES IN THE GREAT WAR

1. AD, P-A, IM94, report by special commissioner to prefect, March 16, 1915.

2. In a recent local-history project, Xiberoans with an interest in the Great War examined more than 1,500 letters written by Xiberoan soldiers to their families (Ikherzaleak 2006). Very few of them were written in Basque, but many contained Basque phrases (R. Elissondo 2007: pers. comm.).

3. Seven and a half percent of the soldier's letters included passages in Basque. The phrases typically contained information that censors forbade soldiers to convey.

4. Mobilized in Pau in 1915, one soldier met a Basque recruit who did not speak any French. The Frenchman observed in his diary that events would soon force the Basque to learn it (E. Weber 1976: 78).

5. From the 1790s into the Second Empire and early Third Republic, the French often responded to military conscription by evading the draft and deserting (Cobb 1970; E. Weber 1976: 295).

6. The customary laws (*foruak* or *fueros*) of the other historic Basque territories make the same or a similar stipulation.

7. E. Weber (1976: 544) cites the report (MR1228, 1840), in the files of Mémoires et reconnaissances, Archives du Ministère de la Guerre.

8. AD, P-A, IM95, report by minister of the Interior to prefect of the Basses-Pyrénées, August 12, 1917.

9. In August 1914 these active regiments belonged to the Seventy-First and Seventy-Second Brigades in the Thirty-Sixth Division of the Eighteenth Army Corps (Rocafort 1997: 16).

10. There is no evidence that networks of clandestine Pyrenean guides existed during the Great War. During the German Occupation, however, Basques operated highly organized intelligence and escape networks across the Pyrenees.

11. AD, P-A, IM95, report by prefect to minister of the Interior, Pau, December 1, 1914.

12. Ibid.

13. Ibid. Soldiers on leave and convalescents required special authorization from the regional military commander, as well as testimonials from two fathers with sons at the front from the applicant's natal community (R. Elissondo 2007: pers. comm.).

14. AD, P-A, IM94, report by special police inspector in Baigorri to subprefect in Maule, January 7, 1917, on Pedro F. of Errazu.

15. Ibid., report on desertions by subprefect in Maule to prefect, December 7, 1916.

16. Ibid., report by subprefect in Maule to prefect, January 25, 1918.

17. Ibid., report by subprefect in Maule to prefect, February 13, 1917.

18. Ibid., report by inspector to subprefect in Maule, July 23, 1917.

19. AD, P-A, IM95, folder on *insoumis,* report by minister of the Interior in Paris to prefect, March 14, 1917.

20. Ibid., folder on complicity in desertion, report by subprefect in Maule to prefect, December 6, 1916.

21. AD, P-A, IM94, subprefect in Baiona to prefect, December 17, 1916.

22. Ibid., report by subprefect in Maule to prefect in Pau, January 12, 1917.

23. Ibid., folder on Ginestoux.

24. Ibid., report by special commissioner to prefect, March 16, 1915.

25. Ibid.

26. AD, P-A, IM352, report by special commissioner in Hendaia to prefect, March 23, 1916. Pourcher (1994: 432) cites a report by the subprefect of Maule, December 19, 1916. In the borderland commune of Urepel in neighboring Behe Nafarroa, only 5 of the 250 men called up for military service did not desert.

27. AD, P-A, IM95, report by subprefect in Maule to prefect, December 7, 1917.

28. On several occasions, Charlie Chaplin attended parties given by one Maule industrialist (M. Etcheverry 2003: pers. comm.).

29. Jean Ybarnegaray was the first president of the French Federation of Basque Pelota and the founding president of the International Federation of Basque Pelota (founded in Buenos Aires in 1929).

30. Interview by Joël Rocafort (1997) with Mme Marie-Louise de Poutier, in Biarritz (date of interview unknown). I met Mme Poutier in 2004, shortly before her death in a car accident.

31. AD, P-A, IM94, letter from Captain Miguras of the Forty-Ninth Regiment to Captain Dosman in Hendaia, March 18, 1918.

32. AD, P-A, IM95, letter from mayor of Sare to prefect, March 20, 1918.

33. AD, P-A, IM94, letter from subprefect of Baiona to prefect of the Basses-Pyrénées, November 30, 1918.

34. Ibid., report by subprefect in Maule to prefect, July 25, 1917.

35. Further archival research is required to compare desertion and evasion rates among the Basques with those of other borderland people in France.

36. AD, P-A, IM94, report on Ybarnegaray by subprefect in Maule to prefect, March 12, 1918. On April 12, 1955, the French government finally passed an amnesty law that allowed First World War deserters to return to France (Rocafort 1997: 496).

4: THE ROOTS OF DIVIDED MEMORIES IN MAULE

1. The Xiberoan cultural and local history association, Uhaitza, undertook the first trans-Pyrenean research project that culminated in a social history of the Swallows and their memories (Inchauspé 2001). The book was produced in conjunction with another trans-Pyrenean association, Ainarak (the Swallows), which launched a second project on relations between Xiberoa and the valleys of Erronkari, Zaraitzu, and Aescoa in Nafarroa and the valleys of Ansò and Fago in Aragón in 2005–2006.

The project aims to produce a history of the Navarrese and Aragonese immigrants in Xiberoa. In June 2006 the project sponsored a week of seminars in Maule on the narratives of former Swallows, oral histories of Spanish Republicans, and a series of presentations on the popular culture of the Pyrenean borderlands (A. Barbe-Labarthe, J. Larroque 2007: pers. comms.).

5: CLASS CONFLICT, DISPLACEMENT, AND FEAR OF THE OTHER

1. In the departmental archives (AD, P-A, 1M20), a file indicates that the first factory strike in Maule took place in 1912. Conflict between sandal-factory workers and their employers also occurred in other French Basque communities during the First World War, but the strikes in Maule were the longest and most violent.

2. AD, P-A, 1OM20, on "conflict in the Maule sandal industry."

3. Ibid. Although this file contains detailed information about the "worker conflict," documents are not numbered.

4. Ibid.

5. Ibid.

6. Ibid.

7. Ibid.

8. Passed in 1928, the Loucheur Law enabled citizens to obtain state-sponsored loans and subsidies for home ownership and was regarded, by some politicians, as a means of combating the communists by making them property owners (Wakeman 2004: 126). In Maule a few privileged workers built their own houses with Loucheur subsidies (Ikherzaleak 1994: 106).

9. *Le Journal de Saint-Palais,* November 18, 1928.

10. AD, P-A, 1OM20.

11. *Le Journal de Saint-Palais,* August 11, 1929.

12. AD, P-A, 1OM20, on "conflicts at work."

13. In March 1939, in the Chamber of Deputies, Ybarnegaray called the Spanish Republicans and communists who sought refuge in France "plunderers, firebrands, dynamiters, assassins and executioners" (Dreyfus-Armand 1999: 46).

14. AD, P-A, 1M47, report 299, February 5, 1937.

15. AD, P-A, 1M278, circular from prefect to all mayors in the department.

16. *L'Indépendent des Basses-Pyrénées,* February 7, 1939.

17. *Le Patriote,* February 9, 1939.

18. AD, P-A, 3Z83; petition dated September 14, 1939.

19. Bérard went on to serve as one of Vichy's ambassadors to the Holy See (Paxton 2001: 175, 340). His young protégé, Jean-Louis Tixier-Vignancour, became director of Vichy radio in 1940. Tixier-Vignancour received more than one million votes in the French presidential election of 1965 (ibid.: 333).

20. Bundesarchiv, Berlin, v237/1/17. Complément rapport sur délégation au camp de Gurs.

21. AD, P-A, 54W31, report 1868, from special police inspector Bats to subprefect, July 22, 1941.

22. In seeking motives for his father's denunciation, the son of Pérez drew upon his late mother's interpretation of events (R. Pérez 2004: pers. comm.; M. Rodrigo Nicolau 2005: pers. comm.). According to Vitorina Olaverri (R. Pérez 2004: pers. comm.), the factory owner wanted to punish his former employee for inciting co-workers to strike in the 1930s.

23. AD, P-A, 30W13, D file on collaboration.

6: XIBEROANS UNDER VICHY

1. In December 1945 Émile Ducommun stood trial on charges of intelligence with the enemy and endangering the security of the French state. He was acquitted (AD, P-A, 30W13).

2. AD, P-A, 54W31, report from special police inspector Bats to subprefect, July 27, 1940.

3. Ibid., report from Bats to subprefect and special commissioner in Pau, July 27, 1940.

4. AD P-A, 54W31, report 1945, Bats to subprefect, August 4, 1941.

5. Fitzpatrick and Gellately (1997: 12–13) cite parallel examples from Stalinist Russia and Nazi Germany. Most civilians who wrote to the authorities "with grievances, complaints and requests" sought to "to achieve some private purposes of their own through their letters."

6. AD P-A, 54W31, report 1945, includes the letter of denunciation. Darlan served as commander-in-chief of Vichy forces and became head of French North Africa. He was notoriously anti-Semitic and anticommunist.

7. The Légion Française des Combattants brought together rival veterans and often suffered from internal rivalries in many parts of France (Gildea 2002: 139).

8. Exhibition on Maule under occupation organized by the local association, Ikherzaleak, and presented at the Collège de Saint-François, Maule, in the summer of 2004.

9. AD, P-A, 54W31, CDN2694, letter from subprefect to prefect, August 2, 1941, replying to prefect's letter of July 24, 1941; CD1482, July 22, 1941, letter from prefect to subprefect.

10. AD, P-A, 54W31, report 1868, inspector to subprefect, July 24, 1941.

11. AD, P-A, 54W37, under M. The first prefect of the Basses-Pyrénées, Émile Ducommun, stepped down soon after the Germans occupied the Free Zone.

12. AD, P-A, 37W14, CD3493, subprefect to prefect, August 29, 1941.

13. Ibid.

14. AD, P-A, 37W6, various correspondences about Manuel S. by Herbille, the inspector, and Manuel's father.

15. AD, P-A, 37W14, report from inspector Bats to subprefect, September 23, 1941.

16. AD, P-A, 37W28, CD4264, report from subprefect to prefect, September 26, 1941.

17. AD, P-A, 37W6, CA7178, letter from Manuel S. to subprefect, October 24, 1941; CA6891 and 4690, letters from Herbille to subprefect, October 17, 1941.

18. AD, P-A, 30W88, CD601; prefect to departmental head of press censorship, January 31, 1942.

19. AD, P-A, 37W14, CA2063, February 24, 1942, report by Inspector Carbou to subprefect.

20. AD, P-A, 37W14, report 414, CA8103, Carbou to subprefect, December 1, 1941.

21. AD, P-A, 37W14, report 669, CA912, Carbou to subprefect, January 24, 1942.

22. AD, P-A, 37W27, report 1056, inspector to subprefect, April 13, 1942. Pierre Béguerie avoided the event. Some Maule socialists accused him of being "Doriot's man," owing to his brief association with fascism in the 1930s (Béguerie n.d.: 17).

23. AD, P-A, 37W14, report 1176, CA3246, Carbou to subprefect, March 25, 1942.

24. AD, P-A, 37W14, report 1316, CA4258, Carbou to subprefect, April 24, 1942.

25. AD, P-A, 37W14, report 2066, CA10438, Carbou to subprefect, September 23, 1942.

26. Ibid.

27. Mme Maitena Etcheverry, owner of the Hotel Bidegain, kindly gave me copies of the letters.

28. AD, P-A, 37W115, CA3723.

29. AD, P-A, 37W14, report 1896, CA8574, Carbou to principal commissioner in the Pau prefecture, August 22, 1942.

30. AD, P-A, 37W6, report 292 by inspector to subprefect, August 25, 1942; CA1838.

31. AD, P-A, 37W27, CD2352, "administrative internments," Elizondo file.

32. AD, P-A, 37W14, report 1614, CA6279; report 1623, CA6532, Carbou to subprefect, June 23 and 24, 1942; report 1890, CA8435, August 22, 1942.

33. The Armistice Commission, based in Wiesbaden, sent a delegation of German officers to Pau soon after France surrendered in 1940. The delegation left in June 1943 (AD, P-A, 30W2).

7: THE GERMAN OCCUPATION AND RESISTANCE IN XIBEROA

1. AD, P-A, 37W14, report 2394, CA12205, Carbou to subprefect, November 25, 1942.

2. AD, P-A, 37W114, HC/HP, CD10283, subprefect to German customs office in Oloron, December 20, 1942.

3. The SD was a branch of the Gestapo, with headquarters in the Béarnais town of Oloron. A French division of the Waffen SS and twenty men in the pro-Nazi Anti-Bolshevist Legion (LVF, Légion de Voluntaires Français contre le Bolchévisme) occupied a château in Moumour, a smaller town nearby.

4. AD, P-A, 37W114, report not numbered, subprefect to German commander in Oloron, December 30, 1942.

5. Hoping to involve Spain in an attack on Gibralter, Hitler met with Franco in October 1940 in Hendaia, a Basque coastal town in Lapurdi (Paxton 2001: 74).

6. No accurate figures on the number of fugitives are available for Xiberoa. Poullenot (1995) provides useful information about clandestine guides and the numbers of people deported and arrested for evasion, resistance, and other activities.

7. AD, P-A, 37W115, CA41, subprefect to prefect, February 1, 1943.

8. AD, P-A, 37W115, CA3334, inspector to subprefect, April 1, 1943.

9. AD, P-A, 37W115, CA3334, and CA4369, inspector to subprefect, May 5, 1943.

10. AD, P-A, 37W15, CA2965, CD101, Inspector Carbou to the subprefect, March 23, 1943. All quotes in the paragraph are taken from this file.

11. Information taken from file, note 10.

12. AD, P-A, 37W15, CA859, report 172, Carbou to subprefect, January 23, 1943.

13. AD, P-A, 37W15, report 122, CA859, Carbou to subprefect, January 23, 1943.

14. AD, P-A, 30W13, D files on suspected collaborators, testimony of Rose Blasquiz.

15. Franco created the Spanish concentration camp at Miranda de Ebro in 1937 for Spanish Republicans and later used it for STO evaders, resisters, Allied soldiers, and intelligence/escape network operatives.

16. AD, P-A, 30W13, D file. The Maule people denounced by Roger D. in 1943 testified against him at his trial in January 1946. The German interpreter for the Gestapo in Hendaia did so as well.

17. AD, P-A, 37W15, CD2805, report 433, subprefect to principal commissioner in Pau, March 21, 1943.

18. AD, P-A, 37W15, CD1233, report 176, inspector to principal commissioner, March 1, 1943.

19. AD, P-A, 30W9, D file on collaborators.

20. AD, P-A, 37W114, reports on German military and civilian personnel, reports 580/3, CA3697, 620, CA3896, by National Police and Carbou, April 13 and 19, 1943.

21. AD, P-A, 37W115, no report number, May 24, 1943.

22. AD, P-A, 30W3, B file on collaboration.

23. AD, P-A, 30W13, D file on collaboration.

24. The Americans appointed General Giraud as head of Vichy's North African forces in December 1942. He changed political direction from support for Pétain to a pro-Republican stance in March 1943. Although American intelligence reports indicate "no support at all among the resistance movements" for Giraud (Sweets 1976: 79n.), he retained the loyalty of former members of the French Armistice Army, created after the 1940 armistice agreement between Germany and France.

25. AD, P-A, 37W15, CD5870, subprefect to prefect, October 2, 1943.

26. AD, P-A, 37W15, CA8072, report 1223/3, Carbou to subprefect, September 23, 1943.

27. Vichy abolished the *conseils-généraux* on October 12, 1940, and replaced the councils with departmental administrative commissions whose members were typically right-wing notables (Gildea 2002: 176).

28. AD, P-A, 37W115, file on arrests, individuals wounded, and individuals killed by the Germans; Lieutenant Tamise's report, head of the Maule gendarmerie, September 24, 1943. The file contains a letter from Souhy to the prefect, September 23, 1943. Ybarnegaray was liberated in April 1945. In 1946 the French High Court of Justice sentenced him to national degradation but annulled it owing to "service to the Resistance" (Eusko Ikaskuntza 1998: 204).

29. AD, P-A, 37W15, report 763, CA4772, Carbou to subprefect, May 19, 1943.

30. AD, P-A, 37WII5, unnumbered report on individuals killed by a French Waffen ss patrol based in the château in Moumour. Mme Jaureguiberry of Barkoxe reported that the patrol also included members of the LVF, a French regiment created in 1941 to fight alongside German troops on the eastern front (R. Elissondo 2007: pers. comm.).

31. AD, P-A, 37WII4, report 269, 276, Carbou to head of the Intelligence Service in Maule, May 24, 1945.

32. Ibid., reports 269, 276.

33. The Basque couple owed their freedom to Eugène Goyheneche, for whom three goals became paramount during the German Occupation of the northern Basque Country: to protect the three northern Basque provinces from harm; to protect southern Basque refugees from the French and German police; and to consider the possible consequences of a German victory (Jacob 1994: 118).

34. AD, P-A, 37WI5, JT/HP, CD5870, subprefect to prefect, October 2, 1943.

35. It was one of three in the Carrère battalion operating in the Basses-Pyrénées (Céroni 1980: 122). The CFP operated in the Ariège, the Pyrenees, parts of Gers and the Landes, the Lot and Lot-et-Garonne, and Tarn-et-Garonne. Poullenot (1995: 196) estimates that some six thousand men were recruited, whereas Kedward (1994: 294) gives a much lower figure of three thousand.

36. Charged with "administrative failure," the director of the camp was himself interned in another Vichy camp. For an account of the raid, see the testimony of Arlette Dachary, who worked at Gurs from March 1941 until December 1945 (AMCB 1995: 143–44).

37. AD, P-A, 37WI5, CA3127, 278, Carbou to commissioner, May 3, 1944.

38. AD, P-A, 37W6, CD1721, Larbonne to subprefect, April 18, 1944.

39. AD, P-A, 37WI5, report 373, CA3560, Carbou to police commissioner in Pau, June 15, 1944.

8: THE TRAGEDY OF OSPITALEKU

1. AD, P-A, 37WI72, elections 1939–46, under St-Blaise.

2. Maurice Malharin kept detailed records for the Xiberoan CFP during the Occupation. His son, Jojo Malharin, kindly lent me his late father's CFP archives in the summer of 2004.

3. Aurelian M. was of Spanish origin and an ex-Communist Party member whom the Gestapo twice arrested for helping fugitives obtain false identity papers. A. M. appears on a Vichy list of "individuals to be arrested in the event of serious troubles" (AD, P-A, 37WII5, no CD number, March 7, 1943).

4. AD, P-A, 37WI5, CA3616, report 381, Carbou's monthly bulletin, June 15, 1944.

5. AD, P-A, 37WII5, arrests, wounded, and killed by the Germans, report on St-Blaise, not numbered.

6. AD, P-A, 54WI3, first deputy mayor of Ospitaleku to prefect and subprefect, July 1, 1944.

7. AD, P-A, 54WI3, "juifs"; report 199, by Carbou to subprefect, February 9, 1943.

8. Aimée Larlus was the "first neighbor" from Ospitaleku with whom Marie-Louise Lasserre Davancens and her mother were deported.

9. As part of the CFP commemorations of Xiberoa's (and France's) liberation in August 1944, Robert Elissondo recorded the testimonies of four people who witnessed the German raid on Ospitaleku on June 27, 1944: Jean François Aguerre, a farmer in Moncayolle; Marie-Louise Davancens, daughter of Ospitaleku innkeepers; Jean Erbinarteguy, who lived on the Barcus/Ospitaleku border and was fourteen years old in 1944; and Marcelle Barreix, who lived in the center of the hamlet and was six years old at the time of the raid. I am most grateful to M. Elissondo for having given me their testimonies, which he transcribed from tapes made in June 2004. He also gave me a copy of his father's own unpublished memoir, "Comment ma famille traverse la guerre" (1989), which includes detailed recollections of events in Ospitaleku on June 27, 1940.

10. Robert Elissondo recorded Marie-Louise Lasserre Davancens on tape (June 2004) and also helped her write down her memories of deportation and her return home. Their joint work was printed and distributed locally in Xiberoa. I heard her oral testimony during a visit to her house in Oloron (February 2005), for which I am most grateful to M. Elissondo.

11. In his account of resisters' ill-fated attempt to liberate the small town of Saint-Amand-Montrond, Todorov (1996) uses Max Weber's ethics of conviction and of responsibility in his analysis of the tragedy that occurred.

9: RESISTING DIVISIVENESS THROUGH RITUAL IN URDOS

1. AD, P-A, 37W30, report 328 by Carbou on primary schoolteachers in 1942 to principal commissioner in Pau, March 3, 1943.

2. AD, P-A, 37W30, report 932 on "suspect schoolteachers," March 31, 1941.

3. AD, P-A, 37W30, a "national security" report. The prefect ordered the teacher to leave Xiberoa on April 15, 1941, and relocated him in a community in the Landes. The teacher had several aliases, which annoyed the prefect and the police charged with tracking his movements.

4. AD, P-A, 37W14, CA12205, report 2394 by Inspector Carbou to subprefect, November 25, 1942.

5. AD, P-A, 37W14, report from unidentified administrator in Maule to subprefect, on arrival of Germans in Upper Xiberoa, November 23, 1942.

6. AD, P-A, 37W, 115, file on people arrested, wounded, and killed by the Germans in 1943–44.

7. The application of la jonchée to sexual liaisons between Basque women and German soldiers is discussed in Ott 2006.

8. Testimony of Eloi Eiherabarra given to Dr. P. Durban, August 1964.

9. AD, P-A, 37W115, file on citizens arrested, wounded, and killed by the Germans in 1943–44.

10. This account of the Doyart-Garat tragedy is based upon fieldwork and classified documents in the departmental archives.

11. AD, P-A, 37W115.

12. During fieldwork I discussed the Garat case with numerous people who had lived in Urdos during the Occupation. I knew the son of Pierre Garat, who inherited the Garat house, but he did not wish to discuss the case with me.

13. In a nearby community, people placed small wooden coffins on the doorsteps of local collaborators to symbolically express their deep disapproval of the individuals' immoral, treacherous actions. Gildea (2002) also reports the use of such coffins to achieve popular justice in the Loire.

14. For an overview of the relationship between justice and the pardon, see Abel 1996.

15. This chapter expands the analysis presented in Ott 2007, which won the Millstone Prize (awarded by the Western Society for French History) in 2007.

10: DENUNCIATION, RUMOR, AND REVENGE IN SUSTARY

1. In order to protect the privacy of individuals and their families, I have changed the names of people and places cited in this chapter. I use the real names of informants who provided personal communications.

2. "Good tongues" is an ironic play on the French expression, *les mauvaises langues,* "bad tongues," slanderers and people quick to speak ill of others.

3. AD, P-A, 30W23, files on suspected collaborators tried by the French Court of Justice.

4. AD, P-A, 37W172, election results for 1939 and 1945.

5. AD, P-A, 37W114, foreigners in the "reserved zone," report by German Kommandatur in Oloron to head of German police in Paris, June 25, 1943.

6. AD, P-A, 37W172.

7. AD, P-A, 37W15, report 39 on "foyers of trouble," CA403, Carbou to principal commissioner, January 19, 1944.

8. AD, P-A, 30W23, testimony of the town crier.

9. AD, P-A, 30W23, letter from notary to Mme Etxart's lawyer, November 11, 1943.

10. Ibid.

11. Ibid., testimony of Dr. Idiart, February 7, 1945.

12. AD, P-A, 37W, CD10283. Although both German and Vichy officials agreed that the border required surveillance, they disputed each other's authority over the French police in such matters.

13. AD, P-A, 37W30, Vichy police inspector, Special Information, in Maule to subprefect in Oloron, August 5, 1940, September 26, 1940, March 31, 1941.

14. AD, P-A, 30W13; 30W23. Their retention in post may have arisen from the short-lived support for de Gaulle by the first Vichy-appointed prefect for the department of the Basses-Pyrénées.

15. AD, P-A, 30W23, testimonies of Lieutenant Hammer (tribunal in Pau, March 28, 1945), M. and Mme Urruty (February 28, 1945).

16. Ibid., testimonies of Idiart to Sustary police (February 7, 1945) and Sabalot (February 6, 1945).

17. Ibid., testimonies of Sergeant-Major Labat in the gendarmerie to Sustary justice of the peace (February 9, 1945); of Hammer to police at Gurs (September 20, 1944); of Mme Urruty to tribunal in Pau (February 28, 1945); report by minister of the Interior, Pau (November 30, 1944).

18. Ibid., Labat's testimony to Sustary justice of the peace, February 9, 1945.

19. AD, P-A, 37W114, CD3835, subprefect to German head of security in Sustary, May 31, 1943; CA8064, Carbou to subprefect, September 23, 1943.

20. I am very grateful to Robert Gildea for having corresponded with me about intracommunity relationships forged between Sustary citizens and German soldiers.

21. AD, P-A, 30W23, Mme Sabalot to Sustary police, February 6, 1945.

22. Ibid., Mme Etxart to regional police at camp Idron, October 3, 1944.

23. Ibid., notary to lawyer of Mme Etxart (November 11, 1943).

24. Ibid., Sergeant-Major Labat to justice of the peace, February 9, 1945.

25. Ibid., Hammer to tribunal in Pau, March 28, 1945.

26. Ibid., Mme Sabalot to Sustary police, February 6, 1945.

27. Ibid., Mme Urruty to tribunal, February 28, 1945.

28. Ibid., Mme Sabalot to police, February 6, 1945; Mme Etxeberry to police, February 6, 1945.

29. Ibid., Mme Bordachar, testimony in Sustary, February 9, 1945; Mme Uthurru to Sustary police, February 19, 1945.

30. Ibid., Mme Urruty to tribunal in Pau, February 28, 1945.

31. Ibid., Mme Etxart to regional police at Idron, October 3, 1944.

32. Ibid., letter from M. Harbustan to president of the Purges Commission, Pau, September 30, 1944.

33. Ibid., president of the Purges Commission to divisional police commander, Pau, October 28, 1944.

34. Ibid., Mme Etxart to regional police at Idron, October 3, 1944.

35. Focusing on the connection between gossip and communication, Robert Paine (1967: 279) shows how judgments are executed and broadcast through gossip.

36. AD, P-A, 37W15, report 39, CA403, Carbou to principal commissioner on "foyers of trouble," January 19, 1944.

11: THE DIVISIVENESS OF LIBERATION

1. A semiofficial organization created in 1951, the Comité d'Histoire de la Deuxième Guerre Mondiale, consisted of historians who collected data on the Occupation, including oral testimonies and memoirs about the period in France (Atkin 2001: 6; Gildea 2002: 10).

2. I have used unpublished CFP documents compiled by the late CFP resister Maurice Malharin and approved by General Pommiès in correspondence during 1964. I am grateful to Jojo Malharin for having provided access to these papers. The Secret Army's version of events is given in the pamphlet "Libération de la Soule, Août 1944," printed in 1944 and, in slightly revised form, in 1984.

3. Testimony of Lavalou and Bercut in *L'Étoile noire, bulletin de liaison de l'Amicale du CFP-49th RI,* 1964, no. 16.

4. Ibid.

5. Unpublished report, "Operations of the CFP," undated, page 10, from Malharin papers.

6. Reported by the editor (Pierre Udoy) of the local newspaper, *Le Miroir de la Soule,* June 11, 1994.

7. AD, P-A, 37W18, report 521, CA5166, monthly bulletin, September 6, 1944.

8. During the summer of 1944, "a sudden German arrival or return was a permanent threat and a frequent reality" in many parts of France (Kedward 1994: 208).

9. Unpublished report, "Operations of the CFP," undated, page 9, from the Malharin papers.

10. At the end of 1941, the Spanish Communist Party selected a number of Spanish militants in the French Resistance to form groups of guerrillas (Guérilleros) in southern France. Most of the resisters came from the legendary Fourteenth Corps of the Spanish Republican Army (Dreyfus-Armand 1999: 162).

11. Unpublished report, "Operations of the CFP," undated, page 13, Malharin papers.

12. AD, P-A, 37W18, commissioner of General Intelligence to principal commissioner of Pau, report 2448, September 18, 1944.

13. Ibid., Sub-Lieutenant Herbelot, Maule Gendarmerie, CA6019, October 11, 1944.

14. Ibid., Carbou's monthly bulletin on "public opinion," report 521, CA5166, Maule, September 6, 1944.

15. Ibid., Carbou's monthly bulletin, report 577, CA6389, October 25, 1944.

16. Ibid., commissioner of General Intelligence to principal commissioner of Pau, CA2468, September 29, 1944.

17. Ibid., commissioner of General Intelligence to principal commissioner of Pau, report 2448, September 18, 1944.

18. Ibid., Carbou's monthly bulletin, report 530, CA5563, Maule, September 20, 1944.

19. Ibid., Carbou's monthly report, report 594, CA6615, November 3, 1944.

20. Ibid., Sub-Lieutenant Herbelot, Maule Gendarmerie, report 6803, November 11, 1944.

21. Ibid., Carbou's monthly report, report 546, CA5874, October 4, 1944.

22. AD, P-A, 30W23, H file.

23. Ibid., Harbustan to divisional commissioner of mobile police, Pau, October 24, 1944.

24. Ibid., Harbustan to president of Purges Commission, Pau, September 30, 1944.

25. Ibid., butcher to tribunal in Pau, February 8, 1945.

26. Ibid., retired tax collector to president of Purges Commission, November 12, 1944.

27. Ibid., Ressel to police at camp d'Andenes, February 15, 1945; Hammer to tribunal in Pau, February 28, 1945.

28. Ibid., Mme Boullion in undated testimony; Mme Sabalot to Sustary police, February 6, 1945; Mme Uthurru to tribunal, February 28, 1945; Duclos to Judge Alibert, Pau, February 10, 1945.

29. Ibid., Mme Etxart to tribunal in Pau, March 2, 1945.

30. According to the 1936 census, the department of the Basses-Pyrénées had a population of 413,411. Of the 525 people convicted by the post-Liberation courts, 108 were women (Poullenot 1995: 273, 277). Thirty-nine of those women, including Mme Etxart, went to prison.

31. AD, P-A, 30W23, letter from Jacques Fonlupt-Esperabert to Spotti, divisional commissioner for mobile police, October 28, 1944.

32. Ibid. Although the state of "national indignity" sometimes entailed a ban on residence, the Court of Justice did not apply this discretionary measure to Mme Etxart (Novick 1968: 148–49).

33. This account of events is taken from a circular distributed by the Secret Army on August 26, 1946. M. Joanny kindly gave me a copy in July 2004.

34. AD, P-A, 30W23; letter from former head of Xiberoan Secret Army, Borgès, to Mme Etxart's uncle, February 12, 1945.

12: UNEASY COMMEMORATIONS

1. AD, P-A, 37W172, election results, 1939–46, for the cantons of Maule and Atharratze.

2. Ibid. The hamlet, Roquiague, had one hundred people, some of whom sheltered CFP resisters and Jews during the Occupation.

3. The citation is quoted in the Secret Army's account of events in the summer of 1944, "Libération de la Soule" (1944 and 1984 versions). The War Cross is kept in the town hall.

4. I do not know the outcome of the case.

5. Mme Udoy, editor of Le Miroir de la Soule, kindly gave me the document in 2004.

6. Kedward (1994) makes a similar point in relation to miners' strikes in France.

7. Military report (FFI, Sector 4, Lieutenant Daugreilh, report on the engagement at Montory, August 30, 1944), kindly provided by M. Joanny, 2004.

8. Letter from Pierre Béguerie to Mayor Champo, August 27, 1964, kindly provided by Jojo Malharin.

9. CFP accounts of Xiberoa's liberation appeared in that newspaper, Le Miroir de la Soule, in installments during the 1980s and again in the 1990s. In a monograph devoted to the role of the Corps Franc Pommiès in the liberation of southwestern France, a journalist-historian attributed the liberation of Maule entirely to the efforts of the CFP and presents an account of the German surrender entirely different from that of the Secret Army (Lormier 1990).

10. Le Miroir de la Soule published the documents in installments during 1984.

13: REMEMBERING THE RESISTANCE IN POPULAR THEATER

1. The play, "William II and the Campaign of France, 1914–1918," included representations of trench warfare, the bombing of the cathedral in Reims, and the miraculous arrival of Jeanne d'Arc at the Battle of the Marne (Lauburu 1987: 45). The oldest known *pastorale* was written and performed in 1750.

2. It is customary practice to perform a play twice. It may never be performed again.

3. Personal communication with Jean-Louis Davant, July 2004. I am most grateful to M. Davant for his help and interest in my research.

4. I am grateful to M. Davant for having shown me her letter.

5. The article appeared in the regional newspaper *La République des Pyrénées,* no. 17280, August 30, 2001: 2.

6. He was referring to the denunciation of a son by his own father.

GLOSSARY

Xiberoan Basque and French terms are in italics; terms that have been adopted into English and proper nouns are in roman type.

aizo (*voisin/e*):   Neighbor.

ardüra: Responsibility.

arrotzak: Strangers, outsiders.

asto-lasterka (*la course à l'âne*): Donkey race, a form of popular justice in which the moral community forced adulterers (or other wrongdoers) to ride backward on donkeys through the streets.

bardin-bardiña: Equality (especially between husband and wife).

barreatu: Disordered.

berdürak (*la jonchée*): "Spreading the greenery" between the houses of adulterers.

la Coutume de la Soule: Xiberoan customary law.

etxe: Basque house.

habitus: Lived environment, consisting of durable practices, rules, obligations, and values imposed by both legal and popular justice upon a community.

hebenkua: "Here person," someone born and resident in a particular Basque community.

herri: Basque community.

indarra: Physical strength; power (jural, procreative, spiritual); authority; intangible essence in an inhabited house.

insoumis: Defaulting recruit.

Iparralde: The "northern side" of the Basque Country, including the three Basque provinces located in the French state.

legetarzün (*legalité*): Legal justice.

lehen aizo (*premier voisin*): First neighbor.

manex: Non-Xiberoan Basque; black-faced sheep.

maquis: Organized resistance group.

maquisards: Resisters who belonged to an organized resistance group.

mihigaixtoak (*les mauvaises langues, les langues de vipère*): Literally, "bad tongues," people who engage in malicious gossip.

Milice: Paramilitary movement created by Vichy in January 1943 to repress dissent and to pursue Jews, STO evaders, resisters, and others deemed to be undesirable by Hitler.

notables: Prominent figures in the villages and towns of Xiberoa, owing to their wealth or their professional or family connections.

	Under Vichy many notables remained loyal to Pétain, though not always to Vichy, and often played key roles in the LFC.
olha:	Shepherding syndicate in Upper Xiberoa; hut used by the syndicate during the period of summer transhumance.
ots, aipü (la rumeur publique):	Public rumor.
le pain bénit:	Bread blessed by the priest and given as a gift of life to a household's first neighbor.
passeur:	Clandestine guide who helped fugitives of the Vichy and Hitler regimes cross the Pyrenees into Spain.
patrons:	Factory owners in Maule.
pays:	Territory inhabited by a certain group of people who may share particular practices and traditions and a particular language; territory inhabited by people who reside in a particular nation, region, province, town, or village; place to which a person belongs by birth.
Silviet:	Xiberoan democratic assembly formed under Xiberoan customary law.
xokhoa (le coin):	Sociophysical space to which a person belongs.
züzenbide (légitimité):	Popular justice; what is deemed to be right, legitimate, justifiable.

BIBLIOGRAPHY

PRIMARY SOURCES

Manuscript Collections, Departmental Archives of the Pyrénées-Atlantiques (formerly the Basses-Pyrénées)

The following series relate to judgments made by Basque moral communities in the eighteenth century:

(i) B5380, folio 38

(ii) B5365, folio 89

The following series were used in relation to Maule and Xiberoa (1912–46):

(i) 27W, folio 5, individual dossiers relating to judgments, collaboration, denunciations; folio 4, relating to collaboration and the Milice.

(ii) 30W2–13, individual dossiers relating to judgments, collaboration, tribunals.

(iii) 30W113, Court of Appeal in Pau; rehabilitations and amnesties.

(iv) 54W31, on Maule 1940–42, community matters such as "political refugees" and "strangers under surveillance."

(v) 37W115, on individuals arrested, wounded, and killed by the Germans.

(vi) 37W113, 114, 115, post-Liberation reports on German military and civilian personnel.

(vii) 37W19–20, reports on Maule industry in 1945.

(viii) 37W13–14–15, Vichy police reports on Maule and Xiberoan politics and society.

(ix) 37W17, post-Liberation reports, mainly by gendarmes regarding Spanish maquis operating in Xiberoa.

(x) 37W18, post-Liberation reports on public opinion in Maule, suppression of court martials in October 1944, armed Guérilleros Espagnols.

(xi) 37W6, reports on communists in Xiberoa during German occupation.

(xii) 37W16, post-Liberation reports on the Légion Française des Combattants and political parties in Xiberoa.

(xiii) 37W23, dossier on Mme Etxart. Accusations of collaboration, individual testimonies.

(xiv) 54W13, reports on Jews in Xiberoa (1941–43).

(xv) 37W30, reports on "suspect civil servants" in Xiberoa (1940–41).

(xvi) 30W88, reports on "daily life and religion" in Xiberoa during 1942.

(xvii)   37W27–28, reports on arrests of clandestine guides (1942–43), the *patron*-worker conflict in Maule, and communists active there.

(xviii)   10M10, labor conflicts in Maule (1919–38).

(xvix)   10M20, labor conflicts and strikes in Maule (1912–37).

(xx)   37W172, elections in Xiberoa (1939–46).

(xxi)   1M278, instructions from prefect to mayors.

The following series relate to Basques in the Great War:

(i)   1M94

(ii)   1M95

Archival and Private Papers for the Secret Army and Corps Franc Pommiès in Xiberoa
M. Joanny kindly provided numerous unpublished documents for the Secret Army (Sector IV), as well as private papers written by family members. M. Jojo Malharin kindly lent his father's extensive files on CFP military activities and post-Liberation correspondence between Pommiès and the Maule mayor, Jean-Pierre Champo.

Manuscripts, Memoirs, and Oral Testimonies
Aguer, Arnaud. 1960. Memoirs of the German Occupation of Xiberoa, published in *Le Miroir de la Soule* (in bimonthly installments during 1960), Maule. Available to the public only with permission of the editor of *Le Miroir*.
————. 1964. Unpublished memoirs about the Occupation and Resistance.
Aguerre, Jean François, Robert Elissondo, and Marie-Louise Lasserre Davancens. 2004. "L'Hôpital St. Blaise, été 1944." Unpublished testimonies.
Arricar, Curé Doyen of Atharratze. n.d. Eyewitness account of the German surrender to Clement de Jaureguiberry, August 20–23, 1944; given to me by Dr. M. Joanny.
————. 1962. "Une page d'histoire." *Autour du Clocher,* March, page C. Bimonthly parish newspaper.
Ayerdi, Gilda. 1999. "Témoignage de deux combattants de l'ombre." Unpublished thesis, Université de Pau et des Pays de l'Adour.
Barbe-Labarthe, André. n.d. "Mon journal de guerre et de captivité." Unpublished journal written from August 1939 until September 1941. Copy obtained from the late M. Labarthe and his daughter Marie-Rose, July 2004.
Barreix, Marcelle. 2004. "Témoignage." Unpublished memoir, recorded by Jean François Aguerre and Robert Elissondo, Ospitaleku.
Béguerie, Pierre. n.d. "Témoignage." Unpublished memoir, Béguerie family, Sohüta.
Dihigo, Marie Claire. 2004. Unpublished testimony recorded by J. F. Aguerre and R. Elissondo.
Elissondo, Laurent. 1989. "Comment ma famille traverse la guerre." Unpublished memoir, collected from his son, Robert Elissondo, in Sohüta, January 2005.
Hastaran, Fantxoa. 1998. "À la croisée des cultures: Mauléon, cité basque multicul-

turelle à la recherche de son identité." Unpublished thesis, University of Bordeaux III.

Huerta (Barrenne), Odette. Unpublished memoir and scrapbooks about the experiences of her brothers in 1944–45 and their deaths.

Jaureguiberry, Clement de. 1950, quoted in "Libération de la Soule" (1984), Tardets: Amicale des Anciens de la Résistance du Secteur IV.

Jaureguy, Pierre. 1944. "Titres de Madame Sagardoy Danielle." Unpublished document collected in Xiberoa, June 2003.

Lassus, Henri. 2004. "La Libération de Mauléon (témoignage)." Unpublished memoir of a former resister in the Secret Army, collected in Maule.

"Libération de la Soule." 1984. Account of resistance activities undertaken by the Secret Army and the Corps Franc Pommiès in July–August 1944, written mainly by Clement de Jaureguiberry, leader of the FFI (Region 4). Oloron-Ste-Marie: Imprimerie du Haut-Béarn. Collected in 2003 from M. Joanny.

Malharin, Maurice. n.d. Unpublished testimony.

Zunzarren, Denis. 2004. "De Mauléon à Brunete." Unpublished testimony recorded by Robert Elissondo, Ospitaleku.

Interviews by Author
The following list of informants spans the period 1976–2007. In all but a few cases, I became well acquainted with these individuals and saw them repeatedly at various stages of my fieldwork. An asterix marks those whom I met only once but with whom I spent several hours.

Georges Althapignet*
Pierre Amigo
Renée Amigo
Gregoire Ardatx
André Barbe-Labarthe
Michel Béguerie
Antoni Bidegaray
Lambert Blasquiz*
Felix Bormape
Anna Carricart
Borthol Carricart
Junes Casenave
Denis Cassard
Pierre Cocosteguy*
Piers-Paul Dalgalarrondo
Marie-Louise Lasserre Davancens
Jean-Louis Davant
Jean Deville*
Jean Duhau
Joseph Elgoyhen

Maddy Elgoyhen
Robert Elissondo
Christian Espeso
Maite Etchecopar
Maitena Etcheverry d'Abbadie
Felix Eyheralt
Maddy Eyheralt
Maienna Eyheramendy
Paul Fagoaga
Adrien Gachitegui
Madaleine Garat*
Anna Grissou*
Johanne Harrmora
Grabile Harispe
Jean Haristoy
Grabile Harriguileheguy
Johanne Hastoy
Jean-Baptiste Hondagneu
Odette Huerta
Maienna Idiart
Gregoire Iladoy
Kattlin Irigaray
Jean de Jaureguiberry
Rufino Jaureguy
Margaita Joanny
Ambrosi Jonnet
Jean-Pierre Jonnet
Louis Labadot*
Borthol Larbonne
Jeanetta Larbonne
Louis Larrandaburu*
Joël Larroque
Joseph Lascombes
Marie-Louise Lascombes
André Laufer*
Gisèle Lougarot
Jean Lougarot
Jean Loustau
Jojo Malharin
François Meyer*
Madalon Rodrigo Nicolau
René Osquiguel
Román Pérez

Jacqueline Pinède
Dominique Prebende
Georges Recalt*
Dominique Salaber
Maienna Salaber
Pethi Salaber
Rosemary Siedenburg
Maddy Udoy
Emile Vallés

Newspapers and Bulletins
L'Etoile noire, bulletin de liaison de l'Amicale du CFP-49th RI, 1964.
Le Glaneur d'Oloron, 1939.
L'Indépendent des Basses-Pyrénées, 1939.
Le Journal de Saint-Palais, 1928, 1929.
Le Miroir de la Soule, 1962, 1964, 1984, 1994, 1996, 2004.
Le Patriote, 1939.
La République des Pyrénées, 2001.

SECONDARY SOURCES

Abel, Olivier, ed. 1996. *Le pardon: Briser la dette et l'oubli.* Paris: Éditions Autrement.

Adereth, Maxwell. 1984. *The French Communist Party, a Critical History (1920–1984).* Manchester: Manchester University Press.

Altaffaylla. 2003. *Navarra 1936: De la esperanza al terror.* 6th ed. Tafalla: RGM.

AMCB (Association Mémoire Collective en Béarn). 1995. *Le Béarn à l'heure de la guerre d'Espagne, Récits et Témoignages.* Bizanos, France: Imprimerie Bihet.

Amouroux, Henri. 1981. *La grande histoire des Français sous l'occupation: Les passions et les haines.* Paris: Éditions Robert Laffont.

Arendt, Hannah. 1962. *Midstream* 8 (September): 86–87.

Arette Lendresse, Pierre. 1988. *Léon Bérard, 1876–1960.* Biarritz: J & D Éditions.

Arnould, Claire. 1999. "L'Accueil des refugiés en Béarn et en Soule de 1936 à 1940." In *Les Espagnoles et la guerre civile,* ed. Michel Papy, 338–50. Biarritz: Atlantica.

Assier Andrieu, Louis. 1987. "La communauté villageoise." *Ethnologie française* 16, no. 4: 351–60.

Atkin, Nicholas. 2001. *The French at War 1934–1944.* London: Pearson Education.

Augustins, Georges. 1986. "Un point de vue comparative sur les Pyrénées." In *Les Baronnies des Pyrénées,* eds. G. Augustins, R. Bonnain, Y. Péron, and G. Sautter, 201–14. Paris: Éditions de EHESS.

Aulestia, Gorka. 1995. *Improvisational Poetry from the Basque Country.* Reno: University of Nevada Press.

Aytaberro, Suzanne. 1983. *Pour que vive la croix basque.* Paris: Librairie Minard.

Bidart, Pierre. 1977. *Le pouvoir politique à Baigorri, village basque.* Baiona/Bayonne, France: Éditions Ipar.

Bourdieu, Pierre. 1977. *Outline of a Theory of Practice.* Cambridge: Cambridge University Press.

———. 2002. "Habitus." In *Habitus: A Sense of Place,* eds. Jean Hillier and Emma Rooksby, 27–34. Aldershot, UK: Ashgate.

Bray, Zoe. 2004. *Living Boundaries: Frontiers and Identity in the Basque Country.* New York: Peter Lang.

Brossat, Alain. 1992. *Les Tondues: Un carnival moche.* Levallois-Perret, France: Manya.

Burke, Peter. 1997. *Varieties of Cultural History.* Ithaca: Cornell University Press.

Burrin, Philippe. 1995. *La France á l'heure allemande 1940–1944.* Paris: Seuil.

———. 1996. *France under the Germans: Collaboration and Compromise.* New York: New Press.

Capdevila, Luc, François Roquet, Paula Schwartz, Fabrice Virgili, and Daniele Voldman. 2005. "Gender and the Second World War." In *Vichy, Resistance, Liberation,* ed. H. Diamond and S. Kitson, 51–58. Oxford: Berg.

Cappelletto, Francesca. 2003. "Long-Term Memory of Extreme Events: From Autobiography to History." *Journal of the Royal Anthropological Institute* 9: 241–57.

Casenave-Harigile, Junes. 1976. *Santa Grazi pastorala.* Oñati, Spain: Jakin.

———. 1989. *Hiztegia.* Atharratze, France: Hitzak.

Cavaillès, Henri. 1910. "Une fédération pyrénénenne sous l'Ancien Régime." *Revue Historique* (105), 14–39.

———. 1986. "Une fédération pyrénéne sous l'Ancien Régime," *Lies et Passeries dans les Pyrénées.* Tarbes, France: Société d'Études des Sept Vallées 1–67.

Céroni, Marcel. 1980. *Le Corps Franc Pommiès.* Vol. 1. Toulouse: Éditions du Grand-Rond.

———. 1984. *Le Corps Franc Pommiés.* Vol. 2. Montauban, France: Dupin.

Christian, William. 1969. *Divided Island: Faction and Unity on Saint Pierre.* Cambridge: Harvard University Press.

Cobb, Richard. 1970. *The Police and the People: French Popular Protest 1789–1820.* Oxford: Clarendon Press.

———. 1983. *French and Germans, Germans and French.* Hanover, NH: University Press of New England.

Cordier, Eugène. 1859. *Le droit de la famille aux Pyrénées (Barège, Lavedan, Béarn et Pays Basque).* Paris: Auguste Durand.

Davant, Jean-Louis. 2001. *Xiberoko Makia.* Ozaze, France: Ideki.

Desplats, Christian. 1982. *Charivaris en Gascogne.* Paris: Berger-Levrault.

Diamond, Hannah. 1999. *Women and the Second World War in France 1939–48.* Harlow, UK: Pearson Education.

Diamond, Hannah, and Simon Kitson. 2005. *Vichy, Resistance, Liberation.* Oxford: Berg.

Douglass, William. 1969. *Death in Murelaga.* Seattle: University of Washington Press.

———. 1975. *Echalar and Murelaga.* London: C. Hurst.

Douglass, William, and Jon Bilbao. 1975. *Amerikanuak.* Reno: University of Nevada Press.

Dreyfus-Armand, Geneviève. 1999. *L'exil des Républicains Espagnols en France*. Paris: Éditions Albin Michel.

Dutourd, Jean. 1955. *The Best Butter*. New York: St. Martin's Press.

Echegaray, Bonfacio de. 1932. "La vecindad: Relaciones que engendran en el País Vasco." *Revista Internacional de los Estudios Vascos* 23, no. 1: 5–26, 376–405, 546–64.

Estornés Lasa, Bernardo. 1996. *Memorias: Recuerdos y andanzas de casi un siglo*. Donosti, Spain: Editorial Auñamendi.

Eusko Ikaskuntza. 1998. *Eusko Ikaskuntzanen hiztegi biografikoa (1918–1998)*. Donosti, Spain: Eusko Ikaskuntza (Society of Basque Studies).

Eychenne, Emilienne. 1987. *Les fougères de la liberté, 1939–1945*. Milan: Éditions Milan.

Fabre, Daniel, and Bernard Traimond. 1981. "Le charivari gascon contemporain: Un enjeu politique." In *Le Charivari*, ed. J. Le Goff and J.-C. Schmidt, 23–32. Paris: Mouton.

Farmer, Sarah. 1999. *Martyred Village: Commemorating the 1944 Massacre at Oradour-sur-Glane*. Berkeley: University of California Press.

Fauvet, Jacques, and Henri Mendras. 1958. *Les Paysans et la politique dans la France contemporaine*. Paris: Librairie Armand Colin.

Ferro, Marc. 1987. *Pétain*. Paris: Fayard.

Fishman, Sarah. 1991. *We Will Wait: Wives of French Prisoners of War, 1940–1945*. New Haven: Yale University Press.

Fitzpatrick, Sheila. 1996. "Signals from Below: Soviet Letters of Denunciation of the 1930s." *Journal of Modern History* 68 (December): 831–66.

Fitzpatrick, Sheila, and Robert Gellately, eds. 1997. *Accusatory Practices: Denunciation in Modern European History, 1789–1989*. Chicago: University of Chicago Press.

Foix, Abbé. 1922. "Sainte-Engrâce." *Gure Herria* 2, no. 4: 207–15, 339–47, 493–504.

Fougères, Alain. 1938. *Les droits de famille et les successions au pays basque et en Béarn*. Bergerac, France: Imprimerie Générale du Sud-Ouest.

Fraenkel, Ernst. 1944. *Military Occupation and the Role of Law: Occupation Government in the Rhineland, 1918–1923*. New York: Oxford University Press.

García-Sanz Marcotegui, Ángel, coord. 2001. *El exilio republicano Navarro de 1939*. Pamplona: Gobierno de Navarra.

Gellately, Robert. 1997. "Denunciations in Twentieth-Century Germany: Aspects of Self-Policing in the Third Reich and the German Democratic Republic." In *Accusatory Practices*, ed. S. Fitzpatrick and R. Gellately, 185–21. Chicago: University of Chicago Press.

Gildea, Robert. 2002. *Marianne in Chains, In Search of the German Occupation (1940–45)*. London: Macmillan.

Gómez-Ibáñez, Daniel Alexander. 1975. *The Western Pyrenees: Differential Evolution of the French and Spanish Borderland*. Oxford: Clarendon Press.

Gordon, Bertram M. 1980. *Collaborationism in France during the Second World War*. Ithaca: Cornell University Press.

Grenier, Roger. 1998. *Another November*. Hanover, NH: University of New England Press.

Grosclaude, Jean-Claude, ed. 1993. *La coutume de la Soule*. St. Etienne de Baïgorry, France: Éditions Izpegi.

Guillon, Jean-Marie. 1997. "Sociabilité et rumeurs en temps de guerre." *Provence Historique* 187: 245–58.

———. 2005. "Talk which was not Idle: Rumours in Wartime France." In *Vichy, Resistance, Liberation*, ed. H. Diamond and S. Kitson, 73–85. Oxford: Berg.

Halimi, Andrè. 1983. *La Délation sous l'Occupation*. Paris: Éditions Alain Moreau.

Halty, Dominique. 1985. *Cambo sous l'Occupation Allemande*. Cambo, France: Imprimerie San Juan.

Hawthorne, Melanie, and Richard Golsan, eds. 1997. *Gender and Fascism in Modern France*. Hanover, NH: University Press of New England.

Heiberg, Marianne. 1989. *The Making of the Basque Nation*. Cambridge: Cambridge University Press.

Hérelle, Georges. 1922. "La représentation des Pastorales à sujets tragiques." In *Bulletin de la Société des Sciences, Lettres, Arts et d'Etudes Régionales de Bayonne*. Bayonne, France: A. Foltzer, 198–361.

Hillier, Jean, and Emma Rooksby. 2002. *Habitus: A Sense of Place*. Aldershot, UK: Ashgate.

Idiart, Roger. 1987. "Réflexions sur la pastorale souletine." In *La pastorale: Théâtre populaire basque en Soule*, 107–22. Bayonne, France: Lauburu.

Ikherzaleak. 1994. *150 ans d'espadrille à Mauléon*. Mauléon, France: De Arce.

———. 2006. *Mémoires de la Soule, 1914–1918: Une petite vallée du Pays Basque dans la guerre*. Mauléon, France: Ideki-Ozaze.

Inchauspé, Vèronique. 2001. *Mémoire d'Hirondelles*. Buziet, France: Éditions Uhaitza & Ikherzaleak.

Itçaina, Xavier. 1996. "Sanction morale, fête et politique: Le charivari à Itxassou au XIXieme siècle." *Revue Historique de Bayonne, du pays basque et du Bas-Adour* 151: 435–50.

Jackson, Julian. 2001. *France: The Dark Years 1940–1944*. Oxford: Oxford University Press.

Jacob, James. 1994. *Hills of Conflict: Basque Nationalism in France*. Reno: University of Nevada Press.

Jiménez de Aberasturi, Juan Carlos. 1996. *En passant la Bidasoa: Le réseau 'Comète' au pays basque (1941–1944)*. Biarritz: Éditions J & D.

Kapferer, Jean-Noël. 1995. *Rumeurs*. Paris: Seuil.

Kedward, H. R. 1985. *Vichy France and the Resistance*. London: Rowman & Littlefield.

———. 1994. *In Search of the Maquis: Rural Resistance in Southern France, 1942–1944*. Oxford: Clarendon Press.

Kelly, Mike. 1995. "The Reconstruction of Masculinity at the Liberation." In *The Liberation of France, Image and Event*, ed. H. R. Kedward and N. Wood, 117–28. London: Berg.

Kidd, William. 2005. "From the Moselle to the Pyrenees: Commemoration, Cultural Memory and the 'Debatable Lands.'" *Journal of European Studies* 35, no. 1: 114–30.

Koestler, Arthur. 1948. *Scum of the Earth.* New York: Macmillan.

Koreman, Megan. 1997. "The Collaborator's Penance: The Local Purge, 1944–45." *Contemporary European History* 6, no. 2: 177–92.

———. 1999. *The Expectation of Justice: France, 1944–1946.* Durham, NC: Duke University Press.

Laborie, Pierre. 1990. *L'opinion Française sous Vichy.* Paris: Seuil.

Lafourcade, Maïté. 1998. "La frontière franco-espagnole, lieu de conflits interétatiques et de collaboration interrégionale." In *La Frontière des origins à nos jours,* ed. Maïté Lafourcade, 331–45. Toulouse: Presses Universitaires de Bordeaux.

Lagarde, Anne-Marie. 2003. *Les Basques, société traditionelle et symétrie des sexes.* Paris: Harmattan.

Laharie, Claude. 1993. *Le camp de Gurs 1939–1945.* Biarritz: Éditions J & D.

Larrieu, Dr. 1899. "Mauléon et le pays de Soule pendant la Révolution." In *La tradition au pays basque.* Paris: Bureau de la Tradition Nationale.

Larronde, Jean-Claude. 1994. *Le Mouvement Eskualherriste (1932–1937).* Vitoria-Gasteiz, Spain: Fondation Sabino Arana.

———. 1995. *Le bataillon Gernika: Les combats de la Pointe-de-Grave (avril 1945).* Bayonne, France: Éditions Bidasoa.

Lauburu. 1987. *La Pastorale.* Baiona, France: Association Lauburu.

———. 1998. *Jean Baratçabal raconte, la vie dans un village basque de Soule au debut du 20e siècle.* Baiona, France: Association Lauburu.

Lefébure, Antoine. 1993. *Les conversations secrètes des français sous l'Occupation.* Paris: Plon.

Lefebvre, Thèodore. 1933. *Les modes de vie dans les Pyrénées Atlantiques Orientales.* Paris : Librairie Armand Colin.

Lormier, Dominique. 1990. *Le corps franc Pommiès.* Toulouse: Grancher.

———. 1991. *Le livre d'or de la Résistance dans le sud-ouest.* Toulouse: Grancher.

Lougarot, Gisèle. 2004. *Dans l'ombre des passeurs.* Donosti, Spain: Elkar.

Lucas, Colin. 1997. "The Theory and Practice of Denunciation in the French Revolution." In *Accusatory Practices,* ed. S. Fitzpatrick and R. Gellately, 22–39. Chicago: University of Chicago Press.

Mark, Vera. 2005. "Truth, Lies and French Popular Memory: A Cobbler's Tale." *Cambridge Anthropology* 25, no. 1: 31–51.

Marrus, Michael R., and Robert O. Paxton. 1995. *Vichy France and the Jews.* Stanford: Stanford University Press.

Milo, Daniel. 1997. "Street Names." In *Realms of Memory: The Construction of the French Past,* vol. 2, ed. P. Nora, 363–89. New York: Columbia University Press.

Moreau, Roland. 1972. "Batailles de jadis au Pays Basque: Le Sillon, le Modernisme, l'Intégrisme, l'Action Française." *Gure Herria* 2 and 3: 65–82, 182–90.

Nora, Pierre. 1992. "General Introduction: Between Memory and History." In

Realms of Memory: The Construction of the French Past, vol. 1, ed. P. Nora, 1–20. New York: Columbia University Press.

Novick, Peter. 1968. *The Resistance Versus Vichy.* New York: Columbia University Press.

———. 1985. *L'Épuration française, 1944–1949.* Poitiers: Éditions Ballard.

Nussy Saint-Saëns, Marcel. 1955. *Le païs de Soule.* Bordeaux: Clèdes et Fils.

Ostrum, Meg. 2004. *The Surgeon and the Shepherd: Two Heroes in Vichy France.* Lincoln: University of Nebraska Press.

Ott, Sandra. 1986. *The Basques of Santazi.* Ethnographic film made with Granada Television for its "Disappearing World" series.

———. 1989. "Mariage et remarriage dans une communauté montagnarde du Pays Basque." In *Le prix de l'alliance en Méditerranée,* ed. J. G. Peristiany, 249–70. Paris: Éditions CNRS.

———. 1992. "*Indarra*: Some Reflections on a Basque Concept." In *Honor and Grace,* ed. Julian Pitt-Rivers, 193–214. Cambridge: Cambridge University Press.

———. 1993a. *Le cercle des montagnes.* Paris: Éditions du Comité des travaux historiques et scientifiques.

———. 1993b. *The Circle of Mountains: A Basque Shepherding Community.* Reno: University of Nevada Press. (Rev. ed. of first English ed., Clarendon Press, Oxford, 1981.)

———. 2005a. "The Old Religion and the Notion of *la Montagne.*" In *Religion et montagne,* vol. 2, ed. Serge Brunet and Nicole Lemaitre, 357–66. Paris: Sorbonne.

———. 2005b. "Remembering the Resistance in Popular Theatre." In *Memory and World War II: An Ethnographic Approach,* ed. Francesca Cappelletto, 65–85. Oxford: Berg.

———. 2006. "Good Tongues, Bad Tongues: Denunciation, Rumour and Revenge in the Basque Country (1940–1945)." *History and Anthropology* (March): 57–72.

———. 2007. "Gift-Giving and the Management of Justice among Borderland Basques during the Occupation (1942–1944) and the Liberation." *The Proceedings of the Western Society for French History* (October): 266–81.

Paine, Robert. 1967. "What is Gossip About? An Alternative Hypothesis." *Man* 2, no. 2: 278–85.

Papy, Michel, ed. 1999. *Les Espagnols et la guerre civile.* Biarritz: Atlantica.

Paxton, Robert O. 1997. *French Peasant Fascism: Henry Dorgères's Greenshirts and the Crises of French Agriculture, 1929–1939.* New York: Oxford University Press.

———. 2001. *Vichy France: Old Guard and New Order 1940–1944.* New York: Columbia University Press.

Peillen, Dominique Txomin. 1997. "Zuberoaren Askapena." In *Gerla eta literatura 1914–1944,* vol. 14, 179–91. San Sebastián-Donosti, Spain: Eusko Ikaskuntza.

———. 1998. "*Frontières et mentalités en Pays Basque.*" In *La Frontière des origins à nos jours,* ed. Maïté Lafourcade, 445–75. Toulouse: Presses Universitaires de Bordeaux.

Peschanski, Denis. 2002. *La France des camps: L'internment 1938–1946.* Paris: Gallimard.

Pollard, Miranda. 1998. *Reign of Virtue: Mobilizing Gender in Vichy France.* Chicago: University of Chicago Press.

Poullenot, Louis. 1995. *Basses-Pyrénées, occupation, liberation 1940–1945.* Biarritz: Éditions J & D.

Pourcher, Yves. 1994. *Les jours de guerre: La vie des Français au jour le jour 1914–1918.* Paris: Plon.

Price, Roger. 2001. *A Concise History of France.* Cambridge: Cambridge University Press.

Régnier, Jean-Marie. 1991. *Histoire de la Soule,* vol. 1. St-Jean-de-Luz, France: Ekaina.

———. 2006. *Histoire de la Soule,* vol. 4. Ozaze, Spain: Ideki.

Rocafort, Joël. 1997. *Avant oubli, soldats et civils de la Côte basque durant la Grande Guerre.* Biarritz: Atlantica.

Rubio, Javier. 1977. *La emigración de la guerra civil de 1936–1939.* 3 vols. Madrid: Editorial San Martin.

Sahlins, Peter. 1989. *Boundaries: The Making of France and Spain in the Pyrenees.* Berkeley: University of California Press.

Schwartz, Paula. 1989. "*Partisanes* and Gender Politics in Vichy France." *French Historical Studies.* 16, no. 1: 126–51.

Société d'Études des Sept Vallées. 1986. *Lies et Passeries dans les Pyrénées.* Tarbes, France: Société d'Études des Sept Vallées.

Soucy, Robert. 1986. *French Facism: The First Wave, 1924–1933.* New Haven: Yale University Press.

Stein, Louis. 1979. *Beyond Death and Exile: The Spanish Republicans in France, 1939–1955.* Cambridge: Harvard University Press.

Sweets, John. 1976. *The Politics of Resistance in France, 1940–1944.* DeKalb: Northern Illinois University Press.

———. 1986. *Choices in Vichy France.* New York: Oxford University Press.

Thomas, Hugh. 2001. *The Spanish Civil War.* New York: Modern Library.

Thompson, E. P. 1991. *Customs in Common.* New York: New Press.

Todorov, Tzvetan. 1996. *A French Tragedy, Scenes of Civil War, Summer 1944.* Hanover, NH: University Press of New England.

Veyrin, Philippe. 1975. *Les Basques.* Bayonne: Arthaud.

Viers, Georges. 1958. "L'industrie et la population de Mauléon." *Revue Géographique des Pyrénées et du Sud-Ouest* 29, no. 2: 97–119.

———. 1961. *Mauléon-Licharre, la population et l'industrie.* Bordeaux: Éditions Bière.

Vinen, Richard. 2006. *The Unfree French.* New Haven: Yale University Press.

Violant i Simorra, Ramon. 1985. *El Pirineo Español: Vida, usos, costumbres, creencias y tradiciones de una cultura milenaria que desaparece,* vol. 2. Barcelona: Editorial Alta Fulla.

Virgili, Fabrice. 2002. *Shorn Women: Gender and Punishment in Liberation France.* Oxford: Berg.

Wakeman, Rosemary. 2004. "Nostalgic Modernism and the Invention of Paris in the 20th Century." *French Historical Studies* 27, no. 1: 115–44.

Weber, Eugen. 1962. *Action Française: Royalism and Reaction in Twentieth-Century France.* Stanford: Stanford University Press.

———. 1976. *Peasants into Frenchmen.* Stanford: Stanford University Press.

———. 1996. *The Hollow Years: France in the 1930s.* London: Sinclair-Stevenson.

Weber, Max. 1958. *From Max Weber: Essays in Sociology.* New York: Oxford University Press.

Winter, Jay. 1995. *Sites of Memory, Sites of Mourning: The Great War in European Cultural History.* Cambridge: Cambridge University Press.

Winter, Jay, and Emmanuel Sivan, eds. 1999. *War and Remembrance in the Twentieth Century.* Cambridge: Cambridge University Press.

Wylie, Laurence. 1974. *Village in the Vaucluse.* 3rd ed. Cambridge: Harvard University Press.

Young, James E. 2003. "Between History and Memory: The Voice of the Eyewitness." *Witness and Memory: The Discourse of Trauma,* ed. A. Douglass and T. Vogler, 275–83. New York: Routledge.

Zaretsky, Robert. 1995. *Nîmes at War: Religion, Politics, and Public Opinion in the Gard, 1939.* University Park: Pennsylvania State University Press.

Zonabend, Françoise. 1978. *The Enduring Memory: Time and History in a French Village.* Manchester, UK: Manchester University Press.

INDEX

Italic page number *130* refers to the photographs after page 130.